EDUCATION, POLITICS AND THE STATE

ALSO BY TED TAPPER

Young People and Society

Political Education and Stability: Elite Responses to Political Conflict

ALSO BY TED TAPPER & BRIAN SALTER

Education and the Political Order: Changing Patterns of Class Control

Education, Politics and the State

The theory and practice of educational change

Brian Salter & Ted Tapper

GRANT McINTYRE

First published in 1981 by
Grant McIntyre Limited
90/91 Great Russell Street
London WC1B 3PY

British Library Cataloguing in Publication Data

Salter, Brian
    Education, politics and the state.
    1. Educational sociology
    I. Title   II. Tapper, Ted
    370.19   LC191

    ISBN 0–86216–075–8
    ISBN 0–86216–076–6 Pbk

Typeset by Computacomp (UK) Ltd, Fort William, Scotland
Printed in Great Britain by St Edmundsbury Press, Bury St Edmunds, Suffolk

Contents

Preface

Our previous book developed a comparatively unexplored research area, the politics of education. Since that book was published government initiated attempts to redefine the educational system have continued relentlessly and in response a number of important texts have appeared. The politics of education is now an expanding research field, one of the few beneficiaries of the cuts in educational spending.

One of the reviewers of our previous book, *Education and the Political Order*, described it as 'a three-legged stool', which in view of the state of the subdiscipline was undoubtedly a compliment. Our primary purpose in writing *Education, Politics and the State* has been to improve on this, to create a firmer theoretical base – an armchair – for our understanding of the relationship between education and politics. The central organizing concepts are change and ideology. We explore the dynamic of educational change in contemporary Britain and relate it to some of the surrounding political and ideological struggles. The main thesis is simple: the dominant bureaucratic apparatus in the shape of the Department of Education and Science increasingly controls the process of educational change. However, some of the related issues this raises are very complex indeed. How does one account for this centralization of educational power? In what ways can that power be exercised? Why are the teachers' unions on the defensive? How will the links between schooling and industry be drawn closer together? How will this affect parents and pupils? Above all, what is to be the future experience of schooling? These are some of the related questions that this book asks and explores.

In pursuing our task we have drawn upon the disciplines of education, sociology and politics; this is therefore very much an interdisciplinary study. Although a specialist text, we have tried to write it in a way that makes it accessible to the non-academic audience. To this end we have erased much of the jargon and many of the asides and footnotes of our earlier drafts. Not enough, we fear, to please all of our potential audience. The empirical chapters should be of interest to those with more precise concerns. We hope, for example, that politicians and civil servants will read the chapters on the Department of Education and Science and the Schools Council, the parents of children in private schools the chapter on public school education, and practising teachers all of the book. Whether they concur with our analysis is another matter.

We have done our best to develop our theoretical perspective in depth, to make our analysis as complete as possible, and to interpret dispassionately all the evidence we uncovered. However, in order to prevent any possible misconceptions we should say we are *not* Marxists, *not* feminists, and *not* part of what is sometimes called 'the race industry' (whatever that may mean). The book stands for what we are and we will leave the reader to his or her own interpretation.

In writing this book we wish to pay particular thanks to the following persons. For comments upon several chapters: Professor T. Blackstone, University of London; Professor M. Kogan, Brunel University; Professor B. Graham, University of Sussex; Mr N. Bowles, Wolfson College, Oxford; Mr S. Steadman, Director of Impact and Take-Up Project, University of Sussex; and Mr C. Parsons, Research Fellow, Impact and Take-Up Project, University of Sussex.

For comments upon individual chapters: Professor L. Hearnshaw, University of Liverpool; Professor L. Stenhouse, University of East Anglia; Dr. I. Goodson, University of Sussex; Mr. F. Sparrow, the Schools Council; and Mr. J. Slater, HMI. For assistance with chapter eight: Mr. J. Cobban, ex-Headmaster of Abingdon School; Professor J. Honey, Leicester Polytechnic; Mr M. McCrum, the former Headmaster of Eton College; Dr J. Rae, Headmaster of Westminster School; Mr G. King-Reynolds, Headmaster of Dauntsey's School; Professor J. Dancy, ex-Headmaster of Marlborough College and currently Professor of Education, University of Exeter; Mr T. Devlin, Director of ISIS; Mr Dorrell, ex-Secretary of the Headmasters' Conference; Mr J. Thorn, Headmaster of Winchester College; Mr S. Andrews, Headmaster of Clifton College; Mr C. Everett, Headmaster of Tonbridge School; Mrs I. Fox, the Polytechnic of Central London; Professor J. B. Mays, University of Liverpool; Dr R. H. Wilkinson, University of Sussex; Dr K. McCormick, University of Sussex; Mr A.

Dingwall, ex-student of the University of Sussex and former pupil of Edinburgh Academy; and the staff of the Independent Schools Information Service. (Unacknowledged quotations from the above are taken from interviews.)

For assistance in typing the manuscript: Betty Fitzgerald, Jane South, Kate Tapper, Elaine Watts and Jackie Wooller. For help in tracing documentary material: the Documents Section, the University of Sussex Library. We should also like to thank the Arts Research Support Fund of the University of Sussex and especially the Arts Accountant, Mr. D. C. Chappell and his staff. For the errors that undoubtedly still remain we take full responsibility.

Brian Salter and Ted Tapper
August 1981

Introduction

The neglect of educational change

At a time when British education is under the greatest stress it has endured for decades, British educational sociology is static. As the demographic and political pressures for change in education mount, educational sociology ossifies into mutually exclusive theoretical camps: comfortable to the inhabitants, maybe, but complacent to some of those of us beyond the perimeters. To the uninitiated it seems strange that the portents of educational change which regularly appear in the nation's press are either ignored or forceably integrated with established theoretical positions and so stripped of much of their meaning. In the wake of the Great Debate has come a burgeoning procession of documents from the Department of Education and Science (DES) and Her Majesty's Inspectorate (HMI) gradually developing, consciously or otherwise, a state conception of how the details of education should be organized and taught. Government cuts, falling rolls and changes in the financing of local education authorities (LEAs) have created an unprecedented level of uncertainty about what the future holds for education. The Schools Council is once again the subject of investigation, this time by the Trenaman inquiry. Higher education is in a similar state of flux. Precisely what effect the University Grants Committee's (UGC) implementation of the cuts will have on the university system is unknown, as is the outcome of the latest moves to centralize the administration of the public sector of higher education. Yet, as the preparation for change become daily more evident, the capacity of students of education to place these events in a unifying perspective in order to understand what is happening with any degree of sophistication remains totally inadequate.

It is the objective of this book to provide such a perspective by developing a socio-political theory of educational change: a theory which shows how the social and economic pressures for change have to be politically negotiated in the context of state institutions which may, or may not, be sensitive to these pressures and which may have their own ideas as to what constitutes desirable change. In developing this theory, we are seeking to remedy the failure of educational sociologists to take educational change, that is change in the way all or part of the education system is organized and administered, as their central concern. Instead, they have either been obsessed with one parochial part of that system (e.g. the curriculum) and neglected to relate it to the rest of education, or they have been concerned with broader social issues (e.g. social mobility, cultural reproduction) where the dynamics of educational change are of secondary importance. This does not deny that, properly orchestrated, each can contribute towards an understanding of why and how educational change occurs in the form that it does. But to assume that their disparate interests will harmonize of their own free will to produce such an effect is to indulge in an unjustifiable act of faith: a laudable gesture but one insensitive to the separatist politics of academia based as they are on the rights of territory.

Academics have a mutual interest in maintaining the boundaries between different areas of knowledge since this means that different academics can claim to be expert in different, if neighbouring, knowledge territories. Authority is thus widely, if not fairly distributed. The broad divisions are disciplinary and within disciplines, certainly in the social sciences, other, smaller territories can be identified as 'schools of thought' or 'theoretical positions'. In this context it is important to note that education is *not* a discipline or knowledge territory in its own right; that is, it does not have a set of constructs that are peculiarly educational. Rather, it is a slice of social reality which has been fought over and partly colonized by insurgents from the territories of psychology, sociology, economics and, more lately, and not convincingly, political science (see Kogan 1978; Tapper & Salter 1978). (Hence we have 'educational psychology', 'educational sociology' and 'the economics of education' though not yet 'educational political science'.) Having secured their positions, the colonists, particularly those from the subterritories of sociology, then view each other with mutual suspicion.

There is therefore a natural inertia against developing a thoroughgoing theory of educational change since this would necessarily require the merging of separate territories. The attempts which have been made, notably those of Vaughan and Archer (Vaughan and Archer 1971; Archer 1979), suffer primarily from the limitation that although the appropriate territories have been included, they remain essentially a federation, rather than a unified state, of ideas. The dynamic of educational change, the force necessary to weld them together, is not identified. Consequently the member states retain much of their sovereignty and much of their tendency to pull in different directions.

In developing a socio-political theory of educational change the chances are that we will encounter considerable resistance not only because our approach is bound to be interdisciplinary but, more important, because we demand the cooperation of schools of thought within sociology which are, according to custom and ritual, normally bitterly opposed. Each guards his territory jealously and strongly resents the suggestion that his framework may supply merely part, rather than all, of the answer on educational issues. To this extent it has become a matter of pride and of routine either to denounce or to puzzle over work which smacks of theoretical eclecticism. After all, why bother to be eclectic when there are pigeonholes available? If the reply to this is that the subject of study, educational change, requires more than existing frameworks can readily offer, we are then faced with the further question of why these frameworks, entrenched though they be, have not engaged in some form of *détente*. Why maintain your theoretical isolation if this means that educational change can be only partially explained? To answer this we must explore the kinds of factors which reinforce the theoretical divisions.

One of the odd things about writing a book on educational change is the discovery that although there are no systematic theories of educational change already in existence there are plenty of authors claiming they are concerned about it. Indeed, in the current climate of educational theory building the announcement of political commitment to change appears to be the *sine qua non* of theory construction. If you do not wear your political heart on your sleeve then why are you bothering? Whether it is Halsey's social mobility theory, Michael F. D. Young's social control of knowledge approach, the polyglot analyses of the Black Papers or, a recent example, the socialist and feminist perspective of *Unpopular Education*, the same preoccupation is evident with how education can serve certain political ends. They take the political means to these ends to be self-evident (adviser to the Minister of education, teacher radicalism, public opinion, local struggle) and structure their theories accordingly. Naturally this rather cramps their theoretical style, not to mention their capacity for theoretical development, because the focus of the theory is logically subordinated to the political ends and means preferred. Since these are, mostly, immutable, so is the theory.

Tradition is frequently invoked to lend dignity to what might otherwise appear to be unrealistic political ambitions. Hence in *Origins and Destinations* Halsey places himself in that 'indigenous style of social science' which has its origins in Mayhew, Booth and the Webbs:

These writers were concerned to describe accurately and in detail the social conditions of their society, particularly of the more disadvantaged sections, but their interest in these matters was never a disinterested academic one. Description of social conditions was a necessary preliminary to political reform. They exposed the inequalities of society in order to change them. (Halsey *et al.* 1980:1)

Even assuming that the 'description of social conditions' phase is conducted in a reasonably objective manner, unbiased by the underlying commitment to a particular form of social change, there is still no guarantee whatsoever that the mere exposure of social inequities will have any policy impact at all. And given the political commitment behind it, it has to be regarded simply as a first step in a chain of analysis which will provide insights into how the desired educational change can be effected. Otherwise the research is bound to remain declamatory, rather than explanatory, with the researchers unsure of why nothing has changed. As Donald MacRae (1980) observed in his review of *Origins and Destinations*, and Goldthorpe's *Social Mobility and Class Structure in Modern Britain*, 'They appear to be surprised and discomfited by the fact that the agents of social change in which they have invested commitment and passion, have in part failed and in part not been applied. Like so many other social scientists and sociologists, they are almost disgruntled not to be successful legislators.' What is odd is that despite the disgruntlement, the adequacy of the analysis generally remains unchallenged, such is the belief in the desirability of the social goals, and the political means to them, with which the analysis is intertwined. Hence we find Tessa Blackstone (1980), in her review of *Origins and Destinations*, not really even scratching her head:

Although much of this book comes to somewhat gloomy conclusions about the limited success of the educational policies which have been introduced with the aim of achieving greater equality, they should not be interpreted to mean that nothing can be done. *The problem is that so far we have not tried hard enough.* [our stress]

While such faith in education's capacity to affect patterns of social mobility significantly is to be applauded for its perseverance in the face of the evidence, one must wonder at the complete neglect of the array of political and institutional constraints within which educational change takes place.

To ignore these constraints because one's political commitment finds them inconvenient and inhibiting unfortunately does not diminish their effect. It merely gives rise to an over-optimistic and inefficient political strategy based on a too narrow theoretical framework. We should emphasize at this point that it is not the overt political commitment which bothers us since everyone has a right to his own cosmetic; it is the limits which this commitment has tended to place on the understanding of educational change and the possibilities of theoretical overlap.

Dialogue between the different theoretical positions to effect such an overlap is virtually unknown. Bernstein in fact disputes that they have theories at all, preferring to describe them as 'approaches' within which are weak and often non-comparable explanations. It is the ideological stance of one approach which is of importance to the other:

Every new approach [to educational sociology] becomes a social movement or sect which immediately defines the nature of the subject by re-defining what is to be admitted, and what is beyond the pale, so that with every new approach the subject almost starts from scratch. (Bernstein 1973:157)

This common characteristic of successive sociologies of education is also taken up by Bernbaum (1977:41) who notes that while both the 'old' and the 'new' are committed to certain types of social and educational change, what has brought about the 'new' sociology of education has been 'the growing realization of the inefficacy of the remedy' offered by the 'old' school: comprehensive education and destreaming have not transformed the social order. Once a fresh approach emerges it then takes root in a particular institution, or sets of institutions, and then duly ossifies, reinforcing the divisions. The fragmentation of educational sociology at the level of dominant approaches finds a parallel in the colleges of education where there exists a similar commitment to change in the classroom. As a result, the educationalist 'shops around', as Bernbaum (ibid.: 36) puts it, within the field of sociology, choosing those topics which deal with 'critical' educational issues and which offer apparently clear recommendations for action.

The concern that education should act as a vehicle for change has therefore led to a neglect of the theory best equipped to understand the process of change. Social science may not be value free, but at the same time there can be no doubt that the distorting effect of values can be controlled to a greater and lesser extent. Being prepared to consider new theoretical insights and adjust one's theory in the light of fresh evidence should not be considered a betrayal of one's political commitment.

The dynamic of educational change

Although we would claim that our theory of educational change is both more direct and more eclectic than is generally the case in educational sociology, it is nevertheless based on certain assumptions which together establish the parameters of the analysis. It is important that we briefly outline them now since they serve to generate the main questions regarding the dynamic of educational change on which this book focuses.

No institution is an island and education is no exception. Indeed, it is frequently argued that formal education is the convenient expression of underlying economic and social need with political institutions merely serving to interpret and specify the precise form that expression should take. This is a much too facile equation and leads to the often unquestioning application of a kind of arithmetical logic to the economic order–education relationship. A logic which implies that capitalism and the infrastructure supporting it operate like a well-oiled machine. We take a more sceptical view, at least to begin with, and assume that tensions can exist both between economic base and superstructure and within the superstructure itself – that is, between the component institutions of the superstructure, of which the education system is one. Clearly this is not a new idea: Gramsci, for one, having argued for it in the past. Where we differ from Gramsci, however, is in our contention that the tensions are created not simply as a result of passive structural impediments to the economic and social pressures, impediments which alone can distort and redirect that dynamic, but also as a result of a counter-pressure which is essentailly bureaucratic. It is out of the interaction of these pressures that the dynamic for change is born.

The bureaucratic pressure emerges, firstly, from the general need of modern society for rational modes of organizing its increasingly complex systems of social relationships and, secondly, from the specific bureaucratic form of state agencies, which have developed to the point where they are capable of generating and sustaining their own autonomous needs. Generally these two factors are linked to the extent that a state agency organizes and administers a single area of individual or societal need (e.g. health, housing, industry), according to criteria which are presented as rational. The education system is different. For not only does it service individual educational need (theoretically), but it also services the credentialling needs of the social order as a whole through the operation of the examination system. Education is therefore *the* critical institution in the social control function of the state because it can help to produce and to legitimize patterns of social inequality and mobility through its provision of a suitable rationale.

If there were no generally accepted and publicly verifiable definition of merit such as education provides, the movement of individuals within and between the complex organizations of society would have to be arranged according to informal criteria of judgement and, because of the scale and complexity of the movement, would almost certainly break down. This is not to deny that informal cultural criteria of selection operate anyway, but it is within a framework of credentials which can be claimed to be fairly and impartially administered. By organizing knowledge into status hierarchies, and labelling and allocating it in a way which is judged to be rational, education not only controls access to the scarce knowledge resources essential for an individual's occupational and social progress, it also performs an ideological function by persuading people that this process is legitimate. Consequently, if it changes the way in which knowledge is organized and allocated it must ensure that the accompanying ideology changes also.

If the economic order is to be successfully reproduced it is necessary that there be continuity in the sets of social relationships on which the production process is dependent. It therefore becomes part of the social control function of education to assist in the maintenance of these social relationships. Yet at the same time, the rapidly changing economies of modern industrialized societies also require education to supply them with new types of manpower suitably trained or re-trained, and credentialled. There is no guarantee that education can perform these two functions without getting itself into a tangle: the greater the diversity and rate of change of the economic and social pressures placed on education the more chance there is that education will be unable to harmonize the implications of the two. In addition, it has the structural needs of its own organization to worry about.

As part of what Althusser would call the ideological state apparatus education is naturally bureaucratically organized. Bureaucracies have their own preferences and ambitions as to how they structure their activities basically derived from the need for routinized and predictable procedures for the purposes of maximizing the efficiency of their operation – as they see it. In an ideal capitalist world this bureaucratic dynamic would work in parallel with the economic and social dynamics. The organs of the state would judiciously harness bureaucratic power to reproduce those systems of class relations appropriate to the needs of the ruling class. But in the real world there are likely to be dysfunctions: the educational bureaucracy itself and the demands for rational credentialling to which education may or may not respond, can together magnify the importance of the bureaucratic dynamic to the extent that it assumes a development logic of its own, independent of the economic and social pressures. Obviously the three work in harmony up to a point: capitalist society would not survive if they did not. But the extent to which they harmonize will vary. It cannot be guaranteed that the needs of the dominant economic class will be faithfully translated into action by the dominant bureaucracies. The latter may have their own interests to look after.

The implication of this perspective is that educational change must be viewed as a phenomenon which is negotiated in an institutional context under pressure from economic, social and bureaucratic dynamics. Furthermore, that this negotiation of change is constrained by education's need to generate an ideology to legitimate both its own power and the social inequalities it helps to perpetuate: the satisfactory orchestration of economic, social and bureaucratic dynamics to produce educational change has to be consonant with the development in parallel of a suitable educational ideology. Without the protective cloak of ideology, the change is likely to be short-lived.

In our socio-political analysis of educational change we will therefore investigate the way in which the dynamic of change emerges in a number of institutional contexts. The purpose of this approach is to identify the details of educational change by focusing on those structures that intervene between the macrolevels of the superstructure and the microlevel of the classroom. Previous studies have, with the exception of Kogan's work, barely touched on this area, yet it is here that the dynamic is first translated into specific structural form with the eventual accolade of becoming public policy. Understanding and systematizing the way in which this translation effect occurs is essential to any understanding of what is happening in education today.

The organization of the book is in two parts. Part one develops a three-stage theory of educational change which moves from the macroeconomic, social and bureaucratic pressures for educational change through the ideological and legitimating stages which it must negotiate prior to its expression in the classroom. Part two then studies particular aspects of education to refine the theory further and to demonstrate the complexities of the educational change process. But before developing that theory, chapter one provides a review of the understandings of educational change to be found in the sociological literature and identifies the nature of, and reasons for, their limitations. It thus sets the scene for our theoretical initiative. This begins in chapter two with the examination of the broad social forces underlying educational change, their interrelationship and the implications of the movement towards the centralization of educational power. However, the ideological partner of structural change in education cannot be automatically produced as the need arises. Chapter three traces how the emergence of a new educational ideology is an arduous and negotiated process which takes place among the top echelons of the institutions with a stake in education. And even assuming that both the structural and ideological components of educational change are negotiated at the political level, chapter four details how it is still problematic as to how far this is reflected in changing classroom practice and different ways of organizing knowledge.

In part two, we begin the task of showing how the pressures for
change are negotiated within particular institutional contexts. Thus
chapter five explores how the major bureaucracy in education, the
DES, is increasingly establishing its own ideas as to what constitutes
acceptable educational change as it formalizes its own internal
methods and techniques of educational planning. This is followed in
chapter six with the study of a much smaller institution, the Schools
Council, but one nevertheless explicitly in the business of educational
change. Here the emphasis is on identifying the kinds of structural
impediments, both internal and external, to the emergence and
implementation of an educational ideology. This is a particularly
interesting case study in the light of M. F. D. Young's rather
grandiose claims regarding the Council's role as an ideological agent
of the status quo. In chapters seven and eight we push our analysis of
educational change further by taking two examples of educational
ideology, the meritocratic and public schools ideologies, and relate the
way they have, and are, changing in response to shifts in social and
institutional conditions. At the same time, these chapters show that
while ideologies do respond to such conditions it is often in a less than
straightforward manner. While the purpose of chapters five to eight is
to elucidate different aspects of our theory, chapter nine draws them
together in the context of the Great Debate, its aftermath and
implications. This thereby sets the scene for the final chapter where
we conclude by assessing the significance of contemporary
developments and the probable future path of educational change in
Britain.

Part One

Developing the Theory

1

The Politics of Educational Change

Three perspectives on educational change

In view of the vast body of literature on schooling it is surprising to find so little sociological analysis of the process of educational change. As if to counteract this paucity of analysis the desire for change has been considerable; there are few educational sociologists who have not wished to see the experience of schooling change. Indeed it could be justly argued that the moral commitment to change is such that it has prevented some from seeing clearly how their goals could be achieved. In spite of this lack of clarity the field is not entirely bare and it is the purpose of this chapter to present a critical overview of the pertinent literature. The aim is to place our book within the context of British educational sociology and to demonstrate how, with respect to understanding the process of educational change, we intend to add another dimension to that subdiscipline.

Bottomore has implied that part of the answer as to why sociologists have neglected the analysis of educational change lies in the sheer scope of the task. In an introduction to Bourdieu's work Bottomore (1977:viii) has observed that to substantiate the proposition that pedagogic action is a product of the structure of class relations (to use their jargon and to reveal what they consider to be the dynamic of educational change) it needs to be demonstrated how changes in the latter bring about changes in the former. The threads, as Bottomore noted, were complex and so difficult to trace. But more demanding, and potentially less rewarding tasks have taxed the ingenuity of man. In our opinion a more complete answer is to be found in a dissection of the main developments in British educational sociology. Put simply the central concerns have not been conducive to developing a sophisticated theory of educational change.

1 *Education and social stratification*

For much of its existence British educational sociology has tried to illuminate the ties between formal schooling and social stratification. This is true of the work of A. H. Halsey who dominated this phase in British educational sociology. It was firmly believed that the relationship was positive and that schooling was the most viable means of social mobility for working-class children. As such there was a commitment to creating educational experiences which would maximize equality of educational opportunity for individual children. Undoubtedly some educational sociologists felt that this should be the dynamic of educational change and they worked with considerable success to make it so. Both Boyle and Crosland testify to the fact that educational sociologists helped to create a different climate of opinion in the 1960s and that within the DES the traditional dialectic between 'the expansion of educational opportunity' and 'education for investment and efficiency' swung in favour of the former (Kogan 1971:46–7, 123). In fact during Crosland's term of office certain sociologists were formally associated with the Department and one can only assume that this was with the intention of explicitly pushing the fulcrum of the dialectic in the desired direction (Kogan 1971:185, 190). This is not to suggest that the sociologists were initiators of change for they may well have been used either as pawns in an internal departmental power struggle or, more likely, as legitimators of a process that was already in motion.

The desire to establish equality of educational opportunity could be closely associated with the belief that schooling should be expanded for economic purposes. In other words there was no inevitable conflict between the demands of social amelioration and the need for the more efficient performance of the economy. Numerous research studies showed that the 1944 Education Act had not achieved all that some had expected of it. In some localities the percentage of working-class children in grammar schools actually declined because they faced increased competition in the 11 + examination from middle-class children. Perhaps more significant was the wastage of working-class grammar school talent; literally thousands of children with high-measured abilities left school each year without any, or at best negligible, formal qualifications (CACE 1954). This, so it was argued, was a loss of talent that the nation could ill afford, and the problem could only grow in size because the increasingly sophisticated industrial base would require more and more skilled and specialized manpower to ensure its smooth functioning. So to maximize the opportunities for working-class social mobility also enhanced the nation's economic wellbeing. In some versions of this perspective schooling is the most complete expression of those values that are conducive to the spread of advanced technology. In his euology to the multiversity Clark Kerr (1963) placed the institutions of higher education at the heart of technological innovation. It was in the university's seminars, conferences and research laboratories that the technology and organizational strategies of the future were discovered and developed.

Although it is impossible to prove, it seems reasonable to assume that the policy influence of the social scientists working in this field owed much to their ability to marry their moral commitment (i.e. the desirability of increasing equality of educational opportunity) with the politically attractive proposition that schooling should serve the needs of the evolving industrial base. As Halsey himself has succinctly put it (Halsey *et al.* 1980: 5) a concern with common culture, social justice and economic efficiency comprised uncomfortable bedfellows. Uncomfortable as the ensuing accommodations may have been it was a politically potent combination. The way to bring about educational change was to persuade the formal policy makers that the prevailing system was failing with respect to both social and economic ends. In terms of schooling the object of attention was the established institutional arrangements; the aim was to restructure these so that increasing numbers of children were exposed for ever lengthening periods of time to the valued product of formal education. In more precise terms R. H. Tawney (1922) led the attack upon the barrier between elementary and secondary schooling in the interwar years (see Hadow Report 1926), while since the 1944 Education Act the political weight of educational sociology has been directed against the tripartite arrangements for secondary education and in favour of the comprehensive schools.

The prolonged and widespread support for the cause of equality of educational opportunity was dependent partly upon its political appeal (who could oppose the gradual equalization of opportunities for individual social mobility?) and partly upon the simplicity and coherence of its implied ideological base (see pp. 62–5). The determinant of educational success should be the qualities that individuals possessed – intelligence, motivation and diligence. Schooling should be structured to maximize the varying talents that flowed out of these personal qualities. The end product was a carefully differentiated pool of young men and women waiting to take their designated places in an ever more complex, specialized and hierarchical society. The criteria for the allocation of roles was the credentials that individuals had justly earned in an educational system that rewarded those qualities which go to make up merit.

As the 1960s unfolded, this phase in British educational sociology slowly lost confidence; the bedfellows started to squabble. The passing of the 1944 Education Act was regarded in most circles as a very progressive measure. However at the heart of the educational system it bequeathed was the 11 + examination which formed the gateway to the secondary schools. This was the most evident manifestation that schooling acted as a means of role differentiation, no matter what it may also have done for individual social mobility. Both those who believed that the 11 + examination resulted in a loss of talent, as well as those who attacked it because it acted as a means of social differentiation and stratification, could unite behind the cause of comprehensive secondary education. But once that cause was conceded – albeit grudgingly – the consensus disintegrated. There was no further reason for its various fragments to hold together; so they went their various ways to confront one another over an ever increasing number of issues.

In his brilliant satirical essay *The Rise of the Meritocracy* Michael Young (1961) raised a fundamental moral objection to the social order implied by this sociology of education: even if it were possible to create such a society the consequences were far from desirable for the outcome would be social stratification as intense and as potentially divisive as the social inequality of rigid class-based societies. From the United States came powerful empirical evidence that questioned the relationship between education and social mobility. James Coleman's research showed (1966: 20–1) that schooling did not narrow the differences in cognitive ability scores between racial groupings; they remained much the same on leaving as on entering school. Extending the argument further Christopher Jencks demonstrated (Jencks *et al.* 1972: chs. 6, 7) that very few measures of formal education correlated positively with subsequent individual occupational status and income levels. The policy implications of such research were little short of momentous. Coleman proposed that attention should henceforth be directed less at equalizing inputs into schools and school systems and more at equalizing outputs; that now the focus should be upon how to achieve equality of educational results rather than equality of educational opportunity. For Jencks the experience of schooling must be evaluated with respect to its day-to-day influence upon the quality of children's lives rather than what it may do for them when they become adults.

It also became fashionable at that time to question either whether expenditure on schooling helped to stimulate economic growth (see Vaizey 1962; Blaug: 1970; 1968) or whether a technologically-oriented industrial base required more and more skilled and differentiated manpower for its smooth functioning. Collins (1972) has argued that over time powerful occupational groups have used the educational system to reinforce their privileges *vis-à-vis* other groups. They do this by continuously refining and upgrading their entrance qualifications which not only restricts the size of their recruitment base but also determines its social and personality characteristics. The expansion of formal education is, therefore, not so much a response to society's changing technological needs but rather demonstrates the ability of occupational groups to engage in restrictive practices.

In view of the evident rationality that enveloped the campaign for the extension of equality of educational opportunity, these were arguments that were difficult to ignore. Besides sounding either logical or plausible the weight of the empirical evidence was decisive. The proponents of extending equality of educational opportunity had provided the intellectual rationale, much of it in the shape of concrete data, for policies designed to achieve this goal. Without rejecting this model of how the social scientist exerts his policy-making influence, it would be impossible not to engage in dialogue with the new critics, and to change one's policy position if the evidence seemed to suggest that this was necessary.

Perhaps more significant than evidence that can be interpreted to fit a range of predispositions was Michael Young's spelling out in his *The Rise of the Meritocracy* of the ultimate social logic inherent in the ideology that underlay the movement for greater equality of educational opportunity for individuals. Some may ponder why such issues were not raised earlier but as long as the concomitant policies resulted in widespread social amelioration such questions could be conveniently ignored. As the social returns of the strategy declined, as Halsey's own evidence with respect to the 1944 Education Act shows, then the voices of the sceptics inevitably grew louder. Whereas the previous goal had been to establish an educational system which provided equal opportunities for all individuals to develop their talents to their fullest extent, the new aim was to create schooling experiences which would stretch talents. As opposed to providing contexts within which individuals realized their potential the schools were to be the force which created the potential itself. Regardless, therefore, of what else may have changed the ultimate faith in the socially ameliorative properties of schooling had not diminished, indeed quite the contrary, it had been enhanced. In a recent article Halsey (1980) has reaffirmed his own commitment in very positive terms: 'And for a government determined to relieve the handicaps of those who come from poor families, a pre-school programme discriminating in their favour seems to be one of the crucial weapons in the armoury. In that way, education *can* compensate for society.'

Although the faith that schooling can enhance the social opportunities of the deprived is retained, along with the belief – at least in Halsey's case – that working through formal political processes can bring about meaningful changes, the object of attention is somewhat different. Programmes like the Educational Priority Areas and the Community Development Projects probably represent the best examples of this new strategy (Halsey 1972; Lees & Smith 1975). Such programmes attempted positively to enrich the schooling experiences of deprived children; this was seen as a small but purposeful endeavour in positive discrimination. Although compensatory educational strategies could scarcely avoid the implicit assumption that failure in school was a consequence of personal cultural deprivation, the supporters nonetheless felt that if they could create different classroom climates it would be possible both to improve the schoolwork of the children and enhance their long-term social prospects. Rather more optimistically – and perhaps naively – Halsey felt that such programmes could stimulate direct political action in their host communities, which presumably he hoped would lead to an attack upon local problems in general.

In terms, therefore, of changes to the educational system this approach has been more concerned to modify and intensify the experience of schooling rather than to manipulate established institutional arrangements. The stress is upon teaching basic skills, many perhaps of a more social than educational nature. Clearly it is hoped that the end result will be a closing of the gap in educational attainment between those groups that have usually performed well and those that have not. So the traditional ends of the educational system remain intact. Furthermore, with respect to the overall character of the social order it is hard to see how 'equality of educational results for groups' will have different consequences from 'equality of educational opportunity for individuals'. Inequality, assuming that the experience of schooling is a critical determinant, will simply be more equitably shared amongst all social groups. Given Tony Crosland's penchant for radical social change whilst avoiding the embrace of social egalitarianism, it is not surprising that he should be the Secretary of State for Education and Science most closely associated with the educational priority schools (Kogan 1971 : 197).

2 *The new sociology of education*

The extent of working-class access to schooling was the main preoccupation of those sociologists concerned to establish equality of educational opportunity. Their aim was to increase working-class consumption of a desirable commodity − formal schooling. These sociologists told us very little about the experience of schooling itself; what the educational process actually looked like. Besides ignoring what many would consider should be central to the study of education, it has also been claimed that as a consequence they failed to appreciate the basis of working-class educational failure i.e. the very experience of schooling (see Young 1971). The new sociology of education aimed to set the record straight.

There are two broad themes within the new sociology of education. The first concentrated heavily upon patterns of interpersonal relations, the hidden curriculum as it is sometimes known (see Hargreaves 1972; Woods & Hammersley 1977). Educational change to be effective has to restructure these patterns; above all the traditional authority relationship between teachers and taught has to be reformulated. Thus Professor Stenhouse (Humanities Curriculum Project 1970) wanted the teacher to become more of a neutral chairperson who orchestrates discussion than a pedant who dispenses knowledge. If classroom authority patterns were to be effectively changed it was necessary for methods of assessment to be internally controlled, that is by the learning group itself, rather than a remote examination body. Partly in response to this mood the GCE and CSE examination boards adopted mode 3 methods of assessment which were more under the control of the classroom teacher. Although the official rationalizations may suggest that this minimizes the degree to which the learning process is stultified by externally controlled examinations, the question of where educational authority lies could scarcely be concealed.

The second, and interrelated, theme in the new sociology of education concerns the organization of knowledge. In this the most notable British representative is Basil Bernstein (see Bernstein 1971; 1973; 1975). It is argued that not only is the organization of knowledge the main function of formal education but, also, the way in which it achieves that end best defines the social purposes of schooling. For educational change to have any social significance it has to restructure the way knowledge is organized. Both themes in the new sociology of education, therefore, recognize that the experience of schooling has to be remade if educational change is to be effective. By and large the moral commitment to the social amelioration of the British working-class is much the same as for those sociologists who wished to extend and equalize educational opportunities. The focus of attention, however, was different with the new school of sociologists believing that it had found the key to explaining the educational failure of working-class children.

The new sociology of education has bequeathed an ambivalent, indeed confused, legacy to our understanding of the process of educational change. Because attention was centred upon the experience of schooling, and so much of this rested in the hands of teachers, some felt it was possible to introduce socially significant changes from within the school, or even from within the classroom. Given the traditional autonomy of teachers and heads in the day-to-day running of British schools the tantalizing possibility of initiating a grassroots revolution was felt to exist. In the work of Ivan Illich (1973) (although his reference point was not the British educational system) this belief assumed grandiose proportions. Closer to home, the headmaster of William Tyndale Junior School, with a cohort of supportive teachers, set about revolutionizing the experience of schooling within his small empire (Ellis *et al.* 1976). Regardless of what the educational payoffs for the children might have been the end result was a political disaster for the innovating teachers. It has been suggested that the headmaster, Mr Ellis, and those teachers who backed his changes, had come under the influence of the new sociology of education i.e. if one was serious about changing the lives of working-class children then it was imperative to reshape radically the experience of schooling. This should be read as a tentative statement, although the Auld Report is interesting in this context

(1976:paras 130–137, 162–170, 227–230). The crucial lesson of this fracas is that there are severe limits to the innovations that teachers can initiate in schools and that if they transgress those limits they can expect to be attacked by other groups in the community including their colleagues.

Although authority relations within the classroom, and how schools organize knowledge, may be factors that have to be changed if educational innovation is to be effective, these are not variables which can be manipulated entirely at the discretion of the teachers themselves. Knowledge and authority relationships are socially organized; a process in which teachers are merely one of the parties. The key to change, therefore, is to effect a reorganization of those social forces which determine the authority patterns and the structure of knowledge. What this points to is a complex political struggle the outcome of which will be decided by the power of the respective parties. So if one looks for social explanations of the structure of knowledge and of authority relations then likewise one has to find the key to changing the configuration of social forces.

3 Education and social reproduction

Those contemporary theorists who argue that formal education is an agent of social reproduction draw upon two contrasting intellectual traditions, one associated with Marx and the other with Durkheim. Sometimes the two traditions can coexist uneasily within one body of work for the inherent tensions have never been fully reconciled, perhaps not even recognized. Both intellectual traditions, however, credit schooling with the same social goal: to reproduce the class structure of capitalist society with its concomitant inequalities of status, income, wealth and power. What is different is the means by which this is accomplished.

Both Bernstein and Bourdieu (see Bourdieu & Passeron 1977) argue that the educational system perpetuates the pattern of class relations through its transmission of established cultural traditions. Those individuals who are academically successful possess the requisite cultural capital. Knowledge is organized within the educational system in a manner which ensures that only those with this cultural capital will succeed. So it is through its most sacred function – the perpetuation of knowledge – that schooling performs its most important social goal. Because success is seen to be a product of individual merit and personal choice this sensitive social task is effectively disguised.

In contrast to both Bernstein and Bourdieu, Bowles and Gintis (1976) have drawn the relationship between individual qualities, the character of schooling and the structure of the social order in a more direct and simple manner. They have posited a one-to-one correspondence between capitalism's social relations of production and the authority relations that can be found in educational institutions. While educational institutions form a prestige hierarchy that parallels the class structure, so intraschool experiences – although in stark contrast to both Bernstein and Bourdieu they make precious few references to the organization of knowledge – are designed to ensure that individuals will fit neatly into their future productive roles.

The common thread in the work of Bernstein, Bourdieu and Bowles is that the primary social purpose of schooling is to reproduce a class-based society. The end result is an integrated model in which individual inputs, the educational system and the end products of the experience of schooling have a relationship to one another which is structured by those interests which depend upon the preservation of our present class-based society for the perpetuation of their power. Not far from the centre of gravity in both Bernstein's and Bourdieu's models is the educational system itself, and in particular the way that knowledge is organized within it. Although their analysis may not commence with schooling, it is a concept that they take seriously. In Bowles' and Gintis' model the educational system is placed in a position of almost complete dependence; correspondence between schooling and work ensures the maintenance of the social relations of production. Their analysis begins and ends with the all-pervasive influence of the capitalist mode of production.

All these authors stress the importance of disguising the process of social reproduction. For Bernstein and Bourdieu this is contained within the very experience of schooling, for what is supposedly taking place is the translation of objectively defined merit into certified competence. It is as if the patterns of success and failure are natural, a judgement aided by the fact that so many of the critical decisions with respect to educational careers are made by the individual himself so that he appears to choose to fail or to succeed (Bourdieu & Passeron 1977:153). Bowles and Gintis in a parallel line of analysis argue that the process of social reproduction is disguised by ideological camouflages which legitimate inequalities that owe their presence to other causes. This explains their detailed discussion of intelligence testing which they see as a potent means of disguising and legitimating the social production of inequality (Bowles & Gintis 1976: ch. 4). To stress the part schooling plays in the legitimation of inequality opens up different possibilities as to its social ends. Because it legitimates the outcome of the social reproduction process it does not necessarily follow that schooling has any direct responsibility for determining the actual consequences of that process. That may be something which is decided elsewhere and by other means. As we will consider later (see pp. 31–7) to dichotomize the social ends of education in this fashion has important repercussions for understanding the process of educational change.

In spite of the fact that the Marxist intellectual legacy is at least part of the heritage upon which these social reproduction theorists have drawn, their ideas are a close reflection of the functionalist view of social reproduction which lies squarely in the tradition of Durkheim. Durkheim (1977: 168–9) was writing at a time when the varying influences of the industrial revolution were being seriously felt in France for the first time. The moral order of the old society, based upon the Catholic church, was crumbling under the pressures of industrialization. Durkheim believed that all societies needed a firm moral order not simply because he abhorred social chaos but also because he believed that it was impossible for citizens to pursue the good life without the guidance of a moral order. Ideally the moral order held sway because individuals fully accepted the guidance it offered and not simply because it was imposed on them. The new order which was emerging in the France of his day required a thoroughgoing secular morality and he believed that the institution which could best transmit this was the school.

Of course Marxists believe that capitalist society is dominated by a moral order but it is one which reflects the interests of the dominant classes and is superimposed by them upon the whole of society. In the Althusserian view the educational system is in fact the central part of the ideological state apparatus and imposes the ideological hegemony of the ruling class. Contrast this with Durkheim (1956: 69) who not only believed in the need for a moral order but also felt that one existed: 'There is no people among whom there is not a certain number of ideas, sentiments and practices which education must inculcate in all children indiscriminately, to whatever social category they belong.' Durkheim was far too sophisticated not to realize that industrialized societies were composed of numerous social groups and classes, with conflicting interests and moral codes. The question is whether the differences could be contained, or better still subsumed, within a wider moral order. For Durkheim this is not just a possibility but rather a necessity.

For functionalists the problem with Durkheim's ideas is how to combine his stress upon the need for 'common ideas, sentiments and practices' with their own belief in the need for social differentiation. How can a consensual moral order be created if schooling perpetuates that social fragmentation which undermines consensus? The best that can be hoped for is a model of the social order in which, although inequality is pervasive, it is at least accepted as legitimate. And schooling then serves as the main agent of legitimation, which is far from Durkheim's understanding of what its purpose should be.

What should be clear from this analysis of the social reproduction theorists is that rarely have they considered seriously the question of educational change. With respect to the work of both Bernstein and Bourdieu the implication is that, until different forms of cultural capital are valued, the way schools organize knowledge is unlikely to change. In a class-based society what is culturally valued is dependent upon the distribution of class power. So the key to change is to effect a restructuring of class relations, and the related power structure. In similar, although more explicit vein Bowles and Gintis see educational change as a response to capitalism's need for new social relations of production. For example, they claim that the spread of the testing movement within the American educational system was in direct response to capitalism's need for a more carefully differentiated and formally certified workforce. Following precisely the same line of argument, although working within the microsociological tradition, Sharp and Green (1975:224) have argued that the expansion of progressive education in Britain during the 1960s reflected industry's need for workers whose individual qualities had been exposed, monitored and socialized by the schools. Roger Dale, working out of the Open University where Bowles' and Gintis' ideas seem to have been warmly embraced, has extended schooling's service to capitalism even further. He argues that the capitalist mode of production has three basic needs: support for the process of capital accumulation, a context which guarantees its continuing expansion, and the legitimation of its mode of production (Apple forthcoming).

Schooling changes in response to the evolving demands of these allegedly core problems. Given the extent of this service one wonders if schools can find the time, even granted the will, to serve any other social ends!

This side of the revolution the social reproduction theorists can scarcely conceive of any educational change which has important social consequences. All those changes which do take place serve only to stabilize the status quo, albeit perhaps in a new guise. Within itself this is a rather harmless, if absurd, view of the world, but it can and has led to a distortion of the historical record including a devaluation of the efforts of those who have worked to reform educational systems. More significantly their work contains no change dynamic; for all their moral fervour their ultimate message is both pessimistic and conservative. Nowhere is this better illustrated than in Bowles' and Gintis' *Schooling in Capitalist America*. For most of the book we are shown a pliable educational system that responds to the machinations of capitalism. Even the apparently most radical of reformers were either self-deluded or subtle advocates of corporate interests. And yet such is the authors' commitment to the ultimate demise of capitalism and the triumph of socialism that we are left with the picture of a rapidly disintegrating educational system. There is no explanation as to why this should be so, and even more significantly why, in view of all that has gone before, the established interests should not triumph once again – with capitalism and the class structure still intact. These problems stem from the failure to place any intervening stages between the alleged needs of capitalism and the experience of schooling. Either this is felt to be unnecessary (once the needs of capitalism have changed then everything else falls into place) or it is simply not part of the research focus.

It is possible to believe that schooling is strongly influenced by its economic context and yet feel that its institutions have a critical part to play in any struggle for social change (see Young & Whitty 1977). This seems the only way forward for a radical sociology of education; educational institutions have to be incorporated in the struggle for social change rather than seen as merely responding to the revolution which is fought for elsewhere. However, when it comes to making concrete proposals for educational reform self-confessed radicals find it difficult to distinguish themselves from well-meaning liberals. An example of this is Rachael Sharp's recent book (1980:164 ff). The issues which the radicals could fight over are as diverse as the access to educational resources or the social consequences of the prevailing organization of knowledge. Of course this raises questions about the relationship between schooling and society as well as the part intellectuals have to play in formulating and promoting counter-hegemonic ideologies. If schooling is to be incorporated meaningfully in the process of change then this necessitates a rejection of narrow structuralist theory or a functionalist Marxism. But the rebuttal of an arid scholasticism may be a small price to pay if it opens up the possibility of more effective political action.

The political dimension

Each of the three main phases in British educational sociology has contributed something to our understanding of educational change. Those who worked for the equalization of educational opportunities had a clear idea of what the change dynamic should be (but were less forthcoming as to what it actually was) and in time their ideas apparently changed the climate of educational opinion. Thanks to a certain amount of political sponsorship they are credited with at least influencing the move from selective to comprehensive secondary schooling. The new sociology of education leaves a more complex legacy. Its main contribution is its analysis of the experience of schooling, what has to be changed if innovation is to be socially effective. However, with respect to both the organization of knowledge and the nature of authority structures, it has clearly had an impact upon the educational system. In some cases this has amounted to very local and radical experiments conducted by particular teachers and heads, while in other cases broadly based and protracted negotiations have been followed by fairly widespread reforms in curriculum content, teaching methods and modes of assessment. The social reproduction theorists have considered what social pressures stimulate educational change, and have provided some illustrations of how these are eventually manifested within schooling, but they have said little about the change process itself i.e. how the social forces are translated into educational forms.

The purpose of this book is to provide a more complete view of the process of educational change. Chapter two presents our synopsis of that process with the following chapters developing in some detail its main features. If the purpose of educational sociology is to demonstrate how schooling links the individual to society then we see our contribution as adding a political dimension to that chain. Indeed it is our contention that without the inclusion of a political dimension any understanding of how the links have been constructed is defective. Dale (Apple forthcoming) has written,

Those political scientists who have focused on education have confined their studies very much to education politics rather than the politics of education. By this I mean that they have concentrated much more on studying the effectiveness of education systems and forms of education government in achieving goals presented to them, rather than on the relationship between the production of goals and the form of their achievement. To put it another way, political questions are bracketed out and replaced by questions about processes of decision making; politics are reduced to administration. The focus is on the machinery rather than on what powers it, or how and where it is directed.

We agree with this critique and consequently intend to transcend the rather descriptive analysis of the formal decision-making machinery which has generally passed for the politics of education. But unlike Dale we are more sympathetic to the view that the machinery is capable of self-generation and so determining for itself where it will be directed. Ironically Dale's faith in the dirigiste powers of 'the capitalist mode of production' results in a structuralist analysis which in fact denies the importance of politics. If the outcome is predetermined, no matter how uncertainly Dale may draw the threads together, then politics is vanquished and political analysis is largely descriptive.

This is not to suggest that our understanding of the political dimension is simply a pluralist struggle for power with an uncertain conclusion. Margaret Scotford Archer (1979:2) has written, 'Education has the characteristics it does because of the goals pursued by those who control it' and that 'change occurs because new educational goals are pursued by those who have the power to modify previous practices'. The end result is that the forms schooling assumes are 'the political products of power struggles'. These are little more than commonsense statements and as such would be generally approved. What we need to know is where educational power is located and what social forces determine this. In other words we need to determine the social dynamic of change.

Archer's own work provides two good illustrations of the danger in

analysing educational change without providing some understanding
of the determining social forces. She has argued that private schooling
in England undermined the movement towards comprehensive
secondary education as some direct grant grammar schools joined the
private sector, and that it counteracted the trend towards the
distribution of educational resources according to meritocratic criteria
by restricting entry mainly to those who could afford to pay the fees.
However, as we will later argue, the private schools have been forced
to embrace meritocratic values in spite of the restrictiveness of their
social intake (see pp. 168–78). Their appeal to parents is increasingly
based upon the examination successes of their pupils. Furthermore,
this is precisely why most of the direct grant grammar schools joined
the independent sector; many of their heads, teachers and governors
felt that the quality of the educational experience their schools offered
would decline if they became part of the comprehensive system. Of
course their motives may be suspect and their actions misguided or
worse, but equally what we may be witnessing is a struggle for what
the experience of schooling should be, with the private schools
leading the way towards a consensual definition. The essence of our
critique of Archer's work, therefore, is that without presenting a
change dynamic it is impossible to know how to interpret actual
examples of educational change. They remain bits of information to
be disposed of as the author sees fit; usually to be moulded into his or
her ideological predispositions.

The political dimension to the change process has to be placed
within its social context in order to understand the form that it
assumes. Accompanying these developments is a profound
ideological struggle the purpose of which is to promote the new social
ends of schooling and to legitimate the power of those institutions that
are moving into positions of ascendancy with respect to the control of
schooling. The object of attention is of course the experience of
schooling: its institutional arrangements, its hidden curriculum and,
above all else, the organization of knowledge. In its initial phase
British educational sociology combined a modified functionalist
theoretical perspective with a socially ameliorist morality. During its
second and third phases the diversification of the theoretical base has
been accompanied by the shifting of research attention into the
schools and classrooms. At the same time the policy positions have
become more radical, veering both to the right and to the left. Given
our conventional academic careers and little – we are pleased to say –

direct experience of schooling outside higher education (other than as victims) it is not surprising that our work is in the macrosociological tradition. Equally our interest in change, ideology and political negotiation flows out of our professional training as political scientists. As for our policy interests we will leave that for others to discern.

2

The Dynamic of Educational Change

The purpose of this chapter is to explain the increasing centralization of educational power, why the control of the dominant bureaucratic apparatus, the Department of Education and Science, is increasing and will continue to increase. Recently Professor Archer (1979; see also Williamson 1979) has proposed a very different thesis. She believes that the character of educational systems is strongly influenced by their social origins and that England, with its legacy of decentralized authority, will continue to have weak central control. Although we accept that the social origins of educational systems have important consequences for much of the contemporary character of schooling, our model suggests that these are continuously exposed to social forces that either destroy, confirm – or more likely – modify their legacy. Archer undoubtedly would concur, but whereas we believe that the evidence points to a very significant increase in centralized bureaucratic power, she concludes otherwise. To some extent the difference between us is more artificial than real. She concluded her research at just about the time that most of ours commences. We have drawn upon a more recent historical record, one which we believe substantially modifies her thesis. Archer also makes cross-national comparisons, and in these terms England may continue to have a decentralized educational system. We are more concerned with the national historical record, and it is our contention that the present-day Department of Education and Science now exercises substantially more control than its predecessor, the Ministry of Education which was created by the 1944 Education Act.

We are, however, very similar to Archer in as much as we believe that the dynamic for educational change is politically controlled. Much of the Marxist-inspired literature writes as if educational change in western industrialized societies is controlled in the interests of capitalism (Bowles & Gintis 1976); as those interests change so the experience of schooling is modified accordingly. It is part of our thesis that schooling is constrained by the needs of capital but if these needs are to influence the process of educational change they must be expressed in effective political terms. It is during this stage that the tensions, even contradictions, in the needs of capital will be revealed. We contend that the state bureaucratic apparatus has assumed the task of helping capital to define what its needs may be, of reconciling the tensions inherent in the definition of those needs, and demonstrating in more precise terms the ways in which schooling must change if these needs are to be met. Although certain Marxist writers have argued that the state apparatus has expanded its power, it is implied that the purpose is to ensure that the needs of capital can be better fulfilled by the educational system. This grossly misinterprets what is happening for the state apparatus has a degree of autonomy such as to negate the simple-minded determinism of some Marxists.

There are three parts to this chapter. In the first part we examine the interrelationship between the social determinants of educational change. In the second part we outline how shifts in the relative importance of these determinants have affected the distribution of educational power. In the third part we examine the various forms that educational change can take which is by way of mitigating somewhat the monolithic nature of the change process that we have been portraying so far. This third section brings us closer to the work of Archer who, in our opinion, has not proposed a theory of educational change but rather analysed the forms of educational change. As this is a book about educational change in contemporary Britain we have drawn most of the illustrative material from this context. However, as many of the western industrialized societies are facing very similar social and economic problems we believe the analysis has a wider applicability. Although – in deference to Archer – any such wider perspective must take into account the social origins of educational systems.

The social determinants of educational change

1 *The social ends of education*
The 1870 Education Act marked the first serious attempt of the state to construct an educational system. Although political support for this

initiative was by no means universal, it was widely believed that
continued economic prosperity was dependent upon it. As the first
industrialized nation, Britain throughout the nineteenth century had a
clear economic lead over its rivals but this was declining as the
century progressed. Some argued that our comparative decline was
because other nations, for example Germany and the United States,
had developed formal systems of schooling which resulted in a more
qualified, and better disciplined, labour force. So throughout its
history one of the main functions of schooling has been to produce a
labour force which will help the nation to hold its own against its
economic rivals. The continuity of this theme should provide some
measure of detachment from, even scepticism towards, the current
heated interest in how schooling can be reshaped to meet more fully
the needs of industry.

The quality of the labour force can be evaluated with respect to two
broad considerations − its technical competence and its discipline.
Schooling is meant to provide the requisite numbers of qualified
individuals (or if not qualified in precise terms for the labour market
then to have received the schooling which enables them to acquire the
necessary skills) for those areas of the economy where there is a
demand for them. So ideally the educational system is required to
provide the labour market with appropriately credentialled
individuals in the correct proportions. A disciplined labour force is
one which is prepared to accept the established social relations of
production i.e. it abides by the authority relationships which exist
within the workplace. For it makes little sense to train a labour force
which has the technical competence to ensure that the economy runs
smoothly but fails to do so because it is constantly questioning the
way that economy is socially organized.

A strong theme in much of the literature is that schooling has been
constructed more in the interests of producing a disciplined than a
technically competent workforce (Simon 1974:ch. 2). Drawing upon
the American experience Bowles and Gintis (1976:ch. 4) have argued
that for its successful reproduction capitalism requires a workforce
that is differentiated according to individual personality
characteristics, styles of self-preservation, ascriptive traits (e.g. sex,
race and age) and credentials, rather than according to individual
cognitive capacities and technical skills. They draw, therefore, a sharp
distinction between the technical and social relations of production.
We would like to hypothesize that they are not that clearly divided,

with credentialling providing a bridge between the two. Although it is obvious that social and personality factors intervene at the beginning of most processes of accreditation, it is equally obvious that both characteristics will be further refined as the process develops. Furthermore, credentials are likely to be a better measure of future job performance than cognitive capacity because, besides measuring at least in part this capacity, obtaining them also requires a variety of other qualities. Jencks (1972:180–185) has shown that the individual's formal qualifications do have a positive correlation with his occupational status and income if for no other reason than the fact that entry into (if not success within) different jobs is so often dependent upon the possession of credentials. He has also examined the comparative worth of credentials (1979:187–190). Formal qualifications become a means of differentiating between individuals with respect to various qualities and they act as a bridge between the social and technical relations of production by partially measuring cognitive capacity and predicting competence in the performance of technical skills. Although this is a debatable point, many employers believe formal qualifications have this predictable quality (Hussain 1976).

It is possible to reach different conclusions as to how well the British educational system has performed in producing both a technically competent and disciplined labour force. However, there is little support for the proposition that it has done consistently well in both respects. It is a common charge that schooling in England has placed a high value upon areas of knowledge that are of only marginal importance to the efficient operation of the economy, above all of its manufacturing sector. Moreover these high status knowledge areas have been embedded most firmly in those institutions, at all levels of the educational system, which have the most prestige. The traditional public school ethos is infamous for the attention it lavished upon the classics, and British universities have been castigated for their devaluation of applied sciences. The alleged consequence is that large numbers of highly talented individuals never think of pursuing a career in industry and the despised entrepreneurial spirit languishes for lack of replenishment. It is also possible to document periodic shortages in the provision of skilled manpower at all levels of the occupational hierarchy.

In contrast to this apparent failure to meet consistently the labour market requirements of a constantly changing, advanced technological society, it is generally conceded that the British educational system has provided a disciplined labour force. This is usually expressed in terms of the successful fulfilment of its social control function, i.e. schooling socializes individuals into accepting the authority patterns that are part of the social relations of production. The public schools, for example, did help to reconcile the interests of the bourgeoisie and the aristocracy, while the provision of state elementary education in the nineteenth century helped 'to civilize' the proletariat. The result has been a social order which is surprisingly stable.

Alternatively, it could be argued that schooling has failed with respect to both functions; we have a workforce that no longer has the technical competence to compete in the international market and we have forms of social control that make it difficult to rectify this state of affairs. Whereas some see social stability and harmony others see social stagnation and an outdated deference or, even worse, class attitudes which constantly fuel destructive conflict. Even if there is no inherent tension between reproducing the social and technical relations of production there is no guarantee that they can be harmonized in a manner which ensures that the mode of production, whatever form it may take, operates effectively. As long as there are no continuous economic or social crises then this state of affairs can be tolerated almost indefinitely. However, a protracted crisis of either nature calls into question the character of the educational system. This is not to suggest that educational change is capable of resolving such crises but given the historical responsibilities of schooling for these matters then such a response is inevitable.

The repeated economic crises, coupled with the nation's more long-term comparative economic decline, have finally triggered off this kind of response. Musgrave (1970:15–29) has argued that periods of educational consensus are usually followed by shorter periods of turmoil within which the major parameters of a revamped system of education are forged. Consensus then reasserts itself. We are now experiencing one of Musgrave's periods of turmoil. As yet it is difficult to state in precise terms what will emerge (although in our concluding chapter we consider what the prospects are), but there are repeated official pronouncements to the effect that schooling should serve the needs of industry more effectively (DES 1980, 1981a). Presumably this means discovering what those needs are and restructuring schools in the supposedly appropriate manner – neither of which is an easy task! However, if this is a serious endeavour – and we are persuaded that it is – then one of a number of things must occur. Schooling could be reshaped to enhance the technical competence of the workforce by reinforcing the general acquisition of basic skills and/or by providing specialized programmes for selected individuals. Alternatively, attention could be paid to improving the social attitudes of the workforce with the intention of improving (that is from the employer's point of view!) the social relations of production. The most likely outcome is the striking of a balance between these two objectives which would be accomplished most efficiently by programmes designed to achieve both ends at the same time. This means discovering what employers actually want (which may be different from what the economy needs if it is to perform effectively) and this is by no means an easy task (CPRS 1980).

It cannot be guaranteed, to use Musgrave's phraseology, that the new consensus that emerges after the period of turmoil will ensure a more positive relationship between schooling and the needs of the labour market. The attempted redirection is accompanied by a power struggle in which the different parties have their own interests to defend. Not only are some of these interests resistant to change (in the present confrontations teachers at all levels of the educational system have been very reluctant to budge) but also the likelihood of securing complete agreement as to the direction in which schooling should move is minimal. In such circumstances the likely outcome is a patched up series of compromises which ensure a tentative political peace but which leave the social and economic problems unresolved. Equally even complete victory for one party or the other may not lead to a solution (leaving aside the possibility that schooling may have only a minimal part to play in their resolution) for there may be no consensus as to what industry expects from its recruits or that such expectations can be defined in terms which changes in the experience of schooling are capable of meeting.

Although much of the political pressure for an expanding educational system was based upon economic and social considerations, this was coupled with more idealistic considerations concerning the welfare of the individual. In the previous chapter (pp. 14–19) we referred to that tradition in the sociology of education which supported the expansion of schooling with a view to improving the opportunities for working-class social mobility. At its very best an expanding commitment to public education was seen as desirable because it was believed that if citizenship in a mass democracy was to be fully meaningful it required schools to make it so. The commitment to expansion has not been accompanied by as much interest in the direction of growth. For the most part schooling has developed, especially in the fields of further and higher education, in response to the demands of its clientele (known rather perversely as social demand), with financial constraints acting as the final check upon growth. Nowhere is this better illustrated than in the expansion of the universities. The Robbins Report (1963:48–9) strongly supported the principle that all those who were minimally qualified for a university education should receive one and that universities should develop in response to this social demand. However, during the 1960s the universities were never capable of providing all the places demanded of them simply because they lacked sufficient financial resources. This did not represent positive financial control of demand as the meeting of commitments was determined by political muscle rather than by the need to fulfil planned goals.

Schooling, therefore, has been required to fulfil contradictory goals. On the one hand it has to ensure a technically qualified and disciplined workforce (and as we have argued these ends do not necessarily harmonize), while on the other hand it is required to provide programmes that meet the demands of its clients. Although we are uncertain as to what will emerge from the struggle to link schooling more closely to the needs of industry, it is evident that the principle of expansion in response to social demand will be severely curtailed. Even when the principle prevailed, periodic economic crises meant that its complete fulfilment was curtailed. Furthermore, the ultimate logic of the principle – that schooling should meet all the demands made of it no matter how esoteric they may be – could lead to absurd demands that few would be prepared to meet. At a time when educational budgets are being cut, and schooling is being directed tentatively along a new path, it is inevitable that the principle of resource allocation by social demand should be eroded.

The erosion of the principle could take different forms. The universities are being required to cut their student intake, and given the dictate that the misery should not be shared equally, some courses (the UGC has pointed its finger at the social sciences) will be more affected than others. If the course is not eradicated, or competition to gain admission severely intensified, this represents a direct attack upon the principle of resource allocation by social demand. Certain local education authorities, in response to the cutting of their budgets, have forced their schools to offer a more restricted curriculum. The schools can extend this only if pupils are prepared to pay for the additional options. Although there are legal complications surrounding such manoeuvres, if these can be resolved there is no logical reason why many subjects should not take their chances in the market place. It is possible that some subjects may be forced right out of the state system with the consequence that those parents who value them may have to opt for private schooling. A softer erosion of the principle occurs with the more 'positive' guidance of individual choices. In the present climate probably only a very resilient sixth-former can contemplate with complete equanimity reading for a sociology degree, even if he is confident of obtaining a place. Sixth-formers in effect are being warned off the social sciences.

In a protracted economic crisis of the three main social functions of schooling – providing qualified individuals for the labour market, acting as an agent of social control and serving as a resource for private consumption – it is the latter which is most threatened. Not only is it the principle which appears to offer least assistance to the resolution of the economic crisis but it also interferes – unless carefully guided – with the fulfilment of the two other principles. If employers need a disciplined workforce then the social control function will continue to be of importance. What needs to be spelt out is the precise social attitudes that are required, how these are to be related to the credentialling process, and how both can be expressed in forms of schooling. Although this is a very complex and lengthy process, it is shifts in the balance between these major social purposes of schooling that result in the most fundamental educational changes.

2   Demographic trends

The post-Second World War expansion of the British educational system owed much to the fact that the size of the school population was increasing steadily. In similar fashion the present contraction is partially a response to a declining school population. We are suggesting that it is difficult for educational policy-making to ignore the implications of demographic trends. The cutbacks in the budgets of the universities (while the number of home-based applicants is increasing) demonstrates that this is not always true, but we would see this as the exception rather than the rule. To work against the demographic trend (either to expand or to restrict the educational system in opposition to what the number of students dictates) usually means paying a political price that few governments, except in special circumstances, would be prepared to make.

Of course, neither expanding nor contracting an educational system necessarily means that the purpose of schooling will be reformulated; it may result in the provision of more, or less, of the same experiences. However, the contemporary falling enrolment, coupled with more meagre educational budgets, provides an ideal context for the redefinition of educational goals. The only way this could have been avoided was either by ignoring the differential impact of declining rolls, (for example, higher education has yet to be affected by them and, although this is about to change, has not experienced the same resource constraints as the schools), or by deciding that the burden should be distributed as evenly as possible. However, neither of these alternatives was politically feasible. As already stated it is much easier, all other things being equal, to cut those segments where rolls are declining. The fall in numbers helps to disguise the fact that budgets are being cut so that, although the overall expenditure may be smaller, the allocation per pupil may actually be higher. Furthermore, in view of the assumed importance of schooling for the functioning of the economy, it would be absurd to argue in the context of economic crisis that all that was required was less of the same. This would be a recipe for repeating the mistakes of the past.

3   *The political input*

If the political commitment of a government to a particular policy is high then it is unlikely to be resisted even if it should run contrary to the logic suggested by demographic trends and/or the need to readjust the social goals of schooling. A good example of this is the respective attitudes of the two major political parties to the independent schools. Both parties have deep-seated ideological predispositions on this topic and they feel compelled to act on these when in office. The present Conservative government introduced the assisted places scheme to enable parents, who might not have done otherwise, to send their children to independent schools. The Labour party is currently formulating proposals which it believes will lead to the final demise of the private sector once the party is returned to power. Neither the Conservative government's policy nor the Labour party's proposals have much bearing upon the pressing issues that today's educational system faces; they are monuments to their ideological traditions. We have seen the trimming of the present government's assisted places scheme (another partial victim of the cuts in educational spending) and only the most blinkered partisan can believe that the Labour party's proposals will not suffer a similar fate. Ideological commitments may be the life-blood of a political party but when it is a question of translating them into precise policies which governments are prepared to enact they have to compete for resources with what may be more pressing considerations.

During the current readjustment of educational goals both the main political parties have lent, at least while in office, their support to the process. The Prime Minister of the day, James Callaghan, initiated the Great Debate with his Ruskin College speech and ever since the DES has led a purposeful quest for a new experience of schooling geared more closely to the needs of the labour market. The present government, headed by Mrs Thatcher, has overseen the emergence of more concrete proposals, perhaps most notably in the field of curriculum development and in the restructuring of higher education, that is in both the university and polytechnic sectors.

The input of the politicians, whatever their formal power may be, consists essentially of providing general rhetorical support for the inevitable logic of the policy-making process. They simply lack the skills, time, resources and inclination to involve themselves in working out the detailed implications of demographic trends or what it means in specific educational terms to set new goals for schooling. If they hold office it is the civil servants who do this for them; if they are not ministers then they may all too often be trapped by slogans. If the political parties have defined policy positions these risk being squeezed out by more potent determinants of educational change, especially if they should run counter to the policy logic of these determinants.

Traditionally educational issues have not figured prominently in party conflicts. By the mid-1960s the dominant position within both the Labour and Conservative parties was a liberal consensus that supported an expanding educational system which enhanced the quality of individual lives and which improved the character of the social order, including the productive capacity of the economy. No such cross-party consensus exists at the present moment, certainly not one which is as dominant, but equally – with perhaps the exception of private education – few issues sharply divide the parties, and it is possible that a new consensus will emerge about the way schooling is to be restructured to meet its wider social obligations.

The location of educational power

Most of the literature on the distribution of educational power in Britain has painted the following picture (see pp. 88–91). Education was a centralized service administered locally in which three dominant power centres interacted; the DES, the LEAs and the teachers' unions of which the National Union of Teachers (NUT) was the most significant. Although other interests might be consulted from time to time, this was with reference to specific issues; in fact the established parties had a vested interest in excluding other groups from their incorporation in the policy-making process. The three parties established well-defined spheres of influence which were at least tacitly agreed to by the other parties. This explained the outrage of the teachers' unions when the DES established, without following the informally agreed procedures, the Curriculum Study Group (CSG). The Department had indeed broken the rules and was forced to back down. When matters of common interest had to be resolved lengthy negotiations followed to ensure consensual action. As Manzer (1970) has shown this did not prevent bitter conflicts from emerging but these were the exception. Finally all the parties recognized the importance of creating a favourable climate of public opinion; it was within this supportive environment that they could get on with the job of running an expanding educational service.

Although the DES had ultimate administrative control of the system, and the LEAs as employers of the teachers had considerable formal authority, the rule was that only in a crisis, and then only as a last resort, were the statutory powers used. Thus the DES usually supervised, rather than controlled the LEAs, while the latter preferred the teachers to be constrained by professional norms rather than bureaucratic regulations. In practice this meant the LEAs could develop, within broadly defined parameters, educational systems that they felt best suited their local circumstances, while it was unusual for anyone to question how individual teachers controlled their classrooms.

In this book we will present a very different understanding of the distribution of educational power in Britain (see, in particular, chapter five). We see the DES as increasingly dominating the other educational power centres. It is not a question of the DES removing either the teachers' unions or the LEAs from the policy-making arena; it has neither the authority nor the wish to do this. What it is doing is defining more carefully, and pulling in more tightly, the parameters within which the other power centres operate. In the past power was distributed pluralistically; more or less equal partners worked within a consensus, which they helped to refurbish, and reached decisions in which all of them could at least concur. Now the other power centres are forced increasingly to work within confines established by the DES; they are less like independent power bases with considerable freedom of action and more like subordinate authorities exercising diminishing influence through procedures that others control.

The shift in the balance of power is manifested in various ways. Neither teachers nor the LEAs have retained their sacrosanct spheres of influence. To assist in the extention of its influence the DES is not above introducing other parties into the policy-making arena. So to the great annoyance of the NUT (TES 1980:4) the Professional Association of Teachers (PAT) has been given a seat on the Burnham Committee which negotiates teachers' salaries. Not surprisingly in the search for a closer relationship between schooling and the needs of the labour market representatives of various segments of British industry have been consulted. LEAs and schools have been requested to pay more attention to the interests of parents, to include them in the governing bodies of schools and to provide them with more information about the character and performance of schools. Besides bringing in other parties, the DES is also prepared to act in a much more dirigiste manner than hitherto. This does not rule out consultation but the Department no longer acts as an aggregating body, searching for a consensus of opinion. It is prepared to state its own view of what the experience of schooling should look like (see, for example, its *A Framework for the School Curriculum*) and wait and see how others react to this. Of course it may modify its perspective in response to those reactions (see its more recent publication, *The School Curriculum*) but this is a very different style of operation than the quiet, behind-the-scenes consensus building to which we became accustomed.

As we have argued previously, educational policy has not been a traditional arena for fierce political party conflict. Up until the mid-1960s policy emerged out of a consensus-seeking pluralism. Since the mid-1960s, very much as a result of the pressure for

comprehensive secondary education, it has proved more difficult to
maintain a coherent educational establishment. There was a shift
from a consensus-seeking pluralism to conflict pluralism. In our
opinion this latter phase is now drawing to a close. We are moving
into a new era of consensus, one that is bureaucratically defined and
imposed.

As our chapter on the Department of Education and Science will
demonstrate, the above statements describe an emerging situation
rather than one which already exists. In certain respects the DES is
one of the weaker Whitehall departments exercising *less* control over
the LEAs than even some Chief Education Officers believe to be
desirable (Fiske 1980). In the absence of direct administrative control
of the educational institutions it will continue to work through
intermediary bodies like the LEAs and the UGC to make its influence
felt. Although on occasions this may enable the Department to deflect
criticisms, it is a less than satisfactory means of making its influence
felt. It is also not the sole master of its own house. In response to the
increase in youth unemployment the Youth Opportunities
Programme (YOP) of the Manpower Service Commission (MSC) has
expanded rapidly. As a consequence much of the training (it could
scarcely be called education) that many young people receive is
outside the auspices of the DES, which creates the possibility of
bureaucratic conflict. Finally, even within its own confines, it is not a
tightly knit bureaucratic organization. There are approximately five
hundred members of Her Majesty's Inspectorate who, however
pretentious it may seem, jealously guard their tenuous independence
from the rest of the Department (see pp. 109–11). This is important
because the inspectors are the Department's field officers and as such
can act as a two-way channel of communication. If the Inspectorate is
not fully in sympathy with departmental thinking then there is no
telling what may happen to the messages.

In spite of all these reservations we wish to stand by the thesis that
the central bureaucratic apparatus is steadily increasing its power.
What accounts for this state of affairs? The answer is that the
Department can respond more quickly and positively to the shifting
balance between the determinants of educational change than the
other traditional power centres. It has always been responsible for
monitoring the input of the political parties i.e. it translates party
programmes (which have in the past been little more than short
statements in a manifesto) into governmental policy. It is also better

informed than other institutions about the direction of demographic trends; it is therefore best able to predict the areas of expansion and contraction.

In the present-day redefining of the educational system the increasing power of the DES stems from its ability to provide some substance as to what the new goals of schooling should be and how the educational system should be reshaped to fulfil these. The teachers' unions have been very reluctant to enter these negotiations mainly because they fear that the consequence will be an erosion of the classroom authority of teachers and they see it as their task to defend this. This is especially so given the fact that redefinition is occurring at a time of contraction and this is one of the weapons used to bring about change. At the same time it is difficult for the LEAs to act in a concerted manner; they are split along political lines and they lack the close continuous institutional ties which would enable them to formulate general policy positions. In any case this is not part of their brief. This leaves only the Department, although we accept that both the Treasury and the Department of Environment have an interest in at least the amount, if not the direction, of expenditure, and that the MSC will play its part in reshaping educational goals, if not the form schooling will assume to achieve these.

The Department is best placed to initiate and orchestrate the discussions which will lead to the formulation of educational goals, to create those committees which carry the process one step further, to disseminate the findings that emerge from these committees, and to present the official response to the wider public reaction. At the same time it can put pressure on the local education authorities, schools and teachers to push the experience of schooling in the desired direction. How else can one interpret the Departmental documents on the common curriculum, the moves to reform the examination system, the impending legislation that requests schools to make more information available to parents, and the circulation of a question-naire to LEAs requesting information about the curricula their schools have adopted? In its past fulfilment of the social control function, the purpose of which was to legitimate social inequality, a decentralized educational system with considerable teacher autonomy probably helped the schools to achieve the goal more effectively. In the words of Bourdieu (see pp. 74–6) the process of social reproduction was disguised by teacher autonomy. But if schools are to serve the needs of industry effectively it makes no sense to·allow

competing definitions of what those needs may be or to permit
schooling to fulfil them in different ways. What is required are
universally agreed definitions which the experience of schooling
relates to in a standardized manner.

In its book on the recent history of the British educational system
(*Unpopular Education*), the Centre for Contemporary Cultural Studies
alleges that schooling is being restructured to meet the needs of the
capitalist economy. This is most clearly enunciated in their chapter on
the MSC. But nowhere is there a coherent statement of what those
needs may be and how schooling can be restructured to meet them.
All the evidence suggests that, although the reshaping of the
educational system may be in direct response to economic crises, it is
the DES which is leading the way in determining what the
educational response to this should be. The drafting of James
Callaghan's Ruskin speech, which initiated the Great Debate, was
strongly influenced by the Department, and the regional meetings
which followed this speech were organized by departmental officials,
as were those subsequent 'invited audience' only get-togethers (see
pp. 201–8). What may be emerging are new partnerships which will
replace the old triumvirate of Department, LEAs and teachers'
unions. But although it may be relatively easy to define the new
educational goals in very general terms, it is likely to prove much
more difficult specifying them in ways that can be met by the
experience of schooling. Which still begs the question of whether
schooling is that malleable, or whether those who are responsible for
initiating educational change will manage to get it right. A perfect
illustration of the latter difficulty is the UGC's attack upon the new,
technologically-biased universities of Aston, Bradford and Salford,
while supporting the expansion of the applied sciences across the
university sector at large. As part of its rearguard action the
University of Salford has persuaded many leading companies to rally
to its defence. If only the process of educational change were quite as
simple as some would lead us to believe!

What then is the dynamic of educational change? It is that policy
which emerges from those increasingly bureaucratically controlled
negotiations which are a response to the interaction between the
developing goals of schooling, the changing pattern of demographic
variables, and the nature of political (primarily political party) inputs.
Accompanying the dynamic is an intense ideological struggle, the
purpose of which is to redraw the relationship between the individual,

the experience of schooling, and the social order. What is required are ideological themes that are appropriate for the emerging social order. Just as the state bureaucratic apparatus can manipulate the institutional context within which the change process occurs so it can, but with probably a slimmer chance of securing equal success, dominate the ideological debate. Even those who may be excluded from the institutionalized negotiations by which policy emerges still have channels through which they can express their views. How effective these will be is another matter.

Change, therefore, occurs within three interrelated arenas. The first is the redefinition of the social ends of education and the restructuring of the experiences of schooling designed to achieve them. The second is the allocation of resources which will flow in the direction of those schooling experiences which apparently achieve those goals defined as necessary, and away from those schooling experiences deemed to be either redundant or at least not meriting state support. The third is the struggle between institutions for educational power. Changes within the first two arenas have a bearing upon changes in the third, but it is our contention that this may emerge as one of the more significant consequences of the contemporary struggle i.e. the location of educational power may shift more dramtically than either the goals of the educational system or the experience of schooling or the concomitant resource allocations. This hypothesis is still tentative and awaits the course of events for either confirmation or rejection.

Our understanding of the dynamic of educational change owes much to what Ranson (1980:14) has termed neo-systems theory for we have attempted to identify 'the key functional problems and dilemmas of the social system as the central explanatory axis' of change. But given the fact that these problems and dilemmas have to be resolved politically we also realize the importance of resource-dependency theory in shedding light upon the process of educational change. While neo-systems theory is crucial to understanding the dynamic of educational change, resource dependency theory (how institutions acquire resources and create mutual dependencies in the pursuit of their interests) makes sense of the process by which that dynamic is translated into educational forms, that is both of institutional change and of the experience of schooling.

Forms of educational change

Musgrave (1970:15–29) has made the obvious, but important observation that educational change is not all of the same type. We would draw a distinction along two dimensions: changing the institutional character of schooling, and changing the experience of schooling within educational institutions. For example, although the move towards comprehensive education has altered the structure of secondary education, whether it has also brought about new educational practices is more doubtful. With respect to the latter the change has been more localized, depending upon the initiative of, amongst others, individual teachers and heads. This suggests a contrast between centrally directed changes which have a general institutional impact and local initiatives which aim to change educational practice. More recently, the DES has opened up new possibilities by leading the fight for a common curriculum which could have a significant impact upon the experience of schooling. Change which is general in terms of its institutional scope and which completely reshapes the character of schooling is rare and invariably occurs gradually, a process which Archer (1979:617) has referred to as incrementalism. It seems fairly certain, for example, that raising the school-leaving age from 15 to 16 (which modified the institutional character of secondary schools) stimulated an accumulative change in pedagogical practices. In the face of a common problem, how to educate those who had previously left school at 15, the stimulus for curriculum innovation was high and it was to be expected that apparently successful models would be transferred between secondary schools.

Combining the two kinds of change results in the following categorization:

not. useful

TYPES OF EDUCATIONAL CHANGE

Impact upon the Institutional Character of Schooling	*Impact upon the Experience of Schooling*	
	Total	*Restricted*
General	Revolutionary	Reformist
Specific	Privatized	Localized

A great deal of educational change may be carried out entirely within the institutions of schooling themselves; concerning such items as the renegotiation of resource allocations, or a modification of teaching practices, or a reconstruction of administrative procedures. Alternatively local interests may negotiate directly with the educational institutions to provide courses that they require. In these cases a trade-off is likely to occur with the local interests providing the resources (or at least ensuring that they are forthcoming) and the educational institution offering its services in return for these. The potential gains for the latter are heightened goodwill amongst those who may have considerable local power, an increase in resource allocation over which internal discretion as to its distribution may be high, and more educational prestige as a result of offering possibly innovative courses. In some cases local interests have actually been instrumental in founding and funding educational institutions which were then meant to provide appropriate services for their creators. The growth of the civic universities throughout the nineteenth century is an example of this, and if some are to be believed (Thompson 1970), Warwick University is a comparable twentieth century expression.

The scale of the operation will influence the process of change. Where it is a question of internally initiated change the negotiations may be confined to the educational institution itself. The process is one of negotiation between the interested parties, teachers, administrators, governors and possibly students. The resources are varied: the formal powers of the respective parties, their numerical size, their prestige and the support they can muster. On occasions the internal negotiations can break down with the consequence that the issues are highly publicized, new issues are drawn into the conflict and external forces cannot be excluded from the debate. A most dramatic example of the latter are the conflicts which erupted in certain art colleges in the 1960s. These usually commenced with precise problems, for example renegotiating the status of fine art, but ended up by questioning the total character of higher education so that controlled internal negotiations quickly became a general mêlée in which all and sundry felt obliged to participate (Hornsey 1969).

Invariably the local education authority will be party to any negotiations for change. At the very least administrative clearance of, if not active support for innovative proposals will be required. Again whether this is more than a formality will depend upon what is being negotiated. As with internal innovation this form of change centres around élite negotiations; the interested parties trade off their respective resources until they reach a compromise which is either of benefit to all of them or some of the parties simply lose out. In some instances the state, usually in the form of the local administrative apparatus, may be actively engaged in helping to reach the compromise while in other cases it may simply approve the deal after it has been made. The difference probably depends upon the level of resources it is asked to provide; the higher the resource commitment the greater its continuous involvement in the negotiations.

The difference between localized and privatized educational change is that whereas the former seeks very precise modifications within the established pattern of schooling, the latter wishes to create a very different form of educational practice within a new institutional context, certainly one which is as free as possible from the restrictions that follow from being part of the state system. Some private schools, of which Summerhill is probably the best known (Neill 1969), fall into this category. The extent to which established practice is challenged in the classroom is a matter for research, but the commitment in theory to building the educational millenium is high.

Privatized educational change usually owes its inspiration to the work of one or more dedicated individuals, which partially explains why it is so restricted in scope. The resources of such individuals are limited in comparison with those of the state and they rely heavily upon the purity of their ideology to sustain the cause. Given their perception of the state such individuals are obviously keen to minimize its influence. If they are serious, therefore, about putting their educational ideas into practice they have to mobilize support amongst sympathetic benefactors (or attract a sufficient number of wealthy parents) or, as is the case with many free schools, work on a very small scale. Free schools may teach children who for one reason or another are excluded (or exclude themselves) from the state schools. Some local education authorities have sponsored experiments in free-school education; where this occurs the privatized model of change will approximate more closely to the localized model. For the most part, however, such change will take place almost unnoticed; quietly ignored by the established authorities who wait patiently for it to run its course.

The dominant form of state sponsored change in Britain has been reformist; it has had a general impact upon the institutional character of education but a more restricted influence upon the experience of schooling. It has restructured schooling (recasting, in Archer's terms

(1979: ch. 4), the extent to which it is unified and systematized) but until comparatively recently has fought shy of trying to reshape the organization of knowledge. Assessment was the main channel through which the state tried to control the latter, and this had the effect of confirming traditional practices and reinforcing the established institutional structure of schooling. However, a notable feature of the current conflict is that the character of the educational experience, almost forgotten by Archer in spite of the scope of her research, is now the focus of attention. Furthermore the impact of this is likely to be felt throughout the educational system. We may be witnessing something of a contradiction in terms – a state sponsored attempt at revolutionary change. But whether its remodelling of the experience of schooling will be that pronounced, or its influence upon the institutional character of formal education that deep or wide. remains to be seen.

3

Ideology and Change

Identifying the dynamic of educational change is one thing. Showing how that dynamic is expressed, or fails to be expressed, in the form of shifts in the educational structure, is quite another. It cannot be assumed that change will occur merely because the dynamic exists. On the contrary, unless other conditions for change are also met, the force of the dynamic will be either dissipated, thwarted or redefined and the potential for change will remain unrealized. It is with these other conditions for educational change, which intervene between the dynamic and its expression, that this chapter is concerned. In particular, we focus on the need of any putative educational change for legitimation through the propagation of a suitable ideology. In doing so we are building on the analysis of the previous chapter in order to detail further the context within which changes in the educational structure must emerge and the constraints which inevitably shape the form of its emergence. Although the discussion is primarily theoretical, it is intended to generate clear themes concerning the functions, mobilization, content and impact of ideology.

In developing these themes, we discuss first the legitimating function of ideology. This is not so straightforward as it may appear since 'legitimation' is a hazy concept and we have to be quite clear about its relationship to changing configurations of power. In the case of *educational* ideology this issue is further complicated by education's social control function: part of this function is education's legitimation of particular patterns of inequality. So educational ideology has the dual function of legitimating a specific power grouping while at the same time acting as an agent of social control. This means that the emergence of an educational ideology is likely to be a difficult process. Secondly, therefore, we explore the institutional context within which ideology is born and defined and consider the role of intellectuals in the formation and promotion of ideology. Different parts of an ideology provide different insights into the political functions it performs and so, thirdly, we develop a typology of the range of elements an educational ideology must contain to carry out its political tasks. Finally, we consider the implications of this approach to educational ideology for our theory of educational change. Throughout this discussion we emphasize the ways in which educational change is problematical and the tensions which exist both between base and superstructure and within the superstructure itself. This should not be taken to mean that all is possible and nothing predictable however. Subsequent chapters will deal with how educational change increasingly takes place within certain parameters of possibility. But for the present it is important to understand the details of the change process itself.

Legitimation and ideology

Weber (1968:953) has noted 'the generally observable need of any power, or even of any advantage in life, to justify itself'. Thus, in the case of education, if the interaction of social, economic and bureaucratic dynamics is to lead successfully to a reformulation of educational power, that change in the distribution of educational power has to be seen to be legitimate. Following Weber, Berger and Luckman (1971:110) argue that,

Legitimation produces new meanings that serve to integrate the meanings already attached to disparate institutional processes. The function of legitimation is to make objectively available and subjectively plausible the 'first order' objectivations that have been institutionalised.

And, also like Weber, they identify two principal components in the process of legitimation: the cognitive and the affective. Hence, legitimation ' "explains" the institutional order by ascribing cognitive validity to its objectivated meanings' and 'justifies the institutional order by giving a normative dignity to its natural imperatives' (Berger & Luckman 1971:119). This approach defines legitimation in terms of its political function on behalf of an authority: legitimation renders an authority valid and thereby fulfils a basic political need ·for its survival. A refinement of this approach advanced by Weber (1968:214) is that individuals or groups may treat a particular claim to legitimacy as valid, and thus confirm the position of the persons claiming authority, even though they do not entirely believe that this claim is valid.

If legitimation is the necessary instrument of power, ideology is the necessary instrument of legitimation. Legitimation cannot occur unless, to quote Berger and Luckman's (1971:141) conception of ideology, 'a particular definition of reality comes to be attached to a concrete power interest'. It is the responsibility of an ideology to supply that definition of reality and to provide the explanatory and justifying meanings on which the legitimation of a particular group interest depends. Without ideology, therefore, a group becomes politically vulnerable and probably unviable. The assumption on which this argument rests is that the distinctiveness of ideology lies in the fact that 'the *same* universe is interpreted in different ways, depending on concrete vested interests within the society in question' (Berger & Luckman: 141; their stress). We would agree with their position here and contrast it with the Marxist concept of ideological monopoly or hegemony.

The straightforward Marxist view of legitimation, ideology and hegemony is that ideas are inevitably class-based: they serve the function of legitimizing the economic and political power of the ruling class and depressing and regulating the aspirations of the subject class or classes. This is because as Marx (1965:39) put it, 'The class which has the means of material production at its disposal has control at the same time over the means of mental production, so that thereby, generally speaking, the ideas of those who lack the means of mental production are subject to it.' Through the manipulation of ideology the dominant class engenders a state of 'false consciousness' in the working class, disguising from the working class its real (i.e. exploitative) relations with the economic substratum of society. Successful ideological resistance by the working class is therefore unlikely since it remains unaware that such resistance is either necessary or possible.

The difficulty with this view is its emphasis on ideology as domination and its dismissive attitude towards ideology as challenge. It too readily assumes that the only political function of ideology worth considering is its contribution to the hegemony of the ruling class. As we shall see shortly, rigid adherence to this tenet has led to

some furrowed Marxist brows, notably Gramsci's. It has also led to
the tendency to use the concept of legitimation in a grand and
sweeping manner. Miliband's treatment of legitimation is a fine
example of the latter. For him (Miliband 1969: 261), the main purpose
of the process of legitimation is to prevent the spread of the
consciousness of an alternative social order through the maintenance
of ruling-class hegemony. This is, unfortunately, not a very dissective
approach and it leads Miliband to list the contribution of most of the
institutions of capitalist society to the legitimation of the social order.
Counter-legitimation and ideological conflict do not appear in
Miliband's model since his notion of inexorable ruling-class
hegemony necessarily excludes them.

Although the assumption regarding the monopoly of ideology by
the dominant class makes for uncomplicated analysis, it also severely
limits the specificity of the analysis. The assumption that a plurality of
ideologies may exist, on the other hand, necessarily promotes more
detailed study even though, in the event, such a plurality may be
shown not to exist. This second assumption forms the basis of our
own approach to ideology and means that we view its function as the
attempted legitimation of particular group interest, both to the
members of that group and to outsiders, while bearing in mind that
this group may be dominant or subordinate, aspiring or established.
Whether or not a particular ideology can be linked to the
establishment of hegemony by a group then becomes problematic; an
area of future analysis rather than a delimiting premise. This does not
deny that in the long term an ideology's success will largely depend
on the economic factors shaping the group's fortunes. But in the short
term no group can survive unless it can legitimate itself and its
activities.

Our concern to operate with a more specific definition of
ideological function is in large part a reflection of our interest in the
political institutions of education and, as we have already argued, the
clear need for more investigation of this part of the superstructure.
Until ideological developments can be tied to definite political
movements in education, discussions of the relationship between
broad economic shifts and educational change will remain little more
than guessing games. No educational change can occur without
ideological conflict between groups anxious to establish fresh
legitimations of their position and possibly a reordering of the power
hierarchy. The more severe the potential power redistribution, the

greater chance that new types of inequalities will arise in society because of it: these too need legitimating if those thus affected by the power conflict and the new inequalities are to retain their respect for the hierarchy as a whole. With the key role to play in legitimizing both the group it serves and the hierarchy it inhabits, ideologies in ferment are inevitably the harbingers of educational change.

By defining what ideas and arguments should be regarded as legitimate and a normal and acceptable part of political discourse, a dominant ideology controls the kinds of issues which are allowed to enter the political arena. This in turn means that such an ideology effectively sets the parameters within which preferred solutions are allowed to emerge. As we argue in detail in chapter nine, it is precisely this quality of ideological control and hence issue definition that the DES was striving to establish in the course of the Great Debate. By seizing the ideological initiative and then pushing it with the overwhelming resources of the educational state apparatus, the Department swiftly gained a political ascendancy which the teacher unions, partly due, admittedly, to their own incompetence, found it impossible to resist.

The mobilization of ideology

Whether or not an educational ideology is successfully mobilized and becomes the public representative of a particular group interest will be dependent, in the first instance, on the institutional context in which it and its host group are situated and, in the second instance, on the promotional resources it possesses in the form of allied intellectuals. Unless both of these conditions for the emergence of an ideology are appropriately fulfilled, both the ideology itself and the educational change it seeks to legitimate will remain stillborn.

1   *The institutional context*
In their writings on ideology, Gramsci (1957) and Hoare & Nowell Smith (1971; 1977) have usefully divided the superstructure of capitalist society into two parts in order to delineate more precisely the realm within which the ideological process takes place. These are political society (i.e. the state and its coercive apparatus – the army, police, prisons etc.) and civil society (i.e. the more private domain of parties, churches, families, education etc.). In both instances the state seeks to exercise its control but whereas in the former this control is

based on violence in the latter it works primarily through ideology. Indeed, Althusser explicitly refers to civil society as the Ideological State Apparatus (ISA) and juxtaposes it to political society, the Repressive State Apparatus (RSA). Furthermore, he is convinced that the dominant ideological apparatus in capitalist society is education; it having replaced the functions of the church in precapitalist society: 'no other Ideological State Apparatus', he remarks (1977:261) 'has the obligatory (and not least, free) audience of the totality of the children in the capitalist social formation, eight hours a day for five or six days out of seven.'

The point and the effect of this distinction is that for Althusser the function of ideology lies in the service of the state. Ideology is part and parcel of the imposition of ruling-class hegemony since it 'is the intermediation of the ruling ideology that ensures a (sometimes teeth-gritting) "harmony" between the Repressive State Apparatus and the different Ideological State Apparatuses' (1977:257). Its contribution is vital to the reproduction of the relations of production, that is, of the capitalist relations of exploitation.

While employing the same distinction between political and civil society, Gramsci is much less inclined to view the function of ideology in civil society solely in terms of ruling-class hegemony. In many ways, this belief in the need for a more flexible approach to the different parts of the superstructure reflects his non-mechanistic attitude towards the base–superstructure relationship as a whole:

The claim presented as an essential postulate of historical materialism, that every fluctuation of politics and ideology can be presented and expounded as an immediate expression of the structure [i.e. base], must be contested in theory as primitive infantilism, and combated in practice with the authentic testimony of Marx ... (Hoare & Nowell Smith 1971:407)

Marx, of course, was at times very hesitant over being too dogmatic about the actual interconnections between materialist conditions and ideological conceptions. As he ruefully pointed out (Bottomore & Rubel 1956:64): 'it is, in practice, much easier to discover by analysis the earthly core of the misty creations of religion than, conversely, to infer from the actual relations of life at any period the corresponding "spiritualized" forms of these relations.' This uncertainty, or more accurately scepticism, regarding any straightforward connections between economic base, state and civil society leads Gramsci to analyse these connections as much from the point of view of the forces opposing ruling-class hegemony as those promoting it. Hence he is concerned with the degree of equilibrium, or disequilibrium, between state and civil society and maintains that the correspondence between political institutions and the popular ideologies that support them may be either stable or precarious (see Boggs 1976:40–1). The correspondence may well exist but it may also be a tenuous one.

We would agree with Gramsci's general point that tensions exist both between base and superstructure and within the superstructure itself. To the extent that the dominant class succeeds in imposing ideological controls upon civil society, in channelling off challenges to its authority or in adapting its ideological stance to compromise with these challenges, it will preserve its hegemony. But it may not: there is no guarantee that it has the monopoly of available ideologies, that it can always fully control the ones it does sponsor, or that it will not be outmanoeuvred by the opposing ideologies of aspirant groups.

The assumption of this argument is clearly that although the origins of ideologies may, in some ultimate sense, be economic, in a more immediate explanatory sense ideologies are autonomous of the economic base. Let us elaborate this point. Ever the political pragmatist, Gramsci (1957:27) observed that the 'economists' failed to understand 'how mass ideological facts always lay behind mass economic phenomena and how at certain moments the automatic drive produced by the economic factor is slowed down, cramped or even broken up momentarily by traditional ideological elements.' He had good reason to know from his experiences with the Italian Communist Party (PSI) that even though the objective economic conditions of a society may favour revolution, it is another, and crucial question as to whether the ideological conditions are also right. In one of his frequent military metaphors he compared the cultural organizations of advanced societies to the trench system of warfare: though shelled they can still put up effective resistance. Economic crisis is not a sufficient condition for revolution (Bates 1975:363).

Although Gramsci is not entirely clear about how autonomous ideologies can be either from the economic base or from the state, he does allow for at least some autonomy in terms of both the ideologies' origins and their maintenance. This is in contrast to Althusser (1977:280) who in a rather throw-away last sentence remarks that 'ideologies are not born in the ISAs but from the social classes at grips in the class struggle: from their conditions of existence, their practices, their experience of the struggle etc.' He thus precludes the possibility of ISAs developing their own ideologies independently of their economic context. This in turn means that he has also excluded the capacity of ISAs to introduce considerable inefficiencies into the operation of ruling-class hegemony through their sponsorship of ideologies which may be functional to their own interests, both internal and external, but not coincide with the interests of the ruling class.

The problem which neither Gramsci nor Althusser face up to squarely is that in our increasingly complex society, group interests, and the ideologies supporting them, are expressed chiefly through highly bureaucratized institutions, such as those which make up the education system, which are quite capable of establishing their own logic of development in line with their own bureaucratic dynamic. So although Althusser may indeed view the education structure as a monolithic Ideological State Apparatus, we have previously shown in *Education and the Political Order* (Tapper & Salter 1978:ch. 7) how, in its more elevated echelons, education in fact harbours at least two ideologies in conflict with one another and sponsoring two competing definitions of élite group interests. One of these, the traditional university ideal, also illustrates how an institution can develop an ideological inertia and lack of flexibility, highly functional to the internal stability of the group concerned, in that values acquire the sanctity of age and permanence. However, these may also be values which if adhered to too rigidly can also undermine that group's power position and its place within the hegemonic order. For challenges can be mounted to a group's ideological status not only from opposing ideologies requiring a redefinition of the power hierarchy, but also from those which accept the status quo but believe they can perform the hegemonic function more efficiently. These ideologies are thus rivals rather than enemies.

In his classic study of bureaucracy Max Weber paid tribute to the capacity of this type of institution to preserve itself when he observed (Gerth & Wright Mills 1964:228) that 'once it is fully established, bureaucracy is among those social structures which are the hardest to destroy'. The permanence of bureaucracy is enhanced by its technical advantages (precision, speed, continuity etc.), the cult of the objective and indispensable expert; its hoarding and control of specialized knowledge; its use of secrecy to increase the superiority of the 'professionally informed'; and its general protective cloak of rational organization and operation. Naturally not all political institutions are fully bureaucratic, but if they are to compete effectively in the struggle for power and the manipulation of ideology this entails that they must have some bureaucratic characteristics. And insofar as they do have these characteristics, and the DES, for us, has all of them, the institutionalization of ideology is bound to place constraints upon an ideology's flexibility and adaptability. The permanence of its institutional context, therefore, is both a political necessity and at times a strategic hindrance.

Unless account is taken of ideology's immediate context, of the protection from the demands of the economic base afforded it by the host institution as well as the direction dictated by the institution's own bureaucratic dynamic, an oversimplified picture of its behaviour is bound to emerge. The tensions within the superstructure have to be seen not merely as a product of disharmony between political and civil society but of the relative autonomy afforded ideology by its institutional home within civil society itself. We will develop this argument further, and in specific terms, when we examine the educational state apparatus in chapter five.

2 *The role of intellectuals*

If the institutional context places limits on the way in which ideology can be mobilized, so also does the contribution made by intellectuals. In *The German Ideology* (1965 : 40) Marx defined intellectuals as 'the thinkers of the [ruling] class (its active, conceptive ideologists, who make the perfecting of the illusion of the class their chief source of livelihood)': that illusion being the view of 'its interest as the common interest of all members of society, put in an ideal form; it [the ruling class] will give its ideas the form of universality, and represent them as the only rational, universally valid ones.' Here intellectuals are cast in the role of the producers of ideology: they have a definite place in the division of labour on which the position of the ruling class rests. But that is really as far as it goes. Nowhere does Marx, or most of his successors, enter into any detail as to how the production of ideas occurs and how the happy coincidence of material interests and supporting ideology takes place. It remains an article of faith resting on the argument that what the ruling class needs it gets.

Apart from the fact that not all would share that faith, it does result in a static view of ideology production since it does not deal with the issue of hegemonic disruption; with the possibility that the intellectuals will not always be able to produce the right ideology at the right time ('right' for the ruling class that is); with the conception of ideology production as problematic. It assumes a natural symbiosis between the ideas produced by the intellectuals and the requirements of the dominant group which becomes unconvincing once challenged by the question of how ideologies change. But before dealing with this question we need first to elaborate further the definition of 'intellectuals' by considering in more detail their political function.

In an attempt to inject more sophistication into the Marxist treatment of intellectuals Gramsci distinguished two types: organic and traditional. Firstly, he maintained (Hoare & Nowell Smith 1971:5), every social group creates within itself 'organically one or more strata of intellectuals which give it homogeneity and an awareness of its own function not only in the economic but also in the social and political fields.' The fortunes of this type of intellectual are inextricably bound up with the fortunes of the group to which he belongs. But traditional intellectuals constitute a separate group in their own right, established over time as the result of the historical continuity of one organic type – Gramsci cites the historical example of the ecclesiastics and that is paralleled today by the universities which stand at the top of the knowledge status hierarchy. The function of traditional intellectuals is more extensive and elaborate than that of organic intellectuals; it has to be because it is the traditional intellectuals who act as the 'deputies' or 'officers' of the ruling class, acting on its behalf to implement the process of social hegemony.

For the traditional intellectuals to retain their superior authority over their rivals, we can add that a hierarchy of cultural prestige has to be maintained with the values that they espouse at its apex and towards which all significant ideological challenges to the status quo must address themselves. While the prestige of traditional intellectuals is assured hegemonic function is straightforward enough and consists of little more than reaffirmation of the dominant ideology. This is generally the case in periods of economic and social stability. However, when the economic base of society is more fluid and fresh types of inequalities emerge, then the hierarchy may come under stress as other groups and ideologies demand, through their own organic intellectuals, a reassessment of their place in the hierarchy, if not a redefinition of the hierarchy itself. Change of some kind has to occur and fresh legitimations of inequality must emerge. In addition, as universities are experiencing substantial cuts in their income, they are becoming acutely aware that their capacity to insulate the traditional intellectuals from outside pressures is strictly limited. The sudden interest in university–industry links, more applied and part-time courses and service to the local community is bound to expose the universities to the organic intellectuals of other groups, particularly of business, who may well demand a redefinition of the cultural hierarchy and concessions from the dominant university ideology. The universities may well find that in order to survive economically they, and their traditional intellectuals, are obliged to find an ideological form more in tune with the needs of the market (always excepting, Oxbridge, of course).

In many ways this idea of a cultural hierarchy dominated by the traditional intellectuals is similar to Weber's notion of status groups characterized by special 'styles of life'; status groups which parallel the class situation but are not synonymous with it (Gerth & Wright Mills 1964:190–4). Both ideas stem from the need to explain how systems of privilege are legitimated, how crude economic and power divisions in society are disguised and maintained by elaborate rationales supplemented by particular styles of life. Hence Weber points out (ibid.:191) how among privileged status groups there are status disqualifications which operate against the performance of common physical labour, against direct involvement in entrepreneurial activity and against the exploitation of literary or artistic activity for income. These are also the types of disqualifications operated by traditional intellectuals as they seek both to reinforce their dominance and demonstrate their manifest exclusiveness by putting as much cultural distance as possible between themselves and less privileged social groups.

However, reaffirmation of the traditional values as a response to challenges from the ideologies of other groups may not necessarily relieve the stress upon the dominant group and the traditional intellectuals if that stress is severe and backed by an uncertain economic future. Ideological adaptation is therefore called for if the existing hegemonic system is to survive, and it is at this point that the manner in which ideologies change becomes critical. The problem faced by traditional intellectuals in seeking to adapt the dominant ideology is more complex than that of other groups wishing to improve their ideological status: for the traditional intellectuals are functionally inhibited not only by the normal institutional constraints, but also by the fact that the hierarchy of cultural status on which their authority rests may well become unstable, should their adaptation of the dominant ideology prove unpopular, that is, dysfunctional, for other powerful groups in the hierarchy. What is likely, therefore, is that significant ideological change in a society, where the hegemony is amended rather than replaced, is preceded by a period of ideological trial, error, conflict and bargaining between the traditional intellectuals as representatives of the dominant group and the organic intellectuals of other groups. In this way room is allowed for the negotiation of a new hierarchy of status after the ideological conflict has been concluded.

The emergence of ideas to legitimize either particular group interests or sets of group interests arranged in a hierarchy of prestige is here construed as an uncertain process with no built-in guarantee of success. It may be that a group will, in the first instance, select ideas that do not adequately suit its interests. However, if the group is to survive as a political entity, reselection will necessarily have to occur. As Weber puts it:

But in time, ideas are discredited in the face of history unless they point in the direction of conduct that various groups promote. Ideas, selected and reinterpreted from the original doctrine, do gain an affinity with the interests of certain members of special strata; if they do not gain such an affinity, they are abandoned. (ibid.: 63)

The production of ideology through the selection of ideas can be a more or less efficient process. The longer it takes, the more at risk is either the position of a group or, if the traditional intellectuals are doing the selecting, the stability of the hegemonic order itself. According to this view, ideas are given a certain, though limited, independent ability to influence both group interest and the direction in which it impels group members. The very acceptance of an ideology imposes constraints on what a group can, and cannot legitimately do. Again quoting Weber (ibid.:63): 'very frequently the "world images" which have been created by "ideas" have, like switchmen, determined the tracks along which action has been pushed by the dynamic of interests.' In the long term, interests are paramount but in the short term if the appropriate ideology is not

Is it saying more than "you have to win arguments"?

forthcoming, a group and its interests may be politically annihilated or a hegemony destroyed.

Argo?

The production of ideology has to be conceived as a tortuous and continuing process if its full complexities are to be realized. To view it merely as the automatic reflection of economic interest or as yet another arm of state domination is a too deterministic and inflexible approach: there are far too many intervening institutional variables supplying ideology with considerable freedom of manoeuvre to permit such statements to stand detailed examination. Furthermore, once produced, an ideology's effect on the power of a group will depend on the answers to a number of questions concerning its operation, to none of which can answers be easily predicted. Firstly, how flexible is the ideology? As we have already discussed, part of the answer to this question lies in the nature of its institutional base. But part also lies in the logic of the ideology itself and in the way in which it relates, or does not relate, to the ideologies of other groups. The more exclusive an ideology, the less able is it to form alliances with others and hence the more isolated is the group whose position it seeks to legitimate. An insistence on purity of belief may benefit the internal cohesion of a group but inhibit its political manoeuvrability by precluding particular modes of ideological adaptation and compromise. The teaching profession is particularly vulnerable in this respect. It was noticeable in the course of the Great Debate that the rigid ideologies of some of the teachers' unions caused them to lose considerable political ground to the DES which was successfully forming ideological alliances with parents and industry alike (see pp. 208–12).

Secondly, there is the question of the political level, or levels, of operation for which an ideology equips a group. We shall deal with this issue again in the following section on the content of ideology, but the point needs to be made here that not all groups are equally ideologically prepared to participate in, or even enter, the same levels of political activity. In this respect a group may have to cut its ambition to suit its ideological cloth and accept that it does not have the ideology appropriate for operating at the highest political levels. From the point of view of the traditional intellectuals, this kind of limitation on the ideologies of new, potentially threatening groups is essential if they are not to be perpetually in a state of siege. For the system of hegemony to prevail ideologies, and their producers, have to be arranged hierarchically, so effectively controlling the access of groups to the different levels of political decision making by defining their aspirations accordingly. In terms of the model of the content of ideology which we develop in the following section, this means that some ideologies will not be so complete and fully realized as will others. Such a hierarchy is necessary because without it the hegemonic system would collapse since too many groups would see themselves as both deserving dominance and as ideologically equipped for it.

The content of educational ideology

Our discussion of ideology so far has been conducted in largely general and abstract terms. However, the content of educational ideology has, by definition, to be examined in specific terms though once again this is guided by an awareness of the political functions the ideology must perform. The model of educational ideology we shall construct is an ideal type from which it is to be expected that the ideologies of the real world will deviate in terms of both emphasis and scope. As we mentioned, some ideologies are necessarily more developed than others in order that there can be a division of political labour regarding the different political levels at which they are equipped to compete. The important analytical objective is to be able to use concepts which are linked and ordered according to their political function in order to distinguish the way in which ideologies differ.

Firstly, behind all educational ideologies lies an idea of the social order, which the ideology both explains in terms of the contribution education can make towards it and legitimates through the propagation of this explanation. The desired society is not always an explicit part of the ideology, however, since one of the more useful aspects of educational ideologies has been their claim to be apolitical, to be concerned with their education of the individual and nothing more, thus disguising their legitimating function by a denial that such a wider function could be part of the specialized activity in which they are engaged. But that the desired society *is* always a part of a fully developed educational ideology, be it overt or concealed, becomes apparent once we consider the second component: the desired product.

In his discussion of education, Bertrand Russell (1926: 38) wrote that 'We must have some conception of the kind of person we wish to

produce, before we can have any definite opinion as to the education
we consider best.' (His discussion, incidentally, contains all of the
ingredients of educational ideology with which we deal here.) For
him the desired product was 'a harmonious character, constructive
rather than destructive, affectionate rather than sullen, courageous,
frank and intelligent' (ibid.: 246). No individual exists in a social
vacuum, however, and to make sense of the desired educational
products we are obliged to envisage the system of social relations in
which they relate one to the other. Clearly, in Russell's case, social
harmony can be assumed to result from the interaction of other-
oriented individuals existing in a liberal and pluralistic social context –
i.e. the desired society. Very few educational ideologies are this
uniform in their portrayal of the desired product. More common is it
to present a distribution of types of persons produced which in turn
can readily assume a hierarchical social order. They may be presented
as a natural fostering of innate capacities which just happens to
produce some individuals with intellectual skills and others with
manual skills. This leads us into the third component: the conception
of human nature on which an ideology is founded.

Within an educational ideology the desired products of education
interrelate in a way which gives rise to the desired society. But for
individuals to be fashioned into 'well-rounded gentlemen' or 'hewers
of wood and drawers of water' there should be some conception of
the raw material being worked upon since this places constraints on
what education is able to achieve. Are human beings innately good or
bad? Do they inherit capacities which are specific enough to
predetermine the lines of their development or are they empty vessels
merely waiting to be filled? The conception of human nature on
which an educational ideology is based represents the final point of
logical regression in its argument beyond which there can be no
discussion. Certain types of education are necessary, it is argued,
because certain individual characteristics are inevitable; they are facts
of life which have to be recognized and dealt with accordingly. Or so
the proponents of particular ideologies would have us believe.

As articles of faith presented as empirical reality, conceptions of
human nature supply the ultimate limitation on the fourth
component: the educational means to the ends of desired individual
and desired society. The educational means are of course the
educational structure and processes, generally the most visible part of
an ideology, and conflicts tend to centre around the extent and form of

institutional differentiation, modes of assessment, curriculum content and teaching methods. Depending on the ideology, these elements are arranged in different ways and according to different priorities to maximize the different individual and societal goals.

The objective of these four components is to be able to legitimize, either singly or in varying combinations, the power of a group, its aspirations for more power if it has them, the political order it prefers and the inequalities associated with that order. Given this political function of educational ideology, its analysis should begin with the identification of the desired society in conjunction with the type(s) of individual preferably produced by education, then consider the conception of human nature constraining both these ideological goals and, subsequently, the educational means to achieving them. In diagrammatic form:

EDUCATIONAL IDEOLOGY: COMPONENTS AND FUNCTIONS

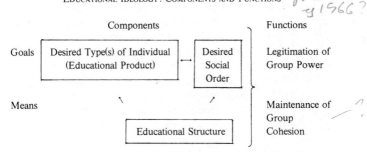

Our model of educational ideology therefore warns against taking the face value of an ideology as the end point of the analysis: the power position of the group has to be considered to discover whether there are any hidden political functions. It is nevertheless true that some educational ideologies are more complex and more sophisticated than others and therefore better able to legitimate the interests of their groups. The lower level ideologies focus almost exclusively on the educational structure and processes (the 'means' component) and are consequently unable, and perhaps do not aspire to promote their group beyond the educational system. But if a group is to stake any claim to a place in the higher echelons of society then it has to possess an educational ideology which incorporates goals as well as means. It has, if necessary, to be able to legitimate in educational terms its conception of what the social order should look like.

Educational ideology and educational change

As a central and highly visible set of institutions in modern society education is obliged to change in the full glare of the public eye. Too many people are likely to be affected by even the more minor or structural shifts for such change to be carried out covertly: not merely those with a direct political interest (teachers' unions, LEAs etc.) but also parents who are increasingly demanding to be consulted over the kind of education their children receive. Furthermore, too much public money is invested in education for significant reallocations of the spending pattern to occur without due public debate. The context within which educational change must occur is insistent upon this change being conducted explicitly and consciously at the ideological level.

Our discussion in this chapter has indicated that there are several reasons why this process of ideological change is a difficult one, why, in the course of their development, group ideologies respond to factors that promote a form of interaction which, in the short term at least, can easily be at variance with the pressures and demands of the economic base. Firstly, the requirements of an ideology's host institution and its place in the hegemonic hierarchy impose considerable limitations on the ways in which the ideology can be used to legitimate a group's position and the manner in which it can adapt to demands for change. The institution's own bureaucratic dynamic may well impose constraints on the type of ideology which is suitable to its projected development. This relative autonomy of institution and ideology both from the economic base and the state results in a system of ideological hegemony which has to be seen as problematic rather than automatic. As a key structure in any such system, education contains ideological tensions in abundance since it includes in the universities many of the traditional intellectuals (the officers of the status quo), many of their opponents ('radical' intellectuals), and at the same time is becoming formally responsible for producing the trained manpower for a rapidly changing technological society.

Secondly, the ideological phase of educational change is rendered more complex by the varying levels of development of the different ideological positions. The capacity of a group to initiate change is limited by the scope of its ideology: how many of the components of educational ideology discussed above does this ideology possess and how convincingly are they interrelated? On the answer to that question will depend the group's ability to compete at the higher political levels where full-blown educational ideologies already dominate. Some groups are better qualified than others in this respect and therefore a hierarchy of groups can be said to exist in terms of the sophistication and quality of their ideologies. And insofar as that hierarchy is a stable one, it is also a system of hegemony.

Thirdly, whether or not a potential educational change can be legitimated will depend on the availability and skills of intellectuals capable of building and maintaining a sound ideological position on behalf of an aspirant group. Such intellectuals may not always be forthcoming and although a group can proceed so far without them, relying on raw power politics, once it is forced into the public arena and made to justify the educational change it is advocating the absence of an ideological cloak renders it highly vulnerable. For that reason, educational change without ideological legitimation may be possible but it will also be short-lived.

Finally, the role of ideology in educational change is complicated by the fact that it has to be functional both for the group sponsoring it (i.e. it must bolster the group's power) and for the broader social and economic pressures to which education is inevitably subject. It is perfectly possible that tension may arise between these two functions: there is no natural symbiosis between the political and socio-economic demands placed upon educational ideology. As we pointed out in *Education and the Political Order* (1978: 142–68), one of the strengths of the DES's economic ideology of education is that it combines a justification for the extension of the Department's managerial power with the idea of education as the servant of the economy. What we will investigate later in this book is how secure that combination is and how it is currently being promoted.

Too vague to mean much

4

Schooling and the Organization of Knowledge

The focus of educational change

We have argued that educational change is primarily a response to the shifting social ends of schooling (see pp. 31–40). Central to this process of educational change are complex political negotiations by means of which innovatory pressures are translated into classroom practice. It is our contention that these political negotiations are increasingly dominated by the state educational apparatus, in particular the DES (see ch. 5). Accompanying the change process is an ideological struggle in which new models of the educated man, the desired social order and the character of the educational system emerge to compete with the established models (see pp. 62–5). So far we have raised a number of interrelated questions: What is the dynamic of educational change? Who or what controls the process of educational change? What are the resources that ensure this control and how are these employed? Besides answering these questions we need to know the precise focus of the change process. What particular aspects of the experience of schooling is the change dynamic directed at restructuring?

Most of the limited attention we have paid to this question has been concerned with the broad institutional features of the educational system. It is reasonable to maintain, however, that such aspects of schooling can be altered without unduly disturbing the educational experience that is being offered. For example, even if comprehensive secondary schools embraced both the full range of the ability and all social classes, it is nonetheless conceivable that the education given to any individual pupil would be scarcely different from that he or she might receive in a secondary school with a selected intake. Seen in this light, if educational change is to be effective it has to alter the kinds of experiences that schools offer as well as the distribution of those experiences amongst their pupils.

This is not to suggest that those who try to control the process of educational change will necessarily intervene directly in the daily affairs of schools. Control of the experience of schooling can be indirect, it may occur within parameters which define unacceptable, rather than acceptable practice. However, if the guidelines as to unacceptable practice are sufficiently detailed then the room for manoeuvre will be very restricted. A central aspect of the history of the British educational system has been the teachers' struggle for professional autonomy. One measure of their comparative success has been the extent to which they eventually achieved *de facto* control of the day-to-day affairs of the school. The consequence is that external social pressures upon the experience of schooling have been felt indirectly, through, for example, the pervasive influence of the socialization of teachers and the powerful constraints that follow from the presence of external examinations. In recent years more direct and explicit forms of state intervention, expressed most emotively in the struggle for a common curriculum, have emerged. We appear to be moving towards a centralized definition of acceptable practice accompanied, – inevitably – by more explicit control of the experience of schooling.

Scarcely ten years ago Davies (1971:273) could reproach British educational sociology with the claim that, 'Unfortunately what is often taken to be the sociology of education is not primarily about education at all – but about selection and stratification, socialization and organizations'. In Davies's opinion how educational institutions 'manage knowledge' should constitute the central focus of educational sociology. Since then, under the guise mainly of curriculum studies, British educational sociology has in fact been inundated by research into the management of knowledge. So much so that at times it is difficult to escape the impression that the trivial reigns supreme as one ex-teacher after the next, drawing upon frontier experiences and connections, tries to escape the classroom and cocoon himself in an institution of higher education or research establishment.

If the ultimate purpose of educational change is to restructure the experience of schooling, including the management of knowledge within educational institutions, then it is impossible to conclude with such a negative evaluation of the 'new' sociology of education, as it is quaintly known. The purpose of this chapter is, therefore, threefold: to describe more precisely the focus of the change process (the experience of schooling is, to say the least, a vague concept), to evaluate some of the debate as to the most viable strategy of educational change, and to suggest a general guideline for interpreting the social significance of changes in schooling. This chapter will compare two interpretations of the experience of schooling, that of the macrosociologists and that of those who are more concerned (at least initially) to understand classroom practices.

The organization of knowledge

Three aspects of schooling have received most sociological attention: the organization of knowledge (see Bernstein 1971:ch. 11), the organization of educational institutions within which knowledge is transmitted, and the behaviour of those who are responsible for transmitting knowledge (see Grace 1978:191). There is a broad consensus within the contemporary sociological literature that the most crucial aspects of the experience of schooling are a product of the organization of knowledge. The consensus encompasses differing theoretical perspectives, ideological positions and empirical research.

The organization of knowledge has three components: the content of education (what is taught), pedagogy (how that content is transmitted), and evaluation (the methods used to ascertain whether the content has been internalized and understood). Intrinsic to the formal content of schooling is the status of the various ingredients of which it is composed and how these ingredients are distributed amongst pupils. If a clear understanding of high status knowledge prevails, and certain kinds of pupils are more likely to partake of it than others, then this makes for a very special type of schooling experience. Pedagogy consists of both the overall organization of the curriculum as well as the individual styles of transmitting areas of special responsibility. Naturally how the curriculum is structured is likely to influence individual teaching methods. A subject-based curriculum, associated with rigid, externally controlled evaluation procedures, has often been accompanied by a didactic teaching method, while an integrated curriculum, especially if evaluation procedures are internally controlled, is sometimes accompanied by various experiments in 'learning through doing'. Evaluation is composed of not only the highly formalized examinations that have been such a marked feature of the educational lives of English grammar-school children but also by continuous assessment that seems to intrude everywhere.

In the mid-1960s, when British educational sociology started to break away from its preoccupation with the relationship between schooling and social stratification, the focus switched to the formal and informal organization of the school (see Hargreaves 1967; Lacey 1970). In spite of the importance of this perspective, to which we will return shortly, much of the formal organization of educational institutions is based upon the curriculum — what is to be taught, to whom, where and for how long. At the same time the hidden curriculum of the school is heavily dependent upon the character of the formal curriculum. Therefore changes in the internal organization of the school are invariably the companion to curriculum change. Where they are not it is legitimate to question whether they will have much impact upon changing the experience of schooling. This is not to deny that a settled structure and routine can ossify into organizational inertia; the established order guarantees a quiet life so few are prepared to upset the applecart. To do so raises too many questions about the distribution of power and material rewards within educational institutions. But even in these situations it is highly likely that the administrative status quo will be legitimated in terms of the way that it allegedly enhances the organization of knowledge, and likewise the desire for change will have to be justified along similar lines. In educational institutions bureaucratic routine is a precarious legitimation for the maintenance of the established order. So although a few aspects of school organization may have no bearing upon the organization of knowledge, the latter is at the heart of the former.

Besides determining the organization of the school the structuring of knowledge also shapes, at least in the long run, the working lives of teachers, for it defines the status of subject areas; governs the distribution of staff and pupils amongst those subject areas; influences how subject areas will interact with one another so channelling both the formal and informal interaction of teachers; impinges upon how teachers are to be trained, evaluated and what promotion prospects they may reasonably expect; determines the use of nonspecialist personnel; and structures the working routines of both teachers and pupils. The essence of our argument, therefore, is that whoever controls the organization of knowledge also controls the experience of schooling. The power that teachers wield is dependent upon the general recognition that they have special authority with respect to the organization of knowledge. This authority, which they share with others in the educational system, stems from their professional training (they have learnt what knowledge is and how to transmit it) and their day-to-day responsibility for managing those institutions which have the task of dispensing knowledge. If this special authority is denied, and actual steps are taken to remove its consequences, then the power of teachers within the educational system is at an end.

Changing the organization of knowledge

If the organization of knowledge is central to the experience of schooling then we need to know how it is changed and how to ascertain the social implications of such changes. The focal point for our analysis is the individual teacher, for the four positions we intend to review each consider in some detail the role of the teacher in the process of changing the organization of knowledge. In view of the teacher's *de facto* responsibility for classroom practice (regardless of where formal control of the curriculum may or may not rest) the widespread interest in the role of the teacher in the change process is to be expected.

1   *The social construction of reality*

One important dimension of the new sociology of education is the claim that the individual's consciousness is shaped partially by the kinds of interpersonal relations that occur within institutions like schools (see Hargreaves 1972). (This is not to deny the role of other social institutions, especially the family.) The school creates various social contexts (in particular the classroom, with invariably one teacher responsible for the education of a number of pupils) within which individuals interact with one another, and in the process views of reality are constructed. The implication is that teachers occupy a very sensitive position in the construction of children's images of reality and, in theory, different teachers can bring about different world views. If this perspective is accepted then the logical conclusion is that teachers are critical to the process of educational change. If consciousness is a product of interpersonal relations, and teachers are not prepared to structure these differently, then any change dynamic will run up against a wall of teacher resistance.

What gives this position a real cutting edge in the British context is the amount of classroom authority that teachers have traditionally exercised. Teachers, and more especially headteachers and heads of departments, have controlled the curriculum, both *what* is taught, and *how* it is taught. Because this authority is generally exercised within socially agreed limits, it is rarely called into question. However, when it is apparently abused one can expect the official position to be firmly reiterated. This is precisely what happened in the wake of the fracas surrounding the William Tyndale Junior School. A radical reorganization of knowledge within that school resulted in a fierce political battle. The subsequent official enquiry, led significantly by a Queen's Counsel, noted that under the powers granted to it by the 1944 Education Act the ILEA had established rules of management which vested control of the curriculum in the hands of the headteacher but *subject to the oversight of school managers*. Furthermore, the Authority retained the right to reinvest, wholly or partly, in its *own* hands control of the school's curriculum (Auld Report 1976: 5–6, 269). In this case, therefore, the ultimate control of the curriculum – clarified only when it came to the political crunch – did *not* reside in the school.

The slow but steady emergence of a common curriculum threatens to limit further the British teacher's classroom authority. Regardless of what is taught, schools will still create patterns of interpersonal relations, but a common curriculum lessens the discretion of the teacher in structuring the classroom context. This would be especially true if the introduction of the common curriculum were to be accompanied by a close monitoring of individual performance levels. What is therefore suggested is the obvious i.e. all the actors, including teachers, are constrained in their social construction of reality. Few would dispute this but there are legitimate differences as to the precise nature of the constraints, what discretion teachers can exercise in interpreting these, and how far they can proceed with this before risking external intervention. After all there may be many William Tyndales that never see the light of day. It is surely precisely this fear that fuels the movement towards the common curriculum.

2 The reproduction of the social order

With the exception of Bowles and Gintis, the social reproduction theorists rely heavily upon how educational institutions organize knowledge to substantiate their belief that the social purpose of schooling is to reproduce the pattern of class relations and its concomitant power structure. Various dimensions form part of this theory. It is possible to pick out very specific aspects of the organization of knowledge that assist the perpetuation of the class structure. For example, one consequence of the schools' alleged failure 'to recognise and utilise the diversity of pupils' cultural backgrounds and experiences' is a restricted definition of what counts as knowledge, and even more so of what counts as high status knowledge (Flude 1974:20). The outcome is that working-class pupils have to compete with their middle-class peers on unfavourable terms for they lack the cultural supports which ensure success in the fields of high status knowledge.

In direct contrast to the enumeration of very precise working-class disadvantages is the sweeping claim that knowledge is socially constructed and the dominant class attempts to perpetuate those constructions of reality which enable it to maintain its power. Whether this is a philosophically sound definition of what knowledge is seems most improbable, but suitably modified it is a central tenet in the work of those who maintain that schools perpetuate social reproduction through cultural reproduction. Bernstein (see 1975) avoids the question of what knowledge is in favour of illustrating how it has been organized within the British educational system. In his early work on sociolinguistics he attempted (1971:239) 'to demonstrate how the class structure affected the social distribution of privileged meanings and the interpretative procedures which generated them'. In his more recent discussion of 'the classification and framing of educational knowledge' Bernstein (ibid.:241) illustrates how the class-based language codes are reinforced by schooling to reproduce a particular class structure. Using the more embracing term of cultural capital, Bourdieu has both extended and clarified Bernstein's propositions whilst reinforcing his basic theoretical position.

For both Bernstein and Bourdieu, therefore, the perpetuation of class power is not simply a consequence of the direct control that dominant classes exercise over the organization of knowledge, but rather how that knowledge itself is structured to value certain cultural characteristics (which they believe are class-determined) over others. The reproduction of the class structure is thereby disguised and legitimized. For Bourdieu the process of social reproduction is further legitimized by the relative autonomy (not independence nor neutrality) he accords the teaching profession. Teachers act as an apparently independent group of professionals, cloaked in the relevant expertise, distributing knowledge to all those who have the capacity to learn.

Regardless, therefore, whether the emphasis is upon very specific aspects of formal schooling, or whether schooling is related to its social context in very broad terms, this sociological tradition sees the management of knowledge, and the part teachers play in that management, as a powerful force for the reproduction and legitimation of social inequality. In the headlong rush to refute (and rightly refute) both the simpleminded claim that knowledge is defined by the dominant class, and the extreme variations in the definitions of knowledge to which this can lead, that point is all too easily overlooked (see Flew 1976:ch. 2; Bernbaum 1977:49 ff.). Even as virulent a critic of 'relativism' as Hirst (1974:50–3) accepts that certain features of the prevailing organization of knowledge do not promote what he terms a liberal education. Not surprisingly, to legitimate the reproduction of social inequality through the organization of knowledge, and with the full cooperation of the teaching profession, is to place social privilege on an exceedingly powerful basis. For many knowledge is a sacrosanct concept and to tamper with its transmission would be tantamount to committing an act of sacrilege.

The social reproduction theorists view the role of the teacher in the process of educational change in a very different light from those who have stressed that reality is socially constructed. They differ sharply as to the constraints that bear down upon the differing actors within the context of the school and classroom. Bourdieu has written (Bourdieu & Passeron 1977:95): 'every transformation of the educational system takes place in accordance with a logic in which the structure and function proper to the system continue to be expressed'. In the light of this one can only wonder if the relative autonomy that Bourdieu accords the professional educators has any significance beyond enabling them to legitimate imposed social goals. This rules out much leeway for individual interpretations of their role and most definitely denies them the political power to resist the demands of the dominant classes.

The macrosociology of Berstein and Bourdieu is reinforced by some of the British empirical research into classroom practice. Keddie (1971:156) has concluded, on the basis of observations collated 'in a large mixed comprehensive school with a fairly heterogeneous social class intake', that, 'It seems unlikely, therefore, that innovation in schools will not be of a very radical kind unless the categories teachers use to organize what they know about pupils and to determine what counts as knowledge undergo a fundamental change.' It is her contention that these categories can thwart the best-intentioned changes both to the curriculum and to school organization. The key question, therefore, is where do teachers obtain the categories which enable them to make sense of their working lives? With specific reference to the concept of ability she has argued that teachers categorize pupils largely on the basis of 'social class judgements' of their 'social, moral and intellectual behaviour' (ibid.: 155). Of course this begs the further question of how teachers acquire their particular social class judgements. Presumably (although Keddie is not forthcoming on this point) the answer would emerge from examining the social origins of teachers, their socialization experiences, their personal aspirations, and views of the social order. One would want to know to what extent they have internalized a defined worldview which they then use to guide their classroom practice.

Sharp and Green (1975: viii), extending and embellishing Keddie's idea that teachers' concepts are a powerful tool of social control, have – on the basis of analysing teaching practice in one 'Junior Mixed and Infants School' – arrived at the extremely provocative conclusion 'that the radicalism of the "progressive educator" may well be a modern form of conservatism, and an effective form of social control in both the narrow sense of achieving discipline in the classroom and the wider sense of contributing to the promotion of a static social order'. In their opinion because progressive education can manipulate a wide range of personal characteristics it is in tune with the forms of social control required by advanced capitalist societies; besides the intellect it monitors 'the social, emotional, aesthetic and even physical' development of pupils (ibid.: 224–5). This suggests a correspondence between schooling and society very similar to what we found in the research of Bowles and Gintis and, not surprisingly, their respective disparagements of progressive education are almost identical. In this very straightforward correspondence thesis the teacher is an instrument of the power structure entrapped within a mechanistic change process. The more he seems to escape the demands of capitalism the more he is in fact subject to its influence.

Whereas Keddie and Sharp and Green have tried to demonstrate how aspects of the experience of schooling result in the reproduction of the class structure, Willis (1977) sees the cultural appeal of working-class life styles as achieving the same end. Those pupils who are 'rejected by' the school turn increasingly to their working-class backgrounds in order to give their lives some meaning and to provide themselves with a sense of personal dignity. And yet it is through this very culture, with its glorification of manual work, that they 'learn to labour'. Willis, therefore, is adding another dimension to the work of the social reproduction theorists by documenting the interaction between the experience of schooling and the pupil's wider cultural context.

To some extent the empirical studies that fall within the boundaries of social reproduction theory have to be seen as part of an ideological struggle within the new sociology of education. Amongst others, Keddie and Sharp and Green, are very keen to assert that teachers have little real freedom of action, and what apparent discretion they exercise serves to aid the process of social reproduction by disguising it. They are intent on attacking what they see as the naivety of sociological phenomenology with its implied belief that through constructing new conceptions of reality schools can act as viable instruments of social change. Such a critique is valid (although few phenomenologists are quite as naive or idealistic as others claim) but in their anxiety to make the point they have linked the school to the social order in a mechanical and simpleminded fashion. Furthermore, they have overstressed the extent to which schools are products of the wider society at the expense of exploring them as social systems with the task of performing certain functions regardless of the societal context. Token concessions are made to the realization that most teachers want to 'achieve discipline in the classroom' but it is then assumed, almost without reflection, that this illustrates how the schools perpetuate a hierarchical social order. But perhaps schools require classroom discipline because without it most teachers find it impossible to teach and pupils to learn. It may also be necessary because without it teachers start to have heart attacks or nervous breakdowns, or alternatively the school disintegrates and can no longer achieve its goals – whatever they may be.

Much of the recent literature reflects a latent impulse to establish an intellectual hegemony: various facets of the new sociology of education pour scorn upon one another, the initial tradition in British educational sociology is vilified because supposedly it has more to say about social stratification than schooling, and the mid-1960s concern

with the organization of the school is rather disparagingly viewed as
an improvement upon the past but still some way from the true path.
We are more catholic in our tastes, refining and synthesizing past
research approaches and theoretical positions, for this is the only way
that the fullest understanding of the relationship between the
individual, schooling and society can be achieved.

3   *The prescriptive educationalists*

As is to be expected much of the literature that describes the
functioning of the British educational system has been written by
teachers and ex-teachers. The experience of teaching seems to be a
legacy that few of them can easily escape. One important manifestation of this is a powerful commitment to the enhancement of the
professional status of the classroom teachers. So regardless of what
the evidence may suggest is taking place, or should take place, it is
widely believed that teachers *must* occupy a pivotal position in the
process of educational change. Up to quite recently this value
judgement was widely held so that with some justification Owen
(1973:70) could write that, 'In Britain ... no one would openly admit
that any change could start elsewhere than in the classroom'. The
continuing strength of this consensus of opinion still influences
interpretations of what is happening to our educational system. In a
book published as recently as 1978 (Grace:218) we read that, with
respect to urban education, teacher autonomy is growing in the move
from 'essentially visible and centralized control to essentially invisible
and diffused control'. Such claims have a decidedly hollow ring in the
light of a steady increase in both the visible and centralized control of
curriculum content in the face of opposition from at least the largest
teachers' union.

The impression is created, therefore, that heads and teachers are
seen as powerful figures in the change process not so much because
they are integral to it but because this is how many, presumably
including the profession itself, would wish it to be. It has to be
remembered that teachers have struggled over a long period of time to
establish a precarious professional identity. Their claim to control the
content and transmission of the curriculum is based upon their view
of themselves as professionally competent individuals who know
better than anyone else the circumstances and capabilities of their
pupils. If this area of responsibility is undermined then the status of
the teacher is jeopardized; he becomes more of a worker operating

within confined and imposed boundaries than a professional defining the dimensions of the work-a-day world for himself.

The contemporary debate on the common curriculum has tested the ingenuity of the prescriptive educationalists, for on the one hand many of them believe that the imposition of a core curriculum makes good educational sense and yet on the other hand they have no desire to see the status of teachers eroded. The squaring of the circle is achieved by establishing clearer national guidelines, making sure that the local education authorities keep abreast of what is going on in their schools, but allowing the classroom teacher to use his own judgement in interpretating the curriculum framework (Becher 1971:10–11; Becher & Maclure 1978:ch. 11). The core curriculum is thus, if this is not a contradiction, individualized. Interestingly this appears to be the present position of HMI. In its recent publication *A View of the Curriculum* (1980: 2–3) the inspectorate sees a need for 'individual curricular programmes' to be established 'within the broadly defined common curriculum' (note not *core* curriculum: for the distinction, see HMI 1977:5–6). Elaborating somewhat it stated, 'In practice that means that the broad definition of the purposes of school education is a shared responsibility, whereas the detailed means by which they may best be realised in individual schools and for individual children are a matter for professional judgement.' In view of the HMIs' close involvement with the grassroots of the educational system this is an expected stance but whether it will be the view that finally prevails is a matter for conjecture.

Lawton (1980:4), a long-term supporter of some form of common curriculum, has offered another suggestion for mitigating the possible impact this could have upon the teacher's professional status. He has argued that 'If teachers are to yield control over curriculum planning ... then they ought to make sure that they make up for this by increasing their influence over examinations.' Precisely how they are 'to make sure' of this given the delicate power balance surrounding the examination system begs a lot of questions, but his proposition does raise the hypothetical possibility of a trade-off in responsibilities in order that the teacher's professional status is left intact. These issues will be resolved through the exercise of political power. It may or may not prove politically expedient to establish internally controlled continuous assessment procedures in return for a greater measure of external policing of curriculum content. However, it should be remembered that there is nothing immutable about professional expertise – as the history of the teaching profession illustrates only too well – regardless of what one may personally think is best for the long-term wellbeing of schooling.

4   *The descriptive educationalists*

The curriculum studies movement has been concerned to monitor precisely how much curriculum change has occurred, to evaluate the effectiveness of the strategies for change, and to ascertain what is the classroom impact, if any, of curriculum innovation. Not so long ago such tasks were part of a growth industry. The consequence is a considerable body of literature that describes the accomplishments of curriculum innovation (see Eggleston 1977; Shipman 1974; Stenhouse 1980). The general picture that these publications give is not especially flattering: there has been less change than the attendant publicity may have suggested, the initial change strategies were not particularly effective, and there is considerable confusion as to how the classroom impact of curriculum innovation should be measured.

Four main models purport to describe the possible patterns of educational change: change as a research–development–and–diffusion process, change as a problem-solving process, change as a process of social interaction, and change as a linkage process (Havelock & Havelock 1973:ch. 1). The fourth model is an amalgam of the three other models, and in the words of Havelock (ibid.:23), the concept linkage acts 'as a possible unifying and integrating idea'. These models suggest different sequences of innovation i.e. it is composed of a number of stages which have to follow one another in a certain order if change is to be effective. Complementing this work, Chin and Benne (1969) have suggested three strategies by which the varying actors in the innovative process can be persudaded to effect change: empirical–rational strategies, normative re-educative strategies, and a power-coercive approach. Clearly different actors are of greater or lesser importance to the change process depending upon what strategy is adopted and what sequence is followed.

Relating these models and strategies to curriculum innovation in Britain, Becher (1971:3) – writing within the context of the early 1970s – could discern the following drift: 'Nevertheless, in very crude terms one can begin to detect an historical shift of responsibility from the centre to the periphery, from the governing administration to the individual institution.' He reflected that this suggested 'some recognition ... of the limitations of an authoritarian or paternalistic approach to the implementation of change' (ibid.:3). His interpretation of the empirical evidence is that unless teachers are involved in the early stages of the innovative process which incorporates them in a meaningful fashion, then effective educational change is improbable. One frequent finding is that teachers interpret innovations 'so that their conventional ways of teaching [are] minimally changed' (McIntyre & Brown 1979:42). Given this interpretative power it is hard to predict the consequences of educational change unless teachers share a common understanding of what is taking place. So like the prescriptive educationalists, the descriptive educationalists stress the critical position of the teacher in the change process. Indeed it could be argued that the descriptive educationalists are in fact prescriptive educationalists hiding behind the facts. Obviously this is too sweeping a claim but one that we believe is not too wide of the mark.

Evaluating the social significance of changes in the organization of knowledge

Bernstein (1975:81) has claimed, 'The battle over curricula is also a conflict between different conceptions of social order and is therefore fundamentally moral.' With reference to the recent controversy in Britain over integrated and collection codes (crudely speaking the distinction between interdisciplinary studies and a subject-based curriculum) he has further argued that disturbances to the classification of knowledge are followed by disturbances to 'existing authority structures, existing specific educational identities and concepts of property' (Bernstein 1971:216). We accept the sociological consensus that the organization of knowledge has social ramifications but would maintain that the extent of these depends upon a variety of contextual factors. For example, the curriculum changes introduced at William Tyndale Junior School under the auspices of the headmaster Mr Ellis clearly affected the school experiences of the pupils exposed to them. However, whether this changed the relationship between schooling and society, even for the individuals involved in the experiment, is another question. The only outcome may have been very confused pupils who failed to establish meaningful relationships to the social order. For one who is keen to acknowledge his debt, it is ironic that Bernstein should have overlooked Durkheim's belief that the experience of schooling has a general social meaning only when it is experienced within a supportive societal framework.

It is our contention that for changes in the organization of knowledge to have any prolonged or general social significance they must be politically negotiated. For example, at William Tyndale Junior School Ellis failed to carry along with him powerful forces, both within the school and the local community, and as a result his changes were short-lived. In an attack on Postman's idealism Keddie has made the same point. Postman claimed that if 'the media of learning' were changed then 'the power relationships and the nature of assessment' would also change (Keddie 1973:16). Keddie, like ourselves, believes that power relationships have to change first. But unlike the social reproduction theorists (including Keddie) we do not believe that the change process is necessarily initiated within the bowels of the capitalist economy and controlled by the dominant economic class.

The social reproduction theorists pitch their understanding of educational change at such a general level that it excludes almost everything other than major shifts in the character of the educational system. However, important changes in the experience of schooling may arise out of very defined stimuli, rather than signify a general social crisis. The raising of the school-leaving age, the abolition of the 11 + examination, the growth of comprehensive secondary education, and the problems posed by the education of immigrant children in the inner-city schools are all examples of middle range problems which have had a considerable impact. Incidentally all of these particular problems have stimulated curriculum innovation suggesting, therefore, that the manipulation of the organization of knowledge may have a limited pedagogical, rather than a broader, social purpose. Furthermore, much of the curriculum change that followed from these challenges was initiated within educational institutions. The process of political negotiations may commence therefore within the school but its ultimate effectiveness is dependent upon its capacity to incorporate powerful others.

The sociologists have generally talked in terms of moral crises, the changing demands of capitalism and the need for new forms of social control, while the educationalists have been inclined to stress the importance of immediate and definitive pressures for change, and place considerable stress on the centrality of one actor, the teacher. But it is necessary to think of the change process at more than one level of analysis. In our model the change dynamic (the extension of state bureaucratic power within the context of an ailing but technologically advanced society which constantly produces new forms of social inequality) assumes its educational forms through political negotiations. What educational authority the various parties exercise is thus dependent upon their ability to translate their potential capital into effective political resources.

Although both descriptive and prescriptive educationalists may appear to have a more realistic view of the process of educational change than many of their sociological counterparts, we are not persuaded of the importance they accord the classroom teacher. Given the formal pattern of educational power in Britain, and the present-day authority of the classroom teacher, it would be absurd to think in terms of the straightforward imposition of centrally initiated educational directives. Even if this were technically possible it would be politically unwise. However, 'imposition' is a very strong word and as we shall demonstrate there is more than one way of skinning a cat. As far as educational policymaking is concerned political negotiation increasingly means an institutionalized power struggle. It cannot be guaranteed, as some would wish, that a reasonable consensus will emerge. Although Manzer's study (1970) of the educational establishment shows that past conflict between its members has been contained, this is not to deny the occasional protracted and bitter guerrilla warfare. In view of the current shift in the internal power balance of the educational establishment, with the DES gaining in influence over the LEAs and the teachers' unions, we can expect the skirmishing to continue unabated.

To conclude the chapter we will consider briefly what this development means in sociological terms. The shift in power marks an end to the old tripartite educational establishment. It is not simply a question of the centralization of educational power, or even the erosion of teacher authority in relation to the DES and LEAs, but rather that a new ballgame with different rules is being constructed. In *The Long Revolution* (1961:14) Raymond Williams argued that three different interests were entwined within the British educational system – the industrial trainers, the old humanists, and the public educators. At present a new, and more powerful interest is busily staking its claim – the educational bureaucrats. Within the framework of a stagnant educational system that is groping towards a redefinition of itself, and drawing upon all the traditional resources of bureaucracy, they are well-placed to win a victory more total than any achieved in the past.

Our review of Bowles' and Gintis' correspondence thesis was highly critical but what we are now witnessing is the political negotiation of a British version of the correspondence thesis. The goal is the production of a certified, hierarchically segregated and flexible labour force which is seen as the best bet to fulfil the nation's future manpower needs given the kind of industrial base that is apparently emerging. This will involve a partial stripping away of the pedagogical disguises through which schooling has helped to reproduce the class structure. Now there is a perceived need to restrike the balance between the economic, social control and personal consumption functions of schooling, and the manoeuvring to achieve this is under way.

To strip away the pedagogical disguises of the social reproduction process means that the educational system must play a more explicit part in furthering and legitimating inequality. Indeed socio-economic inequality will become less of a moral concern, and be seen by many as socially beneficial as well as inevitable. The outcome is likely to be heightened intergroup tensions but these will be controlled by non-educational institutions and by methods other than schooling. In the light of these developments (and if our diagnosis is correct!) then teachers should be sensitized to the growing external pressures upon their day-to-day behaviour (see Taylor 1974:22–3). But this depends on how these are applied. It is just possible that the orchestration of change will be conducted in such a manner as to appease its potential victims to the point that they are unaware that they are indeed victims. Nothing would fit the traditional British image of change more perfectly, and nothing would suit better the interests of those who wield dominant educational power.

Part Two

The Theory in Practice

5

Policy-Making and the State Apparatus

Educational policy making is the process whereby the various pressures for educational change are translated into formal governmental expression. In becoming policy, the dynamic for change takes on specific form and is endowed with whatever legitimacy and power the dominant political structure commands. That much is not in question. Where the difficulty arises is in exploring how the pressures derived from the social control, economic and personal consumption functions of education, on the one hand, and the input from demographic shifts and the political parties, on the other, come together to form policy. What are the structures which regulate, if that is the right word, this process and how do they do it?

In this chapter we argue that the forum in which these pressures for change are politically negotiated is, increasingly, the educational state apparatus: the Department of Education and Science. Furthermore, that this struggle over educational policy takes place in a bureaucratic context which is far from passive in its policy preferences, and which, in fact, sets the parameters within which the policy debate is conducted. We therefore begin with a brief review of existing approaches both to more general and to specifically educational policy-making. This is followed by a consideration of the bureaucratic constraints within which educational change is negotiated and the limitations placed on different types of possible policy outcomes. Do the planning techniques of the British educational bureaucracy bolster the power of the professional civil servant both at the LEA and DES level of decision making? Thirdly, even assuming that the command posts of educational change are being captured by an ambitious bureaucracy, how well-equipped is it to ensure that the resulting policy is effectively executed? Fourthly,

how does the expansion of bureaucratic power square with
education's ideological and legitimating functions? Do the two
always go neatly together or does the management of educational
change present its own problems for the generation of the ideology
necessary to mask education's underlying social functions.

Studies of policy making

Considered in the round, policy making is less a coherent field of
study and more a disparate conglomerate of approaches split along
disciplinary and methodological lines. Definitions of what policy
actually is vary (Lasswell & Kaplan 1950: 71; Robinson 1962: 3) as do
notions of where the process of policy making begins and ends. Some,
such as Lasswell (1956), equate it with decision making and impose a
convenient, if static, taxonomy upon it whereas others, such as Rose
(1969: xi), argue that the 'sense of continuous activity and adjustment
involved in policy-making is best conveyed by describing it as a
process rather than as a single, once-for-all act'. Many of the studies
are over-optimistic in the degree and influence of individual
rationality which they assume to be present in the process but protect
themselves from the consequences of this optimism by focusing on
very narrow case studies. As Heclo (1972: 90) observes, the result is
that 'the inheritance from the majority of policy case studies on both
sides of the Atlantic is a series of isolated episodic descriptions –
particularly of legislative enactments – which are apparently thought
to be of intrinsic interest.'

The treatment of policy by the more substantial areas of political
science is not much more convincing. To the traditional
institutionalists, policy was obviously a product of the formal
distribution of governmental powers and as such held little interest for
them. Similarly the study of parties and interest groups, even when
buttressed by the behavioural approach, failed to treat policy making
with anything more than peripheral concern. Policy was regarded as a
'natural output' of party and interest group activity but questions such
as why one policy rather than another came to be adopted, what the
alternatives were, how policies were sustained over time, how they
affected other policies and why they fell by the wayside, were largely
neglected.

Now some would argue that a unified approach to the
understanding of policy making does exist in the form of the

programmatic policy analysis which has emerged from the management side of economics. To name several of the more well-known examples: output-budgeting (OB), planning–programming–budgeting (PPB) and management by objectives (MBO) (see Bridgeman 1969/70). However, to argue that these approaches assist us in our understanding of the policy process rather stretches the meaning of 'understanding'. Essentially these are techniques designed to increase the efficiency with which policy can be implemented or to aid the efficiency with which choices can be made between policies. Hence they only assist our understanding of how policy is formed if they are already being used. Alternatively, if they are not already in use by a decision-making body then they can only assist in our understanding of how policy *should* be formed according to their own, supposedly rational, criteria. This is because their purpose lies in the *service* of policy not in its *explanation*. They are concerned with the implementation of policy, not with its understanding. It is important that this distinction be clearly established at this stage since we will be examining the programmatic approach and its influence on educational policy making later.

But to return to the limitations of policy-making theory, there is little doubt that the study of educational policy formation has suffered from the absence of a general coherent approach. Three frequently quoted studies of educational policy are those by Jennings (1977), Saran (1973) and Kogan (1975) and in different ways they illustrate the difficulties of the area. The first two concern themselves with local authority education and Kogan deals with the national perspective. Although both Jennings and Saran claim to be using the decision-making approach to educational policy and although both employ the same methodology, that of the case study, the content of their work contradicts these superficial similiarities. While Jennings' notion of decision making is explicitly derived from Agger's seven stage model (1964; see Dahl 1962), Saran relies on the administrative arrangements she finds to exist in the case study for her conceptual framework. Hence Jennings tends to impose a 'rational', and foreign model which leaves one with the uncomfortable feeling that facts have been crunched into place and Saran rarely raises her head above the details of procedural decision making.

Meanwhile, in his national study Kogan (1975: 74–7) applies a model of interest group theory whereby policy is seen to emerge from the activities of a number of groups (e.g. local authority associations, teachers' unions) with the DES acting as eventual arbiter in the situation. Despite the empirical thoroughness of this approach the dynamic of policy formation remains elusive. Thus the initial assumption is that once the interests of the major educational groups have been identified the way is cleared for an explanation of how a consensus emerged to become policy. This is the normal tenet of such an equilibrium model. However, as Kogan (ibid.: 23) himself admits, such a framework is not adequate for the purpose of analysing the complexities of educational policy making.

The sources of policy generation are so difficult to locate, let alone place in any logical pattern, that detecting the changes in values, or the pressures by which change is effected, is more a matter of art than of analysis. The imagery of political science suggests too much precision: such words as 'power', 'structure', 'pressure', 'leverage' all suggest that political activity is analogous with predictable engineering. Softer and more modest imagery is needed.

The primary difficulty lies with the inability of interest group theory to incorporate the forces which lie behind the apparent balancing of rival group interests: hence the issues of process and change over time remain enigmatic. The result, as Kogan (ibid.: 235) observes, is that there is 'no adequate explanatory framework of how local pressures and decision-making add to the national aggregate', 'no clear or linear process of change' (ibid.: 236). Rather, educational change is like a kaleidoscope, 'Colours in a changing pattern move out of view, or get stuck, or change position when the box is tapped' (ibid.: 237).

This then leaves us in the position of asking, with Kogan (ibid.: 238), 'But, how does the DES aggregate the knowlege, feelings, resistances and resource feasibility of the 30,000 institutions, the complex political system that we have described, the press and the intelligentsia?'

One answer could be that the DES does not have this 'aggregating function' at all; or at least, not on any significant scale. Again, the DES may aggregate but only after it has decided which viewpoints should be selected for aggregation. The point to be made is that the adoption of the interest group model by Kogan has placed him in the position where he is obliged to try to make sense of educational policy in terms of its being an output produced as the result of a complex of interest group inputs, or policy preferences. According to this model, the main problem lies in discovering the equation which, it is assumed, governs the way in which inputs are 'balanced' and policy calculated. As we have shown the absence of such an equation then leads to the use of that 'softer and more modest imagery' in order to make sense of what is happening.

Recognition that less easily accessible, but nonetheless influential processes are at work in the formation of educational policy often appears as a discussion of vague concepts such as the changing 'climate of opinion' or 'public opinion'. Thus Parkinson's argument (1970:122) explaining how the Labour party exercised an influence on educational policy-making talks of how the party helped to change the climate of public and professional opinion. Similarly, Kogan (1971:46–7) describes the impact of the 'new educational Establishment' (educational journalists, sociologists and economists of education) on the 'climate of opinion' and of how the Ministry 'moved with the climate of opinion'. And at the local level, Saran (1973:270–1) notes how a CEO responded to changes in 'informed opinion'. Comments such as these are usually linked to a consensus model of policy formation which presents 'policy making in education as a cumulative process, where change rarely occurs until a consensus is reached' (Parkinson 1970:122) and the government as the recipient of the inevitable: 'Public opinion, and especially opinion in the educational world, will usually have been moving in favour of such [policy] changes for many years before they are sanctioned officially by government' (Fowler 1974:21)

The advantage of such a diffuse idea as 'climate of opinion' is that it ostensibly plugs the gap between cause and effect in the group–policy relationship: groups influence, and are influenced by public opinion which in turn influences policy. However, although the felt need for such a concept is a valid one, this particular answer to that need merely raises the generality of the discussion without telling us how and why one type of 'climate of opinion' rather than another is formed. It is a kind of conceptual sop that leaves the question of the nature of the policy dynamic unanswered. It is to this question that we now turn.

The bureaucratization of educational power

British educational policy is increasingly produced in the context of bureaucratic developments which, we will argue, represent preferred policy directions. These developments have, in turn, to respond to the pressures generated by education's functions as an agent of social control and servant of the economy (however badly performed) as well as to the more obvious demands imposed by demographic shifts and changing party governments. As the manager of the arena in which these demands are negotiated, the state apparatus (the DES) is in a position to arrange not only the agenda of the negotiations but also to advise on the financial considerations involved in particular policy outcomes and the changes in the state apparatus required in order to implement certain policies. So although it cannot ignore the social and political pressures to which it is inevitably subject, the Department can nonetheless interpret these pressures in ways which suit its own bureaucratic ambitions. While the bureaucratic medium within which policy emerges very much constrains the content of the policy message produced, we are not arguing that this is a total process – if only because the bureaucratic developments in question are relatively recent and are occurring within a decentralized education system. They nevertheless have an internal logic, are progressive in their encapsulation of the policy-making arena and can in no way be seen as part of a rational balancing of opposing group interests.

An initial and highly visible indication of how the policy-making context in education has altered over the past thirty years is the changing position of the DES. 'For a long while after the 1944 Act', writes Kogan (1973:171), 'the Department considered itself not as an educational planning department, or as leaders on policy, but primarily as a mediator between the "real" agents of educational government – the local education authorities, the teachers and the denominations and the government-wide network of control and economic policy led by the Treasury.' It exhibited a 'persistent reluctance' to take seriously its own role as promoter of educational policy (ibid.) and maintained the prewar functions of the Board of Education which were 'regulatory and quasi-judicial' (1971:170). This passive and retiring posture has now changed. Today we see a far more interventionist-minded DES; one that is prepared to initiate and orchestrate the Great Debate, attack bodies such as the Schools Council, and raise questions about the curriculum and standards of teaching which had previously been regarded as well outside its preserve.

The change in the role of the DES from blushing handmaiden to prima donna has to be seen as the tip of the iceberg so far as the policy-making process is concerned. It is merely a surface indication of rather deeper sea changes in the educational bureaucracy which are reflected in the manner in which policy is shaped and controlled. Nor should it be assumed that this shift in the mode of policy production with the DES playing a more dirigiste part has been accomplished without stress being placed on the capacity of education to act as an agent of social control and to legitimize inequality through the sponsorship of a dominant educational ideology. The more education is seen as an activity consciously directed by one group, the DES, as opposed to the impartial product of a consensus of wise old heads, the more it will need fresh legitimizing clothes to replace the discarded old ones. It is by no means clear that the DES appreciates that for the policy output to carry legitimizing weight it is essential that the policy-making process should itself be regarded as legitimate. Too much haste in changing the nature of that process could well undermine its credibility.

What aspects of educational policy formation do we need to examine to determine the extent to which the new DES stance is indicative of more fundamental shifts? The way in which policy is formed can be said to influence the shape of the policies produced in terms of both the range of structures which have access to the policy-making process and the values that dominate those structures. Together they constitute the parameters within which policy emerges. It is our contention that policy formation in education is becoming an activity encapsulated within a limited set of structures, permeated by bureaucratic values which emphasize the importance of scientific rationality, efficiency and professional expertise. These are the parameters which control the rate and direction of educational change. So how have they developed?

1   *The LEAs*

At the local level both the Maud Management Report (1967) and the Bains Report (1972) gave official recognition to the *de facto* influence which local authority officers have on the formation of policy. As Bains (para. 3.23) put it:

We do not dispute that the major policy decisions must be taken by the elected members, but the officers have a role to play in the stimulation and formulation of policy, and in seeing that the members have available the necessary advice and evaluation to enable them to make the best decisions.

The question which concerns us in the case of education is how far the stimulatory role of the officers pre-empts the influence which the elected members might have on policy and so effectively contains the making of educational policy within the ranks of the full-time professionals and their full-time professional values. Although commentators have noted how in local authorities there is an 'increased amount of politics in educational issues and a haste to imprint party labels on every issue (Jennings 1977:125), it is doubtful whether this extends beyond a ritualistic party opposition to include the realm of policy creation – a much more time-consuming activity. The reasons for this are in the first instance pragmatic.

The amount of information gathering and consultation which has to occur before a policy formally reaches the drawing board at local authority level is substantial. This effectively means that he who has access to, or control over the relevant flows of information can also delimit policy choices because he decides what is, or is not feasible. Despite their varied theoretical positions, all the studies conducted of local educational policy-making agree that the Chief Education Officer, and sometimes his senior officials, have a key role to play in this respect. Some authors are prepared to go further than others in assessing how far this 'gatekeeper' control of information supply subverts the policy-making role of elected members. Birley (1970:171), an ex-CEO himself, is convinced that members 'are not in any sense involved in policy-making if in a complex and far-reaching matter their only function is to consider a report from an officer.' And even though he recognises that members have the unfettered right to say 'yes' or 'no', this, he maintains, 'is a power more illusory than real':

On a complicated issue much of the policy has in fact been determined once the report has been written; the approaches to the problem, selection of facets within it, can settle in advance the lines of decision-making. (ibid.)

Likewise, in his conversations with three ex-CEOs, Kogan (1973:55) remarks that the 'style of education of a whole county or city can be changed with a change of CEO'.

However, others are less sure that the CEO is quite that much of a god-like creature. Although Jennings (1977:46) admits that the flow of information and opinions to members, the timing or pacing of their presentation and the suggestions for consultation can usually be controlled by the CEO, he nevertheless argues that party political control acts as 'a check against bureaucracy and professional syndication in local government'. The CEO has to ensure that any policy he may develop is acceptable to the majority party in the education committee and, in particular, to the committee chairman. Equally we find that Saran (1973:79) sees policy initiative as hinging on the close consultative relationship between CEO and chairman. But precisely who is likely to be the dominant partner in that relationship is not immediately clear. What is clear is that elected members on the whole tend not to have a great interest in educational issues, that detailed policy consideration is left to a small minority of members and that therefore there is little likelihood that a developed ideological alternative exists to counter a detailed proposal put forward by officers and backed by all the trappings of research and consultation (see Jennings 1977:75).

These pragmatic limitations of time, money and resources indicate that a process of enclosure is occurring in local education policy making restricting participation largely to the professionals who have the necessary knowledge and expertise to make 'informed' choices. There may also be a parallel process of co-option of the extended structure designed to provide for contribution and participation by non-governmental groups (ibid.:186), though this is more doubtful. It may merely be exclusion through cosmetic consultation.

If the making of educational policy at the local level is gradually being encapsulated within a professional enclave, how do the officers justify this to themselves, let alone to the public? What are the values upon which this enclosure process rests? Reading the accounts of the experiences of Chief Education Officers one swiftly gains the impression that, with the possible exception of Solomon, there can scarcely have ever before been men and women so amply endowed with a sense of wisdom and justice. After all, as Dan Cook, ex-CEO for Devon, points out, 'it is the officers who have no or very few personal axes to grind' (Kogan 1973:64). They are the impartial men of goodwill, sustained by their sense of service to the community. And if they are empire builders then they are, as Cook (ibid.) protests, 'empire builders for children' – which adults may or may not see as reassuring. The importance of this idea of the CEO and his officers as reasonable men is that it is a value which can manage the tension in educational policy making between 'democracy and efficiency, planning and pragmatism, philosophy and procedures' (Birley, 1970:128).

But like all forms of benevolent paternalism it has its other side; for if the officers are the men of reason, where does that leave the elected members? Or come to that, where does it leave democracy itself? Although this may at first appear an odd question it surely becomes less odd when one considers Birley's remark (ibid.:9) that the planning of educational advance in a free society will always have to contend with the 'persistent amateurism and opportunism that regular, democratic elections foster'; or Cook's opinion (Kogan 1973:46) of councillors that 'By their very nature they cannot be policy makers because they get in the way of the planning process in which elections are an interruption.'

However, despite the antipathy of the professional planner towards the vagaries of formal democratic procedures, this does not mean that he sees himself as the usurper of democracy. Far from it. Indeed he is apt to cast himself in the role of protector of the people's interests. In this respect Kogan (ibid.:45) remarks that what the three CEOs of his study asserted is quite similar to what a group of civil servants also recently asserted – 'that in Britain the permanent official is often concerned with the *sustaining* of the democratic process against the ephemeral and often highly idiosyncratic intervention of individual members of parliament or ministers' [our stress]. For a permanent official to be able to make these assertions with confidence and aplomb it is useful if he has a basis on which to rest his case apart from simply a belief in his own capacities. In other words, if he can legitimize his position both to himself and to others by means of an argument which has apparently 'objective' qualities and does not rely for its conviction on the personal qualities of the individual officer, admirable though these may be.

In the case of local governments, such an argument has emerged to buttress the professional values of the administrator, though it has also generated divisions between administrators. It is called 'corporate planning'. The concept of corporate planning, originally developed in management theory in the form of Output Budgeting (OB) and Management by Objectives (MBO), was initially applied to commercial and industrial organizations and then subsequently to public authorities. In brief, it operates by defining the organization's overall goals, translating these into precise objectives, formulating alternative strategies for achieving these objectives, evaluating these strategies in terms of their capacity to maximize the attainment of the highest priority objectives, costing and implementing the most 'efficient' strategy. Once funds are allocated to a strategy its performance is monitored, feedback and review generated to see how far objectives are being realized, and if necessary the goals, objectives, plans and assumptions reassessed (see Eddison 1973; Stewart: 1971; 1974). The corporate planning process is thus comprehensive, continuous and output-orientated. It is characterized by a concern with the efficiency of the public authority as a whole, a tenacious belief in its own rational virtues and is undoubtedly an ideological force to be reckoned with.

The ways in which corporate planning has been implemented in different local authorities may have varied (Greenwood *et al.* 1969; Norton & Stewart 1973; DES 1974) but its implications for the local policy-making framework of education on the whole have not. Structurally it has meant a much more centralized planning system in an authority (e.g. one coordinated by a policy and resources committee) and the attempted integration of education into that system alongside the other local government services. Education thus becomes accountable to the central objectives of an authority rather than having separate, and separately evolved objectives of its own. And given the concern of corporate planning that outputs should be measurable and preferably quantitative, education finds itself operating within a management system which some would regard as foreign to its very nature. In his feasibility study of a planning–programming–budgeting–system (PPBS – a form of output budgeting) in Gloucestershire Ronald Butt (1972:44) remarked that it was the education programme which posed the biggest problem:

Education perhaps best illustrates how progress in developing output measures depends on being able to define clear objectives. Education is bedevilled at a philosophical level by uncertainty about the objectives of the society for which young people are being educated; and there are doubts among politicians, administrators and teachers about how far the education system should be pursuing any conscious objectives because this involves moulding pupils possibly in ways that do not correspond to parental wishes.

Furthermore, as Sir William Pile, Permanent Under-secretary of State at the DES between 1970 and 1976, has observed (1979: 55), both individual 'outputs' of education (such as self-fulfilment, enrichment of experience, quality of life) and broader social benefits are very difficult to quantify.

The difficulty of tailoring the measurement of educational outputs to the demands and techniques of corporate planning has had three major repercussions. It has led, firstly, to a continuing search for possible means of producing such measurements, for example literacy and numeracy testing; secondly, to a reliance on input measurements, such as teacher-pupil ratios, which are susceptible to quantification; and thirdly, to a dependence on the extrapolation of existing trends (e.g. proportion of school students taking 'A' levels calculated over several years) as a guide to future policy. There can be little doubt that all three place considerable limitations on the kinds of educational policies which are either possible or feasible in the eyes of the corporate planners. For a policy readily to fit the 'scientific' criteria of this mode of rational planning it has, preferably, to be capable itself of quantification so that its costs and benefits, success and failure can be accurately measured. It has to be capable, also, of providing such quantifiable information through the normal administrative machinery of local government rather than through additional, and therefore costly, new methods.

The assumption on which corporate planning, and any other form of output budgeting, rests is that a greater degree of certainty can be injected into human affairs through the introduction of this management technique than was the case before its introduction. Furthermore, that this is a certainty which, because it allows for rational planning amid the chaos of conflicting interests and arguments, is therefore bound to be beneficial to the community. It is this 'certainty principle', allied as it is to an exclusive right of access to, and use of official information which makes corporate planning a useful ideological partner to the paternalistic values of the professional administrator. It justifies his exclusive virtuosity. However, a drawback of corporate planning from the point of view of individual education departments within local authorities is that its call for centralization of the authority planning procedure can cut across existing departmental power interests. Thus although an education department may be able to use its part in the corporate planning operation to identify certain 'necessary' and rationally justifiable policy directions, as an individual department it also has to beware of encroachments on its autonomy by the authority's central policy review body. Some CEOs have opposed corporate planning both because it might erode their power and also because of its delimiting effect upon educational policy options.

Certainty for the administrator may well mean less influence on the policy process for the elected members and outside interest groups. The centralization of the planning procedures in a local authority often diminishes the number of access points available to the councillors and the public – or, at least, diminishes the number of such points which are not officially sponsored and controlled for the collection of filtered information, but which remain vulnerable to the vagaries of public opinion. Hence, the introduction of this kind of management structure is political in that it affects the existing distribution of political power:

To devise a management system which will strengthen the role of officers, or alternatively of councillors, or which will more effectively secure the implementation of government policies, may be a function of the management theorist. Its adoption is an act of political choice. (OU 1974:164)

Of course it is only the political analyst who is describing the introduction of corporate planning as 'an act of political choice'. To those actively involved in local government, corporate planning is frequently perceived as a 'natural' development in the search for more local government efficiency. And it is this supposedly apolitical quality which provides it with a defence against those whose interests and powers it is usurping. The encapsulation of the policy-making process within the ranks of the professionals is presented as both necessary and inevitable in a society where scarce resources must be utilized to their maximum efficiency.

A development which in education reinforces this tendency for corporate planning to erode the powers of elected members, has been the use of projections of existing trends as a means of long-term planning. Its fairly simple quantified format readily fits corporate planning requirements and thus renders it an attractive proposition in the largely non-quantifiable area of education. The significance of this is that its widespread application not only pre-empts resources which might have been allocated to policies other than those stemming from projections but also that it pre-empts the role of the councillor by committing resources prior to his election. He is left to play with only marginal resources, and thus affect only marginal policy changes, in contrast to the full-time officer with his continuing influence over nascent policies subsequently to be integrated with projected trends.

We have dealt with policy making at the local level in education in some detail in order to try and establish the kinds of parameters within which policy emerges and the direction in which these parameters are moving. It now remains to be seen how far the increased role of professional values, output-budgeting techniques, quantifiable options, rationality and efficiency in local policy formation acting at the expense of traditional democratic procedures can be linked to changes in the LEA–DES relationship. Are the two establishing harmonious policy parameters or are they at odds with one another?

The DES

The origins of the Department's shift from 'holder of the ring between the real forces in educational policy-making' (local authorities, the denominations, teachers and parents) to 'enforcer of positive controls, based increasingly on knowledge which the department itself went out to get' (Kogan 1971:30) can be traced back to changes in the DES–LEA relationship in the 1950s. During this period it became obvious that certain basic processes of resource allocation within the educational system could no longer be subject to the whims of decentralized administrative procedures without complete confusion resulting. In particular, more effective centralized influence was seen to be necessary over capital spending on buildings and the prediction and supply of teachers. This led to the setting up within the department of the Architects and Building Branch and the Teachers Supply Branch. Referring to major developments in the Department's forward planning capacity in recent years, Sir William Pile (1979:59) noted that 'These changes reflect the growing recognition than an essential function of the Department, over and above the performance of specific practical and administrative duties deriving from the education Acts, is that of resource planning for the education service as a whole'. He elaborated:

that is, the formulation of objectives, the framing of national policies best calculated to meet these objectives, the undertaking of long term costings of policies in a way that enables ministers to choose their priorities, and the task of effectively presenting the consequential resource needs within central government.

Now there can be little doubt that, given the Department's final responsibility for the administration of education and the increasing demand for education and expenditure on it, the emergence of these more sophisticated kinds of planning mechanisms was inevitable. The question which concerns us is how far the theme of 'administrative necessity' was used to justify the enclosure of the policy-making process; how far the planning process has been internalized within the Department on the grounds that the Department alone has the planning know-how and that, within this, projections about capital expenditure and teacher manpower, for example, have an objective and unchallengeable validity of their own. As Woodhall (1972:63) puts it,

The real weakness of manpower forecasts is not that they are inaccurate, for all long-term forecasting tends to be inaccurate, but that they have been treated as though they are accurate, as though opportunities for substitution, flexibility, or alternative use of resources, did not exist.

The attraction of 'projectionism' is principally that the arithmetic behind it is simple, though there tends to be a lot of it, and that the conclusions which stem from it are easy to comprehend (see Armitage 1973:214–6). So it is not entirely surprising that the methodology of the Robbins Report (1963) was based on projected numbers of students in higher education and that it envisaged a system of rolling planning based on projections made for ten years ahead. In effect, the prestige of Robbins further legitimated the use of projections in DES planning as well as extending the range of its use to include students as well as teachers.

Official government confirmation of the Robbins method for estimating future provision required in higher education appeared in 1970 with the publication of Educational Planning Paper No. 2. This claimed that it was 'a working document intended to assist discussion ... and carries no implication whatever for future Government policy or finance', (1970c: iii), a highly dubious claim in view of the fact that it did not see fit to explore more than the single policy option implicitly contained in its projections. It dismisses the possibility of considering other options in terms which by now have a familiar ring:

There are a considerable number of factors, both internal to the higher education system and external to it, which may have a significant impact on its future development. *In many cases it is not practicable to assess their impact in quantitative terms.* [our stress] (ibid.: 8–9)

In other words the capacity for quantification becomes the key criterion, as in corporate planning, for inclusion as a possible policy option. Behind it lies the confident but dubious assumption that the past is capable of an unambiguous interpretation and that on this sure foundation planning for the future can be built.

The more that official estimates dominate the context in which policies are made, the more these estimates are likely to become self-fulfilling prophecies and, conversely, the more that opportunities to develop the system in different ways will be neglected. Official command of the type of information input for the consideration of policy makers (as in the case of a heavy reliance on the extrapolation of existing trends) will naturally prescribe the parameters of possible policies. There is also an easy symbiosis between the use of projections of student and teacher numbers by the DES and the financial procedures governing department spending organized under the Public Expenditure Survey Committee (PESC). This requires that early each year government departments submit estimates of what they expect to spend over the next five years of each of their programmes to PESC. Given that departments compete with each other for a share of the expenditure cake, the DES is naturally not going to lose the opportunity of supporting its case and its financial projections with parallel figures concerning student and teacher population trends. The 'hard' data culled from the latter thus have considerable political appeal for the DES in the annual round of interdepartmental budgeting warfare, and until it can find an equally authoritative substitute it is not likely to downgrade the importance of projections in the face it presents to the rest of Whitehall.

As a means of estimating the financial implications of existing government programmes the Public Expenditure Survey system obviously suffers from the weakness that it does not cost and compare alternative policy options, as the White Paper 'The Reorganisation of

Central Government' (The Cabinet Office 1979 : para. 50) pointed out. In an attempt to remedy this problem, an output budgeting technique called Programme Analysis and Review (PAR), in many respects similar to the technique of corporate planning discussed earlier, was introduced into government planning in 1970, and the DES (1970b) has been one of the first departments to try and develop it. Like corporate planning, PAR seeks to systematize the process of policy analysis and policy formation along lines which place a premium on being able to assess the budgetary implications of differernt policy developments. The objective is to take a particular programme area such as nursery education and then to set out in a logical and informed fashion the alternative policies and their alternative costs.

Again it has that rational quality with immediate ramifications for the delimitation of the policy-making process. Firstly, some educational policies are going to be more easily costed than others and these are likely to be those already tried and tested and those which can be linked to trend data. Newer and less quantifiable policies are bound to appear experimental and hence more of a gamble. Secondly, the more confident that officials and ministers become that this management technique supplies them with the information required to make rational policy choices, the more policy formation will be internalized within the DES and the more outside interest groups will be excluded from it. Or, to put it another way:

The stronger are formal systems for policy analysis and evaluation in the government of education, the more doubtful becomes the autonomy of teachers and academics in deciding what they shall do, and how. The development of sophisticated management systems in government and in the DES is of interest not just for its own sake, but for its effect upon the balance of power in the education system − even the concept of 'partnership' between DES, the LEA, and teachers. (OU 1974:43)

Consultation with outside groups may take place, therefore, but in the context of choices already defined. Such consultation is consequently likely to be confirmatory rather than initiating in its objectives. However, what this argument does not deal with is the possibility that no matter how systematic the administration of PAR may be, and the indications are that it is not that systematic, that room still exists for the injection of values not sanctioned by the DES into policy making in the form of the education minister's role. How real is this possibility?

The most detailed evidence relevant to this question is Maurice Kogan's conversations with ex-DES ministers Edward Boyle and Antony Crosland in *The Politics of Education*. His general conclusion (1971:41) is that the 'ability of even the most able Minister to create, promote and carry out policies is limited'. Both Boyle and Crosland emphasize the constraints under which a minister operates in terms of policies already in train or being explored, the amount of information to be digested and the continually evolving nature of educational policy. Crosland calculated that it takes about two years to fully master a department but that even so, within these two years 'there will be chunks of the Department and of Department policy which you have not really had time to look at at all' (ibid.:158). Similarly Boyle felt that he did not have control over the vast range of policies of the DES – partly because he did not have time to understand all the various parts of education. (ibid.:137). This feeling is reinforced by the arguments of Lord Crowther-Hunt (a former Minister of State in the DES) concerning the gathering of influence by the bureaucratic élite. Crowther-Hunt maintains that the continual turnover of ministers of education (he estimates that in recent years their stay has averaged 17 months) means that they are rarely in the position of having sufficient independent knowledge to challenge the details of the policy aganda advanced by their civil servants. So when one of the Whitehall official committees (which ministers do not attend) or PAR reports (which are not published) produce their recommendations, it is increasingly difficult for a minister not to accept them (Crowther Hunt & Kellner 1980).

Probably the most influential role one can ascribe to a Minister, therefore, is that of arbitrator of competing policies within the DES rather than the initiator of completely new ones and the imposer of foreign values. This does not deny of course that department policies are heterogeneous rather then homogeneous. What Toby Weaver, ex-Deputy Secretary at the DES, has described as the 'dialectic within the office' ensures that such choice is available (ibid.:123). However, it is our contention that the procedures on which the policy-making process is founded increasingly circumscribe the nature of its possible content and hence the range of choices available to a minister.

For those continually concerned with the generation of those choices, the civil servants of central government, it would seem that there would be little to object to in the enclosure and limitation of policy formation. Indeed, if Locke (1974:71) is correct in his belief that the 'dedicated professional thinks of himself as fair and able to avoid self-interest in a way which representatives of localities or particular interests are not' then there would apparently be much to gain. The OECD report *Educational Development Strategy in England and Wales* was very forthright on this issue:

The feeling exists strongly within the Department that when it comes to planning leading to policy decisions for which resources have to be secured and allocated, such informal methods, utilised by sensitive and fair-minded government servants, are superior to highly structured formal procedures which invite half-baked and politically sectarian opinions, and encourage demagogy, confrontation, and publicity battles, leading to a considerable waste of time. (1975: 31)

If Birley's opinion of CEOs (protectors of democracy) and OECD's opinion of the DES are correct, then local and national managers of education have at least their self-esteem in common. But if the enclosure process means that the civil servant is seen by others to be the initiator of educational policy then his own conception of his role will have to shift accordingly. For although there is little doubt that the professional administrator regards himself as rightly influential in policy formulation, he is accustomed also to being supplied with protection by the cloak of democracy around him. Visibility is really not the name of the game for the civil servant and neither is direct public accountability. In the long term, however, he cannot expect to have both increased power and the same degree of anonymity. Those formerly included in policy formation are bound to demand that the new breed of expert managers be seen and held to be responsible for their actions.

The more activist definition of the educational administrator's role is a necessary corollary of the interventionist DES prepared both to take the lead in policy making and to prescribe its acceptable limits. Although the traditional conception of the department as aggregator and synthesizer of pressure group demands, responsive to the movement of the consensus, is still much beloved by many writers on education including the public self-presentation of the DES itself (see OECD 1975:Pt. 1), it is a conception rapidly being rendered obsolete by the march of events, as the chapter on the Great Debate demonstrates. And just as the Department shrugs off its passive policy stance so must those who administer it. But while shrugging off a self-conception is one thing, rearranging the relationships with others to fit that new conception is quite another and depends, firstly, on the amount of control the DES can exercise over its environment in the construction and execution of policy and, secondly, on its capacity to legitimize new policy. Changing the state apparatus can be a dicey affair.

Controls

Until recently, the department has been engagingly modest in its estimation of its own power. In its contribution to the 1975 OECD report, for example, it argued that the powers of the Secretary of State under the 1944 Education Act and subsequent Acts 'though important are not extensive' and that he 'relies heavily on non-statutory means of implementing his policies, by offering guidance and advice through the issue of circulars and other documents' (8–9). Phrases such as 'adequate consultation', 'foundation of assent' and 'general consensus' are scattered liberally throughout the DES section of the report as the Department insists that it is reflecting an aggregate of existing opinion rather than seeking to mould a new one. Its view of its controls are here fully consistent with its consensus model of educational policy making. As chapter nine demonstrates, this passive public face of the DES has changed considerably in the last few years in recognition of its search for more controls to service more adequately its burgeoning planning function. As it happens the Department's earlier promulgation of a public image where its powers were presented as limited and mainly non-statutory was in any case something of a false modesty.

All LEAs operate within an established network of national policies: the length of school life, salaries paid to teachers, minimum building standards and maximum building costs and pupil-teacher ratios. Any consideration of departmental control must in the first instance recognize that this framework exists and itself sets limits upon an LEA's capacity to deviate too far from central guidelines. Similarly, the much vaunted autonomy of the classroom teacher is regulated by the national system of curriculum control, namely the General Certificate of Education Examination at Ordinary and Advanced Levels, and the Certificate of Secondary Education

Examinations in their various modes. Although the actual examinations are administered by autonomous examining bodies (eight GCE and fourteen CSE) the Secretary of State decides what changes will occur in the system after listening to the advice of an intermediary body, the Schools Council. Beyond this framework of controls, the DES has its financial controls, whatever overlap exists between local and central administrator values on policy making and last, but not least, Her Majesty's Inspectorate.

Although the department does not directly control the capital finance used by LEAs for educational building, it does decide (according to building regulations and cost limits developed by the Architects and Buildings Branch and the annual building programme allocated to each educational sector – schools, further education and teacher training, etc.) which LEA projects will be given the go-ahead and which ones refused. The fact that local authorities must submit educational building plans to the Department for approval means that the DES cannot only apply the standing administrative requirements to the plans but can also use the opportunity, if it so wishes, to exercise political control over changes in local authority provision. The most notable clashes recently in this respect have been those over LEA plans for comprehensivization which have failed to meet DES standards, flexible though these are, on what precisely constitutes a comprehensive system. Given this method of financing the physical context in which education takes place, it is obviously in the interest of LEAs to remain sensitive to developments in DES policy both by keeping a close watch on the numerous circulars issued by the Department and by consultation with its local liaison officer, the HMI.

Even recognizing this ultimate control of capital investment by the DES, it would not do to conclude as a result that LEAs are the easy and obedient servants of the Departmental will. For although Crosland 'was very struck by how much influence, control, power, or whatever the right word is, the Department has' (Kogan 1971: 169), Boyle pointed out (ibid.: 124) that 'there can't be a straight, single control here for the very simple reason that the Ministry directly controls so very little money'. Boyle was referring to the fact that the majority of the expenditure on education by local authorities, that is recurrent as opposed to capital expenditure, comes to the LEA as part of the annual Rate Support Grant (RSG) from which the government finances all local authority services. The RSG is a block grant within which, until very recently, no funds were separately labelled for the use of the education service alone: education had to compete with the other services for its share. At first sight this system may appear to have given LEAs substantial discretion in terms of what they spend on education and how they spend it but, bearing in mind the national guidelines within which LEAs must operate, the true situation is much less clear cut and the arguments continue (see Boaden 1971; Byrne 1974). The picture is further muddied by the 1980 Local Government Planning and Land (No. 2) Act which replaces the single block grant with one awarded on a service by service basis. Precisely what effect this will have on the DES–LEA relationship it is as yet to soon to say. What is, nevertheless, clear, is that considerable variation exists in LEA provision of books, equipment, furniture, in-service training of teachers, school transport etc., indicating that although the DES may control the broad parameters of education so far it does not substantially influence the quality of the day-to-day provision within these paremeters (see Taylor & Ayres 1969).

Nor are its financial controls integrated so as to form an efficient basis for the policy-making process. Reporting the reactions of local authority associations to the 1969 Public Expenditure White Paper, the Education and Arts Sub-Committee of the House of Commons Expenditure Committee stated:

The associations were also anxious about the effect of the [annual] PESC predictions on the biennial Rate Support Grant settlements. They complained that the PESC figures and the Rate Support Grant figures were on a different price basis and could not therefore be related to one another in their present form. The association wished ideally to see a Rate Support Grant and PESC as parts of a single interrelated exercise rather than as two separate and, as they suspected, conflicting operations. (Armitage 1973:39)

Add to this the particular problem of higher education where the responsibility for financial provision lies both with the LEAs (polytechnics), and the University Grants Committee (universities) with its own quite distinct planning procedures and relationship with the DES, and you have a less than coherent financial framework within which to form policy. Recent reorganization of the DES Higher and Further Education Branches responsible for financial planning into a single new 'super-branch', FHE 1, is an attempt to mitigate the problem by bridging the binary divide and reducing the power and isolation of the University Branch. As yet it is too early to know what effect this will have on the co-ordination of DES policy on the universities and polytechnics.

At present, then, the fragmentation of the financial procedures on which the DES relies in its attempts to construct policies leads to tensions between the local authorities and the Department. However, it is worth noting that both would agree on the diagnosis of the reasons for the problem, that is the inefficiencies of the financing mechanisms, and the need for more systematic cooperation. Whether this also means that they would agree on who has what say in a more integrated planning system is open to doubt. For our previous analysis suggests that the DES has already defined what it means by more efficiency in central policy making and it will be a question of how far local authorities are prepared to go along with this definition once its structural implications begin to percolate through. Despite the common professional concern that long-term planning in education should be rationally organized the traditional central–local differences are bound to pose problems. Thus Mrs Thatcher's rather abrupt withdrawal of Circular 10/65 enforcing comprehensivization and its replacement with Circular 10/70 allowing LEAs to decide against comprehensivization if they so wished drew unanimous protest from the local authority associations. As Kogan (1975:100) points out 'it was not what she did but the way that she did it that was objectionable'.

If there is doubt this far about the Department's ability to orchestrate policy change, where does that leave its territorial force, Her Majesty's Inspectorate? How far can HMI be regarded as the willing tool of the DES in its attempts to impose central definitions of desirable policy shift and how far is HMI an independent body with opinions and values of its own? Its position in the educational system as authoritative supplier of information both to the LEAs and schools on the one hand, the the DES on the other, is undoubtedly critical. At the local level, HMIs have the functions of inspectors of schools and colleges, interpreters of Department policy to the LEAs, and are members of numerous committees such as examination boards and regional advisory councils for further education. (The latter is particularly important since HMIs have the singular power to accept or reject new courses.) At the central level, they act as professional advisers to the DES drawing on their network of local contacts, contribute to Department publications and staff Department courses

for teachers. Any move by the DES to systematize further the process
of policy construction is therefore dependent upon HMI to acquire
and to disseminate the right information at the right time. This would
imply that from the Department's point of view the closer the ties
between itself and HMI the better.

Writers on Her Majesty's Inspectorate are frequently at pains to
point out that HMIs are independent-minded people, if occasionally
idiosyncratic. With some pride Blackie (1970:53; and see Edmonds,
1962), an ex-HMI himself, argues that,

An inspector's essential independence is professional. In all
educational matters he is free to hold and to express his own opinions,
and no departmental control can be exercised upon them. This means
that what he says to a teacher or writes in a report is what he really
thinks, and is not in any way trimmed to suit government or
departmental policy.

More realistically he subsequently admits that the 'Department could
not tolerate a situation in which one of its employees was openly and
explicitly hostile to a policy which it was implementing at the behest
of Parliament' (ibid.). Other sources tend to confirm this image of
HMIs operating within very severe constraints set by the Department
and only exercising or voicing their personal judgement in situations
not likely to offend. Thus the Select Committee on Her Majesty's
Inspectorate (1968) concluded that the Department and the
Inspectorate are in fact a very integrated body and the DES in its
pamphlet *HMI Today and Tomorrow* (1970) also down-played the
significance of HMI autonomy:

HM Inspectors are a body of men and women who are ultimately
answerable to the Secretary of State for Education and Science. They
may well be given direct instructions by him. Their appointment is
made on his recommendation. ... It is the duty of the Inspectors, as of
other civil servants, to assist the central government in discharging
the responsibilities that successive parliaments have laid down.
(1970a:9).

As the DES moves further in the direction of policy-making
enclosure, so it must rely more on its internal means of information
collecting rather than on information supplied by external groups. In
this respect the role of HMIs as the field representatives and data

collection agents of the DES is bound to be crucial in its efforts to sustain this move. Precisely how this role is likely to develop and how it relates to the growing activities of the Department's Assessment of Performance Unit is discussed later (see ch. 9). But suffice to it to say here that whatever the Inspectorate still retains is likely to be further eroded in response to the requirements of the new style of policy making; though the myth of autonomy may well be retained as long as possible since it enhances the supposed objectivity of the information on which the Department rests its policy proposals.

The legitimation of the state apparatus

The OECD report (1975:28) on British educational development bravely stated that 'the evolution of education in the United Kingdom cannot be charted without placing the planning function of the Department of Education and Science at the centre of the story.' It summarized DES policy formation as characterized by attempts to:

minimize the degree of controversiality in the planning process and its results; reduce possible alternatives to matters of choice of resource allocation; limit the planning process to those parts of the educational services and functions strictly controlled by the DES; exploit as fully as possible the powers, prerogatives and responsibilities given to the DES under the 1944 Education Act; understate as much as possible the full role of the Government in the determination of the future course of educational policy and even minimise it in the eyes of the general public. (ibid.:42)

Our own analysis of the bureaucratization of educational power in Britain has so far reached similar, though probably less emphatic conclusions. However, our theoretical perspective leads us beyond the recognition that bureaucratic change has and is taking place in the management of education and takes us on to the further question of what ideological change is necessary to support these bureaucratic shifts in the state apparatus given education's central ideological function in society. Our theory insists that if educational change is to be acceptable to the populace at large it has to go through an ideological stage. There are, analytically speaking, two aspects to this stage: (a) the way in which policy is produced and (b) the policies produced. Both require ideological legitimation and, in practice, the nature of this legitimation may overlap the two aspects. Nevertheless, as we will show, the overlap is not so complete as to undermine the importance of the analytical distinction itself.

In the past the process of educational policy production was legitimated by the Department's claim that it aggregated and reflected the existing educational consensus. The major instrument reinforcing this claim was the work of the educational committees appointed either by the Central Advisory Council (CAC) on education, a standing statutory body, or by the DES itself. Major shifts in educational policy have, until recently, always been heralded by reports from such committees (e.g. Robbins, Crowther, Plowden) and their public hallmark has been their independence from the Department, the eminence of their membership, their sensitivity to the broad sweep of educational opinion, their increasing use of 'objective' social science, and, stemming from these others, the authority of their pronouncements. To a large extent these qualities are in fact illusory and the committees are, as Kogan documents, 'far more "in-house", far more a part of official review, than the outward forms seem to suggest' (Kogan & Packwood 1974:23). Committees generally have their terms of reference and membership determined by the Department and their secretariat and research data supplied by the Department (Robbins being a notable exception to the latter). This has meant that, up to now, they have performed the latent functions of enabling the Department to use them both as a jury against which Departmental policies could be tested as they emerged and as a centre for negotiations on policies which had, in any case, to be discussed with the main educational interests before reaching the public stage (ibid.:23).

Nor is the DES in any way obliged to accept the policy implications of a committee's conclusions, though public opinion may force its hand. In his examination of the influence of prewar advisory councils on the Board of Education, Graves (1940:89) cites the example of the report *Books in Elementary Schools* which was widely read, reprinted, yet comprehensively ignored by the board. He concludes that this well illustrates the impotence of an advisory body once it has reported: 'Unless the education authorities are willing to take the matter up, or public opinion is strong enough, a first-class report may disappear almost without trace.' And the Department is only likely to take the matter up if it fits a prior policy decision made internally.

Yet if education committees and their reports are such malleable material, to be promulgated by the DES as policy legitimating instruments as and when it thinks fit, why are such committees used less now than before? Why did Crosland deem it appropriate to disband the CAC after the publication of the Plowden and Gittins reports in 1967 particularly since, as Kogan (1978: 135) underlines, 'since then there has been discontent at the way in which the recently created planning system within the DES seems to feed on its own expertise and knowledge rather than bringing in wider circles of expertise and knowledge', as it had done previously? Crosland's own explanation is revealing: he argues that there is a danger of too many and too lengthy reports – 'And they can slow up action, as Plowden would have done on comprehensivization if I hadn't been very firm' (Kogan 1971: 174). In justifying the phasing out of the CACs, Sir William Pile (1979: 38) observed that if committees of inquiry are to be used then *ad hoc* ones which reach speedy conclusions are increasingly preferred by ministers. The difficulty with placing this premium on decision-making efficiency, however, is that the legitimating function of the committees is neglected. While it is one thing to take a decision swiftly, it is quite another to get it accepted by the rest of the educational system.

As the department adopts a more positive stance towards the rest of the education system, gathers its own information, internalizes its planning procedures and shrugs off its old service image, it has to face the fact that since policy can no longer be deemed to 'emerge' (like those Conservative party leaders of old) by some hidden but natural process of evolution, neither can the ideology necessary to support both the policy-making framework itself and the policies produced. At present the tendency is for the DES to attempt to legitimize its own dominance of the formation of policy by arguing that the planning techniques which it employs are in some sense 'objective' and 'scientific' and allow ministers a fair choice between a full range of policy options. This can be characterized as a low profile approach which will work so long as major educational interests are not unduly offended by the policy biases inherent in the Department's use of these techniques. Even so, the fact that the policies which are produced are directly the DES's responsibility alone, rather than that of a vague consensus, will increasingly place the Department in an exposed position.

If questions are raised about the legitimacy of the means of policy formation employed by the educational state apparatus, this is bound to have an effect in turn upon the DES's ability to manage the tensions between education's social control and economic functions. For these functions to be performed effectively by the educational system, it is essential that any change in their operation (i.e. any new educational policy) is both cloaked with the suitable ideological apparel and viewed as having been produced by legitimate policy-making machinery. As the forum in which these underlying pressures are politically negotiated, along with the inputs from demographic shifts and party policy, the Department undoubtedly comes under considerable institutional stress as it seeks to reconcile the policy implications of these demands with its own bureaucratic needs and ambitions. To relieve this stress, though not to remove it, the DES needs ideological protection: in order to implement successfully its social control and economic functions and to legitimize its policies. Merely claiming that the policies were produced by 'rational' planning techniques is not going to be good enough. We do not live in a rational world. What the CACs and the other committees were good at, and what the DES is still learning, was that assembling of broad societal values into patterns which carried authority – i.e. they were good at producing ideology. Until the Department acquires the art of developing ideological positions to match the policies it sponsors, it will not have fully worked out the implications of its own bureaucratic changes and education's social functions and will remain exposed to attacks such as that of the OECD report. We return to this issue later in chapter nine to examine how far the Great Debate can be considered an attempt by the DES to generate educational ideology.

6

The Schools Council and the Dissemination of Ideology

One of the major objectives of this book is to introduce a positive element of doubt and scepticism into conceptions of the relationship between the class system and educational change. While we do not deny that a dominant or aspiring social group will attempt to use education as a means of propagating an ideology which serves its interests, the extent to which it succeeds is problematic and dependent in part upon the internal and external bureaucratic factors shaping its development. In particular, in the case of organizations of the modern state such as the DES there is no guarantee that as their self-confidence increases they will automatically implement the policies best suited to the interests of the class they ostensibly serve. In addition, it also can be said that no such guarantee exists where an organization is on the margins of the state apparatus and lacks self-confidence, as in the case of the Schools Council for Curriculum and Examinations. It is this latter organization which this chapter examines in order to explore the process of ideology dissemination or non-dissemination as the case may be (see also Lockwood Report 1964; Richards 1974; Lawton 1980:5).

As the national, state-funded, body charged with the development of new curriculum materials and ideas as well as with the recommending of major possible changes in examinations to the Secretary of State for Education, the Council has several advantages as a subject for study. Its prominent position in the educational system could lead one to expect that it would be using its authority to legitimate a mode of organizing knowledge in the schools which would be in tune with the interests of the dominant class. In other words, it would be using its command and manipulation of state resources to propagate an educational ideology (or more accurately a partial ideology since it is concerned chiefly with the curriculum) which reinforced the existing hegemony. Some observers have argued that this is the case and that the Council 'effectively defined for teachers the parameters of innovation' in a way which bolstered the status quo (Young 1976:92). Yet at the same time its vulnerability in the Great Debate on education, the calls from backbench MPs that it be abolished (see Butt 1978:18), suggest that it is still not an accepted member of the educational establishment or an integral part of the educational hierarchy. How can it then be an effective vehicle for any ideology if its own legitimacy is in question?

A second justification for studying the Council is that it is what might be termed a 'middle-range' educational institution, much smaller than a government department but with functions which are national in scope. In this connection Whitty and Young (1976:3) have argued that 'Given the inadequate and abstract nature of many broad theories about the relationship between education and society, it becomes important to identify quite precisely the institutional practices which produce and sustain the constraint within which teachers work.' The Schools Council provides the opportunity to do exactly this and to act as an institutional bridge between macro-theory and the details of the legitimation process.

In the last few years it has come in for a lot of criticism. In the well publicized DES memorandum to the Prime Minister in 1976 (the infamous 'Yellow Book') the Schools Council was attacked for having 'scarcely begun to tackle the problems of the curriculum as a whole' and its overall performance, both on curriculum and on examination, was described as having been 'generally mediocre' (TES 1976:2–3). The report continued:

Because of this and because the influence of the teachers unions has led to an increasingly political flavour – in the worst sense of the word – in its deliberations, the general reputation of the Schools Council has suffered a considerable decline over the last few years. (ibid.)

In response to this, other public criticism, and considerable arm twisting by Shirley Williams, then Secretary of State for Education, the Council reviewed and on 1 September 1978 adopted a new constitution which contained increased lay, industrial and government representation on a reformed committee structure. The full implications of the new *modus operandi* of the Council have yet to be worked out. In this chapter we confine the discussion largely to the pre-1978 Council which funded large-scale national projects, returning to the recent change towards small-scale local funding of curriculum development in a concluding section on its future ideological role. It is important to note, however, how relatively precarious is the position of the Council in the educational system and the insights with which this may provide us.

As a relatively recent addition to an educational structure traditionally resistant to change, the Council could be seen as a new boy who has still to prove his worth. It could be argued that until it has passed through the various *rites de passage* for entry into the education system and had conferred upon it the mantle of educational authority, its capacity for ideology dissemination and legitimation is suspect. This is at least a possibility and one which renders the Schools Council an interesting case for study. For it could well be an institution still in the formative stages of forging both its ideology and its legitimating machinery and hence an institution where this machinery is more visible than concealed.

The institutional context

A major theme of this chapter is that the process of ideology formation and dissemination has to be proved rather than assumed given its essentially problematic nature and that it is in the inter-relationship of institutional structures that the answer to this problem can be found. In examining the Schools Council's contribution to the legitimation of particular structures of knowledge through ideology dissemination, we begin by placing it in its institutional context for, as we shall see subsequently, this context is essential for understanding how legitimation occurs or does not occur. To ignore it, as some commentators have done, is to ignore the range of institutional constraints within which the Council operates and hence, by omission, to endow the Council with unreal amounts of power, influence and legitimating capacity.

The very creation of the Schools Council provides an initial insight into the complexities of its institutional position. Anne Corbett (1973:2) has described its setting up in 1963 as 'an intensely political act' in that those major groups with a formal vested interest in the control of the curriculum at that time (the Ministry of Education, LEAs, and teachers' organizations) fought out a well publicized battle as a result of which the Council was created (see Manzer

1973:59–69). There is little doubt that the conflict was precipitated by what Manzer (ibid.:63) describes as 'a definite departure in the Ministry's (Ministry of Education) conception of its role in the formulation of an important area of educational policy'. It decided unilaterally that the time had arrived for it to become more interventionist. Hence, as a result of the urging of Sir David Eccles (then Minister of Education) that 'the secret garden of the curriculum', as he termed it, should no longer remain immune from central government influence, the Curriculum Study Group was set up in 1962 within the Ministry of Education. Drawn from administrators, HMIs and outside experts, it was envisaged that the group would commission research and make recommendations in the fields of curriculum and examinations.

So far so good. However, while it was one thing for the ministry to alter its own conception of its role, it was quite another for it to get other groups to accept what amounted to a shift in the definition of the power distribution in the educational system. It was unable to legitimize to the satisfaction of the other vested educational interests a restructuring of the process of curriculum control. Nor was the Ministry in a position at that time to redefine what exactly constituted a 'vested educational interest' in order to extend the range of the conflict and perhaps undermine the position of the opposition, the teachers – though the opportunity was to come later in 1977 with the Taylor Report on school management and the opening up of issues of accountability and parental or community involvement in the running of schools. In 1963, however, this possibility was not on and the Ministry soon found itself outflanked by the teachers' unions and accepted the recommendations of the Lockwood Committee for a teacher-dominated Schools Council, publicly financed but independent of government. For the time being, then, more control of the curriculum eluded the Ministry's grasp.

The implications of this mode of creation for the Schools Council's relationship with other parts of the educational system were considerable. Not surprisingly for an institution born of political compromise, it constantly found itself, in terms of both the influence it has and the influence it thinks it should have, surrounded by ambiguities. Nowhere is this more evident than in the Council's pre-1978 constitution which placed great emphasis on what it *cannot* do, though this negative power feature is expressed in positive form as the value of school autonomy. Hence under its constitutional 'powers' the Council's advisory role was stressed: it could 'offer advice *on request* to schools' (SC 1978: para. 3b; our stress). In addition, 'regard shall at all times be had to the general principle that each school should have the fullest possible measure of responsibility for its own work, with its own curriculum and teaching methods based on the needs of its own pupils and evolved by its own staff' (para. 4). Similarly, with specific regard to examinations, its function was 'to assist the Secretary of State to carry out his responsibility for the direction of policy and the general arrangements for secondary school examinations, and to discharge on his behalf, the functions of a central co-ordinating authority' (paras. 13, 14).

Exactly how the Schools Council was supposed to be a 'central co-ordinating authority' in a decentralized education system when its own constitution outlawed such concepts as 'intervention' and 'direction' was, from the outset, unclear. Add to this the fact of teacher union majorities on all the council committees up to 1978, with the exception of finance, on the whole ensuring the protection of 'classroom teacher interests' from significant external interference, and you have the picture of a body very much constrained by its internal structure. The external constraints on its possible influence were, and are equally substantial. Firstly, the validity of the well-worn maxim that 'he who controls the examinations controls the curriculum' means that whatever the Schools Council produces in the way of new curriculum material or ideas for the secondary sector has to be seen in terms of its acceptability to the examination boards. Anything produced without that test being applied is, like it or not, likely to be peripheral to the main business of secondary schools (see Maclure 1975: 142–51). Secondly, the fact that responsibility for the curriculum is, by the 1944 Education Act, devolved to the local education authorities in theory and to the headteacher and his staff in practice, means that the take-up of Schools Council products is dependent upon the Council's acceptability to widely dispersed and localized units of power. Thirdly, even assuming that the Schools Council did move openly in the direction of more positive promotion, it would still need to sell itself in the first instance to those local agencies responsible for in-service training and teaching support activities – teachers' centres, LEA advisers and colleges of education. Fourthly, it has always to remain sensitive to the possibility that the DES may try to increase its own influence over the curriculum as the Ministry of Education did in the early 1960s.

For both internal and external reasons, therefore, the position of the Council in the formal power relationships of British education is essentially a subordinate one. As Nisbet (1973:67) points out:

Its position is vulnerable, in that it is dependent on other institutions for implementing its work. Consolidation of linkages with the other parts of the system on which it is dependent is therefore an urgent priority, and to achieve this, it has still to win their full confidence and trust.

This brings us to the question of legitimation of power.

Even assuming the Schools Council *had* been endowed with certain powers over the curriculum and examinations, it would still have faced the problem of rendering these powers acceptable to the structures in which it is embedded in order to gain their full cooperation. As it is, the Council 'operates within the restraints of the established relationship of authority in the educational system, and has only the power of persuasion' (ibid.). And to legitimize its powers of persuasion it has to establish its credibility in the eyes of the existing authorities on which it is, by definition, dependent for cooperation; a somewhat circular situation to be in. In optimistic vein some commentators (see Richards 1974:335) have asked why the Council has not mounted a serious challenge to the educational status quo. The short answer is that even if it had, none of the powers that be would have felt obliged to take any notice. Why should they? It had first to acquire, to use Stuart Maclure's phraseology (1975:146), 'a mossy respectability', 'to take things a step at a time and build up confidence in the power groups whose association in the work of the Council was vital to success'. It was, therefore, bound to 'prefer discretion to valour' (ibid.).

While the Council's initial strategy (conscious or unconscious) to secure its own legitimacy was inevitably circumspect, it could be argued that once legitimized the Council would then be in a position to adopt a more positive political stance even given the continuing constraints of an ambiguous constitution, the accompanying set of ill-defined goals and a dependent power position. However, an essential part of such a stance would be a fairly well-defined ethos of its own, sustained over a reasonable period of time. And here, once again, the council was ill-equipped. Its 'committee network, the divided secretariat and the policy of staffing by short-term secondment, provide effective constraints on the staff' (Nisbet 1973:47), so that fragmentation has so far prevented the emergence of a coherent ethos. Without this the Council lacks the drive and direction to utilize effectively whatever legitimacy it acquires. Putting it another way, it can be said that the Council did not possess the structural prerequisites for the emergence of its own organic intellectuals capable of generating a Council ideology. Until the roles of thinker and planner became an integral and permanent part of its organization, the Schools Council could not hope to approach the rest of the education system with the confidence of a known and developed ideological position. The importance of this institutional context is that it sets limits on what we have to say subsequently about the details of the legitimation process. It forces us away from grandiose generalizations about the possible legitimizing activities of the Council in the direction of more circumspect, but also more accurate statements.

The implementation of ideology

One of the less hesitant comments on the implementation of an ideology through the legitimation of a particular educational form by the Schools Council has been made by Michael Young (1973:78). He claims that the council 'through its legitimation of curricula that might be characterised in Bordieu's terms as based on class cultures, together with the schools, maintain the class structure of which they are a reflection'. This neat, not to mention circular argument flows from the general position of those sociology of education theorists who focus on the formal processes of social control secured through the management of knowledge (see pp. 21–6). It is not the focus that bothers us here but the level of the generalization and subsequent *modus operandi* to which it gives rise. Young assumes that Schools Council resources produce a particular class effect and then sets out to prove that this is the case, employing an argument largely devoid of an institutional context and a methodology best characterized as idiosyncratic. We would argue instead that it is more fruitful and more rigorous to assume that this class effect is uncertain and then to examine the extent of its presence.

In exploring the way in which the Council acts as a vehicle for an educational ideology or part-ideology, we need to consider three questions:

1 To what extent does the Council have the capacity to legitimate anything?

2 With reference to what groups does it have this capacity?

3 What does it legitimate?

Ideology propagation by an institution, then, can be seen as having the components of capacity, target audience and ideological content – all of which may be capable of having an independent effect upon the process if historical circumstances alter. And far from being a total and homogeneous process, as Young assumes, legitimation may be partial, fragmentary and intermittent.

1   *Legitimation capacity*

To begin with the question of 'legitimation capacity', it is obvious that for an institution to be able to legitimate something to a group, it itself must first be regarded as legitimate by that group: that is, it must be seen as having the authority to ascribe values, be they new or existing values, to particular objects such as parts of the curriculum. Merely because an institution exists is no guarantee that it can legitimate. Now as we have already seen, the extent to which the Schools Council is seen as authoritative by other groups is questionable. Lacking formal powers it has had to build its legitimacy slowly through consultation and cooperation with LEAs, colleges of education and so on.

In the case of examinations its formal authority is in fact less than that of its predecessor, the Secondary Schools Examination Council (SSEC). Whereas the SSEC required exam boards to submit both 'O' and 'A' Level syllabuses for approval, the Schools Council only receives 'O' Level syllabuses 'for comment', though it retains the function of approving revised 'A' Level syllabuses. The CSE boards are independent of the Council – not surprisingly given the vast number of syllabuses which their Modes 1, 11 and 111 generate and the logistic difficulties of monitoring them. Similarly, in performing its statutory function of providing advice to the government on major changes in the examination system, the Council has failed to establish itself as an organization with any political weight. The only Council proposal on examinations so far accepted by the Secretary of State is the A, B, C, D system of grading at 'O' Level. Of the others, the government refused to endorse the Council's recommendations for a twenty-point grading of 'A' Levels in 1972, with the result, as Gerry

Fowler (1975:84) comments, that the 'proposal was in effect dead from that moment, although the Council had approved it six months before'. Likewise, its proposals on 'N' and 'F' Levels (to replace 'A' Levels) were rejected in 1979. A decision on the final form of a common system of examining at 16 + and on the proposed Certificate of Extended Education (CEE – for those wishing to stay on in full-time education after the age of 16 but not wishing to study for 'A' Levels) is awaited. The fact that the regrading of 'O' Levels was readily accepted is obviously a reflection of its comparative insignificance and the lack of challenge it presents to existing arrangements in the curriculum and the process of selection for higher education. Where such a challenge is presented, as is the case with the other proposals, the government's strategy appears to be to delay and attempt to co-opt the decision-making process by appointing its own committees to examine the proposals (the 16 + proposals were examined by a working party under the chairmanship of Sir James Waddell and the CCE proposals by a study group chaired by Professor Keophane). This is scarcely the type of response guaranteed to enhance the status of the Council's advice in the short term though, as we shall discuss later, in the long term a series of decisions favourable to the Council would have had the opposite effect.

In addition, the hostile attack on the Council in the 'Yellow Book', sniping from various politicians in the course of the Great Debate and instances like the defeated amendment to the 1976 Education Bill that the Council be abolished, indicates that it is not yet that secure a part of the British educational hierarchy. For these attacks were not merely on the Council's policies but on its right to exist as a separate institution. Although Young does not deal with this question of the Council's peripheral power position, it is not all clear how the Schools Council can have a legitimating effect *down* the educational hierarchy when it remains a less than fully integrated member of the educational establishment. Unless, of course, it is seeking to legitimate anti-status quo values – which Young firmly denies.

2   *Target audience*
Turning to the question of the 'target audience' of the legitimating process, we find that Young has little to say on this. He goes no further than stating that legitimation of different types of knowledge occurs and does not specify how ideology is disseminated and

channelled in particular ways to particular groups. He does, however, make the negative statement that whether or not the Schools Council has any influence is 'beside the point' (1973:78) — presumably because it legitimates even if it does not influence, though precisely how this can happen and what the relationship between the two concepts is, we are not told. The implication is that legitimation takes place in some vague kind of way merely because the Council exists and that there is no point in tracing the path of its legitimating effect. Our argument, however, is that a more discriminating form of analysis than this should at least be tried even if it should subsequently be found that the legitimating effect of the Schools Council is uniformly distributed across all educational structures: allowance can then be made for its possible differential legitimating impact.

The major target of the council, both in terms of the material produced and the legitimation of certain arrangements of knowledge such as subject divisions, is of course the teaching profession itself. This can be used as an illustration of the hazards of too readily assuming that legitimation inevitably occurs in a uniform fashion. Up to now, the Schools Council has not only felt wary of infringing the autonomy of the classroom but has also not been particularly effective in the distribution of its products (see SC 1974). The reasons for this lack of effectiveness lay as much with its own internal bureaucratic arrangements as with its uncemented position in the education system. Just as analysis of the DES bureaucracy can supply us with indications of its more positive sponsorship of an ideology (see pp. 100–106) so the Council bureaucracy can be shown to have been sadly lacking in the basic mechanisms of ideology promotion.

A clear distinction has to be drawn between the Council and the projects it has funded. Once launched, a project was very much on its own, receiving occasional guidance from its liaison officer at the council 'This', as two ex-members of the Cambridge School Classics Project observed (Grieg & Reid 1978:16–17), 'is a very tenuous connection.' They continued: 'Once the Project started, the practical concern of the Council fell away, to re-emerge only when some money was wanted. Its accountability was construed in the more limited categories of formative and summative evaluation — and even these were seen as something extra to be added on, a kind of ritual blessing to the Project's work, rather than an intrinsic part of the whole operation.' The separation of Council and project has meant that project directors are not assisted and trained in the conduct of what, for many, are the previously unencountered fields of project management, public relations and information dissemination. They remain amateurs, assisted occasionally by Council advisory committees composed mainly of disciplinary experts equally lacking in the skills required and by a sparsely worded *Handbook for Project Directors and Grant Holders*.

In any case, even if there had been a Council policy for inducting new project directors in the skills of project management it would have been a policy very difficult to put into operation. For until 1978 it was the Council's practice to employ its central staff on short-term contracts, supposedly to ensure that fresh blood from the teaching profession was continually flowing through its administrative veins. In fact, the consequent regular turnover of personnel successfully prevented the accumulation over time of expertise about how to run a project and disseminate its products. So although projects were obliged after 1974 to build a 'dissemination phase' into their project proposal, it was not a phase which could be grounded in any systematic fashion in the lessons learnt from the experience of past projects. Different projects pursued different dissemination strategies, with no idea as to which was likely to be the most efficient strategy in their case. Add to this the fact that project dissemination had to negotiate its way through the same complex of educational agencies with which the Council is still trying to establish its own legitimacy, and it becomes reasonable to conjecture that this dissemination was not going to be that successful.

Apart from the flow of Schools Council information through the educational system initiated by the projects themselves and by whatever sales their materials and publications obtain on the open market, there is little other formal promotion from the centre. What there is, is not guaranteed to have much impact. A newsletter is circulated about three times a year to all schools via LEAs in fierce competition with the avalanche of other circulars, publishers' lists, etc. with which schools are inundated. Secondly, brief project profiles are sent annually to LEAs and teachers' centres and others but what happens to them after that depends on the attitude or whim of the recipient. This is entirely in keeping with the non-interventionist stance of the council and its tendency to allow information about its activities to be distributed in a *laissez-faire* or haphazard fashion: to be diffused rather than actively disseminated.

At the same time, it can be argued that to characterize the Council as a non-promotional institution oversimplifies its position. In the report of the Schools Council working party on dissemination and in-service training, it is made plain that:

we believe that projects should follow a policy of positive promotion of their ideas and materials. We recognise that some will see it as the incursion of the market place into the classroom, but all we are saying is that it is wrong to expend public money on educational research considered by the appropriate Council committees to be desirable and then risk wasting it because teachers are unaware of the results. Positive promotion is not the hard sell. (SC 1974 : 11)

This is a fairly definite statement about the value of positive promotion even if the final sentence does introduce a note of equivocation. Furthermore, from 1976 onwards, the Schools Council's own research team began studying the dissemination strategies of projects and the Impact and Take-Up Project was set up at Sussex University to examine what influence Council projects had had on the classroom. It was, however, a rather belated concern which was soon to be overtaken by events in the shape of the new constitution in 1978 and the resulting shift away from national projects to local curriculum development. A concern which was essentially cosmetic since it lacked the resources, political will and organization to translate it into effective action. With its cumbrous committee system, temporary central staff and amateur project directors the Schools Council's ambiguous bureaucracy was very much the creature of the political compromise which gave it birth.

If the capacity of an institution to legitimate particular structures of knowledge to a particular group depends at least partly on its capacity to disseminate information efficiently to that group, then the Schools Council's ability to legitimate a class-based conception of the curriculum to teachers must be seriously in doubt. It has problems enough letting teachers know it exists, let alone ensuring that a coherent philosophy of the curriculum (if it has one) is transmitted to them. At present, its dissemination efforts are too weak and its own legitimacy in the eyes of teachers too shaky for this to occur. For it has to be borne in mind that the ranks of the teaching profession are far from unanimous in their approval of the Schools Council. For some perceive it to be as deeply tarred with the brush of progressivism (and hence non-authoritative) as Michael Young sees it branded with the badge of the status quo.

Most of the statistical evidence available on how far teachers have been influenced by the Schools Council was collected by its Impact and Take-Up Project. For our purposes, that is for the purposes of tracing the propagation of ideology, the results are largely inconclusive since questionnaire surveys (on which the Project mainly relied for its data on the national impact of Council projects) are inevitably unsubtle in their treatment of ideas formation and transmission. Nevertheless, certain figures are worth quoting. Overall, 32 per cent of secondary teachers and 71 per cent of primary teachers said they were making at least some use of ideas or materials from at least one Schools Council project (Steadman *et al.* 1980:8.4). The difficulty here, of course, as the Impact Project's reports reiterate, is knowing exactly what is meant by 'some use'. Rather than pursue that, it is more important to note that in secondary schools, 82 per cent of those using council project ideas or materials reported that they did so after adapting these ideas or materials (ibid. 4.6). This figure confirms the suspicion voiced elsewhere that considerable 'slippage' occurs between the original goals of a curriculum development project and the way in which it is implemented in the classroom (Jenkins & Shipman 1976:72). The Impact Project's observation that generally less than a third of teachers in secondary schools using a project were making 'extensive use' of its ideas or materials would tend to support this view (Steadman *et al.* 1980:1.3). The fact of the matter is that the familiar constraints of lack of time and money, as well as the natural inertia of school organization (ibid.:ch. 6), mean that teachers are much more likely to see Council project materials as a convenient, but occasional resource for teaching rather than as a package to be purchased wholesale. The majority commitment to 'some use' is therefore a natural concomitant of 'slippage' occurring.

If, as would seem to be the case, 'slippage' is taking place on this scale and teachers are viewing Council products mainly as a resource bank, then the argument that the Council is defining the parameters of innovation becomes a highly dubious one (Young 1973:74). Alternatively, even if it is defining the parameters, not many teachers are listening to it. What is more likely is that teachers, like the Schools Council itself, operate within more enduring parameters such as the examination system which limit the extent of curriculum innovation while not bothering to legislate on its details. In any case, it would be a mistake to assume that the Schools Council has a monopoly in this field. Other sources of curriculum innovation abound and are similarly restricted: LEA advisers, subject associations, universities and colleges are quite capable of stimulating their own programme of curriculum development without reference to the Schools Council. But in the last analysis they must all pay due heed to the examination system.

3   *Ideological content*

Our argument so far has focused on demonstrating that the ideological effect of the Schools Council through its legitimation of certain structures of knowledge is open to considerable doubt when assessed in terms of legitimation capacity and legitimation target(s). However, it could be that the Council does have a coherent ideological position and is just lamentably inefficient in its dissemination techniques. But if it has, then it is not one which is a conscious product of policy. Nisbet has pointed out how 'Decisions on development programmes are made on the basis of the quality of the proposals, and there is no intention that funds should be spread evenly across subjects or age-groups, or in any fixed proportions, nor even that amounts spent should reflect in any way the importance of any one area or age' (Richards 1974: 332). This, of course, does not deny that the selection of projects for funding by the Council could well be unconsciously systematic or that the educational environment could produce research applications which reflect the dominant educational values. In the case of the latter, the Schools Council would merely be acting as a channel for the preservation of the existing consensus on the goals of education. However, given the internal fragmentation and inefficiences of the Council's structure which has more the look of a scrambler device than the air of an efficient communication channel, this hypothesis has to be proved by an examination of its products.

The evidence brought forward by those who argue that the Schools Council's publications and materials legitimate existing class cultures is characterized, firstly, by a dubious methodology and, secondly, by a failure to place the evidence in an appropriate institutional context when interpreting it. The result is easy, but unconvincing interpretation. The general argument is that the Schools Council achieves this effect by reinforcing the idea that certain types of child should be associated with certain types of knowledge hierarchies.

These hierarchies are in turn maintained by subject divisions, particular teaching methods and the university-sanctioned examination system. An initial, and as Young (1973:23n) quite rightly says 'very crude' index of support for this thesis is the breakdown of the Schools Council project list according to the subject allegiance contained within a project title. As a result of their calculations, both Young and Richards (1974:330) find that those 'subjects or areas traditionally low in the educational hierarchy remain low in the Council's priorities' although Richards rather whimsically decides to exclude from his calculations projects concerned with 'interrelated studies' – which would have given a somewhat different balance to a table based on school subject. It is in any case impossible to replicate the findings of either Young or Richards (we have tried) since their criteria for categorization are not stated in sufficient detail and there is no generally accepted agreement as to where traditional subject areas, such as Maths and English, end and the more recent additions to the curriculum such as Moral and Social Education, begin. It seems likely, however, that Young and Richards have relied on the Schools Council's own categorization of projects into different curriculum areas in the annual project list without realizing that this categorization is a matter of administrative convenience rather than a rigorous assessment of the subject commitment of individual projects.

A more secure measure of a project's subject allegiance than its title (how do you classify 'History, Geography and Social Science 8–13' or 'Integrated Science', for example?) is its content, and here the arguments begin. For given the fact that the Council has so far funded well over 160 projects, there is plenty of room for judicious selections of material to illustrate quite opposite interpretations. And this is what has happened. In the absence of any commonly accepted methodology for the content analysis of the project's products, illustration has been employed in the place of systematic analysis. Thus, while Young (1973:78) can argue that such documents as those of the 'Young School Leaver' series provide 'legitimacy for existing subject and institutional hierarchies and the assumptions about ability and competence that they imply', Richard Pring (1975:115) quotes 'Society and the Young School Leaver' (Working Paper 11) as one of several explicitly *opposing* 'an imprisonment by the disciplines', 'fragmented type of curriculum', 'an artificial restriction', 'pigeon-holing of knowledge' and 'subject prejudice'. He continues:

In this way, 'integration', as some form of unity amongst the different kinds of knowledge, became part of the accepted premises from which a lot of Schools Council thinking began. Even in curriculum development projects *concerned explicitly with specific subject areas* (for example, 'Art and Craft Education', 'Arts and the Adolescent', 'Project Environment' and 'Religious Education in Secondary Schools') there was felt to be a need to incorporate into their exploratory thinking possible integrative links with other subjects. (ibid.: 116; our stress)

Even a casual perusal of the project profiles (the annual summaries of the projects funded by the Schools Council so far) reveals that this is the case, that many of the projects parade themselves in the integrationist, child-centred language in vogue in the late 1960s and 1970s and adopt a stance which does not legitimate subject divisions. Precisely what the balance is between 'subject-based' and 'integrated' projects must, however, remain an open question until a commonly accepted mode of analysis of the Council's products is developed. What is clear is that this legitimizing content is far from homogeneous in its political implications.

The same scepticism must also be accorded the evidence based on the content of projects' work and advanced to support the argument that the Schools Council legitimates particular hierarchies linking types of child with types of knowledge since this argument is largely based on the same illustrative methodology. It is true that because, as we have seen, the Council largely accepts the constraints of the present examination system those projects explicitly concerned with qualifications will not challenge the notion of hierarchy itself. On the other hand, what the past and present debate over the Council's proposals regarding the CEE, N and F Levels and the common system of examining at 16 + clearly demonstrates is that it is prepared to sponsor attempts to redefine that hierarchy in the teeth of opposition from both examination boards and universities. Merely to argue, therefore, that the Council legitimates the existing hierarchy is far too static a view and excludes the possibility of conflict, development and redefinition in the legitimation process.

In support of the idea that the universities dominate and guide the direction of curricular development thus ensuring the preservation of the existing educational order, both Young (1973: 71–2; 1976: 193) and Richards (1974: 332) present figures showing how by far the majority of Council projects have been based at universities. While we do not quibble with the figures *per se*, it is interesting to recalculate them using the latest (1978) Schools Council Project List according to date of funding as well as institutional base (Table 1).

Table 1
Institutional Base

Date of funding	University	Non-university	Total
1964–1970	60 (80%)	15 (20%)	75 (100%)
1971–1977	37 (48%)	41 (52%)	78 (100%)

(Examination projects are not included in this table which deals exclusively with curriculum development projects.)

Looking at the figures this way, it is obvious that there has been a marked shift away from the universities over the past seven years. The proportion of projects based at a university has dropped from 80 per cent between 1964–1970 to 46 per cent between 1971–1977. For the most part this shift is accounted for by an increasing tendency on the part of colleges of education to sponsor curriculum development projects rather than to rely on the received wisdom of the university-based projects (and the growth of independent research institutes such as the National Foundation for Educational Research). It reflects the spread of expertise on curriculum development from the obvious and only starting point, the universities, to neighbouring institutions. Given the Schools Council's reliance on a *laissez-faire* system of funding, whereby it becomes the responsibility of the educational environment to throw up, if that is the correct expression, ideas for new curriculum projects, it was inevitable that universities would form the starting point. It would have required the kind of intervention outlawed by the Council's constitution for this not to be the case.

However, from Young's point of view, providing this kind of institutional context and explaining why certain actions by the Council did not, and could not have occurred and why certain changes may be now occurring, is more of an apology than an explanation. It is also rather low level empiricism. Far better to make the sweeping statement that the Schools Council 'has confirmed existing educational hierarchies and excluded any real possibility of widespread teacher involvement in the transformation of curricula' (1976:197). Unfortunately, this touchingly assumes that more active teacher participation in curriculum development equals more challenges to the educational status quo and does not deal with the problem of how those at the bottom of the legitimizing hierarchy can escape its influence (which, as Young has argued, is considerable) in order to challenge it. If it is an alternative which could evade the legitimizing process then this needs to be documented rather than merely asserted.

Our own analysis suggests that the role of the Schools Council in the implementation of ideology is far from straightforward. Once the question is approached in terms of an institution's capacity to legitimate its target audience, and the ideological content of its legitimizing message, numerous complexities arise which render an easy assumption of a simple class effect too naive to accept. The Schools Council is hedged in by organizational constraints and inefficiencies, has an uneasy relationship with surrounding educational institutions and finds it difficult to get its message across to its clients, the teachers. This would be the case regardless of whether the Council was the bastion of conservatism or the herald of the revolutionary order.

The future

With the revision of the Schools Council's constitution in September 1978 as the result of DES pressure in the course of the Great Debate, the Council moved into a new phase of its activity. How is this likely to affect its operation as an agency of ideology implementation? Will it become more or less efficient?

In terms of straightforward structural change the new constitution has brought into being three main committees: Convocation, Professional, and Finance and Priorities – and it is the latter committee, with a majority of representatives from the DES and the local authorities, which has the real power. Its function is to 'determine the broad direction and priorities of the work of the Council, taking into account any views or recommendations from Convocation or the Professional Committee and to give advice on these matters to the Secretaries of State, local education authorities and other bodies as appropriate' (SC 1978:78). Effectively this means that although the teachers' unions retain substantial representation on the other two committees, their dominance of the Council has been ended. However, merely because the DES now has more influence over the direction of Council policy is no guarantee at all that the Council's capacity for ideology implementation has increased. In fact, if this influence were to become very visible there is every chance that teachers would shy away from choosing to use Council products. What is probably more important are changes in the Council's style of working.

In a brief leaflet entitled 'Guiding Principles and Programmes of Work' (1979) the Schools Council states that 'One of the most significant changes in working methods which followed [the reconstituted Council] was the Council's decision to determine an overall scheme of priorities and then devise programmes to meet these needs.' Four planning groups, plus the Council's Examinations Committee, have developed five programmes of work to guide the Council's progress in the period 1980–1983. These are: purpose and planning in the schools; helping individual teachers to become more effective; developing the curriculum for a changing world: developing basic skills and preparing for adult life; individual pupils: identifying talents and needs, responding to problems and dealing with difficulties; improving the examination system. As yet, it is still unclear how these programmes will be put into operation (what the mix of central versus local development work will be, for example) but there can be no mistaking the dirigiste tone with which they are set out. On the other hand, and not surprisingly for a political compromise, they appear to contain something for everyone (the leaflet was universally praised by the educational press) and it remains to be seen whether they, like the horseman in one of Leacock's poems, 'ride wildly off in all directions'.

In that the programmes can be seen as a rationalization of the activities of the Schools Council, as an attempt to structure its attitude towards its educational neighbours, it is worthwhile considering what other indications exist of similar bureaucratic refinements in its organization. Since 1978 the use of short-term contracts for the Council's research and liaison staff has gradually been phased out and permanent positions created in their stead. The realization has slowly dawned that hoarding expertise is better than dissipating it and that the previous inflow and outflow of ex-teachers was not of critical use to an institution which is not a school. Routinization of roles is also beginning to occur on a more systematic basis and the responsibilities of central staff defined in a more rigorous manner. These changes are the kind of minimum internal rearrangements necessary to provide the Council with its own sense of professional identity.

But professional identity or not, the Council is still in the position that no matter how sophisticated are its own organic intellectuals and no matter how coherent the ideological messages it produces, its external links nonetheless remain tenuous. For instance, in a leader comment headed 'Ring of Confidence' in 1978, the *Times Educational Supplement* stated: 'The work of the Waddell steering committee on proposals for a common system of examining at 16 + has been essentially an exercise in credibility.' It continued:

What it has done is to give the Schools Council's work (on 16 +) an added ring of confidence, based partly on the authority and weight of its membership and partly on the workmanlike document they have produced – with the strong twin presence of the DES and the HMI very evident in both.

On its own the Schools Council does not yet have the authority and respectability of an institution whose recommendations are more likely to be implemented than not. It must rely on the transferred authority of other major educational institutions, like the DES and HMI, to boost its own legitimacy via the work of bodies such as the Waddell committee. Though the irony with the 16 + proposals, of course, is that even with this extra legitimacy they were still not acceptable as they stood to the new Conservative government. Coupled with the defeat of the Council's N and F proposals this rather leaves it still groping around for that 'mossy respectability'. It is a respectability that is likely to remain elusive while the Council retains its independence of the government machine. Full co-operation and recognition from the educational state apparatus is only likely once the Council's relationship and with the teachers' unions has been sharply diminished and its structure and ideology linked to the DES in some way. The instigation by the government of the Trenaman inquiry into the operation and efficiency of the Schools Council is an indication that the 1978 reform has failed to please its masters and that further concessions may be required to undermine yet again its already peripheral power position. It will be interesting to see in what shape or form it survives, if at all.

At the more general level, it is inevitable that much will depend on the outcome of the wider debate on education, the attempt by the DES to extend its powers, the evolution of the doctrine of accountability and the capacity of the teaching profession to preserve its traditional autonomy. As a fairly weak member of the educational power structure, the Schools Council is unavoidably sensitive and responsive to these wider political and ideological shifts. If, for example, the educational system were to move away from its present decentralized organization, both in terms of values and structure, the Council might well find itself in a position to utilize a more centralized educational model to improve its dissemination efficiency and hence its legitimation capacity. But, for the moment, as an instrument for diffusing and lending status to particular sets of ideas, the Council has decided limitations. To ignore them is to ignore the importance and accessibility of institutional analysis.

7

The Political Demise of Intelligence Testing

Educational change is accompanied by ideological struggle. Using schools to restructure the relationship between the individual and society inevitably results in the emergence of ideologies to legitimate the desired educational experience and new social goals; and these then need to be related to one another for particular individuals. The purpose of this chapter is to examine the emergence of intelligence testing as a means of secondary school selection within the British educational system. We see intelligence testing as one particular, if limited, expression of meritocratic ideology. We have selected this focus because, in our opinion, this has been the dominant ideology within the state educational system. The differential distribution of educational resources between individuals was justified on the grounds that some individuals (because of the merit they had demonstrated) required an educational experience that consumed more than the average share of resources. As a consequence it was these individuals who would obtain the more prestigious jobs. Our focus is upon the political support for ideology, for without this ideologies are vulnerable to attacks which destroy their credibility as instruments of social policy.

It is evident that the meritocratic legitimation of inequality is a complex and slippery notion. Because measured intelligence does not have the predicted association with status, income and power it does not follow that scarce resources are not distributed meritocratically. Intelligence is only one individual characteristic and as even Bowles and Gintis (1976: 103) argue educational attainment 'is dependent not only on ability but also on motivation, drive to achieve, perseverance, and sacrifice' which – in their opinion – ensure that 'the status allocation mechanism acquires heightened legitimacy' (ibid.: 106). Furthermore, it is dubious if measured intelligence is, in the words of

Hogben (1939:29), 'a just measure of all that we commonly mean by the adjective intelligence when we apply it to adults'. For as he goes on to note, 'Probably the intellectual performance of adults depends quite as much on temperamental characteristics ordinarily described by alertness, persistence, curiosity, or a sense of humour' (ibid.: 29–30).

A more fundamental point is to question to what extent the legitimations of inequality in western industrialized societies are simply meritocratic. In Britain the private educational sector is healthy and the purchase of privileged schooling is dependent upon the belief that, within certain constraints, individuals have a right to dispose of their resources as they see fit. Although increasingly constrained by meritocratic ideology, entry into British public schools is still so restricted that they have become symbols of institutionalized class privilege (see pp. 168–78). With respect to the United States Jencks (1972:227) has argued that the distribution of occupational status and income may be more dependent upon random factors, such as luck, than was previously realized. In fact it is part of American mythology that many owe their success to a lucky break, so such speculation may be less outrageous than it first appears.

Nonetheless, from approximately 1920 onwards intelligence tests were used to determine the distribution of educational resources within the state sector of the British educational system (see Rose 1979; Sutherland 1977). Since then they have had a profound influence upon the lives of many thousands of children. Also it is reasonable to see intelligence testing as an advanced, if limited, expression of meritocratic ideology. The tests were the product of a new 'science' – psychology; individuals were awarded a concrete test score computed with the aid of statistical techniques, and – according to some – the scores were largely uncontaminated by environmental influences. Our first task is to consider why intelligence testing was used increasingly to resolve specific educational problems.

Why the need for intelligence testing?

1 *The educational dimension*
Until the 1944 Education Act schooling in Britain was essentially of two types, elementary and secondary, distinguished not by the age of their pupils but by the educational experience they imparted. The

secondary sector, composed of grammar and public schools, offered an academic curriculum which was seen as the expression of high status knowledge. Under the auspices of the School Boards, which had been established by the 1870 Education Act, various forms of post-elementary education took root. This development, however, was crushed by the Cockerton Judgement of 1901 which decreed that ratepayers' money could be spent only on elementary education. In view of the limited definition of secondary education it was inevitable that access to it, and in particular working-class access, would be restricted. The academic nature of the secondary school curriculum was considered to be beyond the capabilities or needs of most working-class children, and neither was it an education that all felt to be worthwhile as many had no desire to enter the growing ranks of blackcoated workers. Furthermore, for the secondary schools to retain their monopoly of what was deemed to be high status knowledge, access to them had to be restricted as open recruitment would have undermined this status. Robert Morant, the first Permanent Secretary of the Board of Education, is credited with much of the responsibility for the perpetuation of this bias but it should be remembered that even as progressive a report as 'The Education of the Adolescent', which appeared in 1926, was concerned to note that its proposals should not be used to cripple 'the development of secondary schools of the existing type' (Board of Education 1926:80).

It was not long before the education authorities, created by the 1902 Education Act, were sanctioning further experiments in post-elementary schooling. As the Consultative Committee's report (ibid.:34–5) on 'The Education of the Adolescent' commented:

This fact in itself seems to indicate the half-conscious striving of a highly industrialised society to evolve a type of school analogous to and yet distinct from the secondary school, and providing an education designed to fit boys and girls to enter the various branches of industry, commerce and agriculture at the age of fifteen.

This committee advocated 'secondary education for all' through the provision of different kinds of secondary schools so that 'selection by elimination' would be replaced by 'selection by differentiation'. With the passage of the 1944 Education Act the proposal became reality, due not so much to the actual tenets of the Act but more to a particular interpretation of them sustained by the Ministry of

Education. What is certain is that the various forms of secondary education stood no chance of achieving an analogous status as long as the traditional secondary school curriculum represented the clearest expression of high status knowledge.

The structure of secondary education in England, therefore, needed well-defined recruitment procedures. Both the traditional model of secondary education as well as the manner in which that model was reformed after 1944 assumed as much. Furthermore, the dominant political pressures which the educational system responded to between the Education Acts of 1902 and 1944 reinforced this. The demand for secondary education expanded relentlessly, in spite of all the economic problems of the interwar period (Bernbaum 1967:39). None of the political parties was immune from the consequent pressures but rather differed in their degrees of sympathy for the state financed expansion of secondary education. In 1907 the Liberal government pioneered a major breakthrough when the Board of Education issued regulations governing the availability of free places in grant-aided secondary schools. With a few exceptions at least 25 per cent of the places available in each grant-aided secondary school were to be designated as free places. In view of the recognition that this figure could be increased steadily, the way was open for the emergence of a state secondary sector that had eliminated entry by fee-paying. Under these regulations a free place was available to each candidate who could profit from a secondary education. In theory, therefore, gaining a free place was dependent upon a qualifying examination; in reality the demand was so intense that the examination was highly competitive.

Whereas with the passage of the 1902 Education Act a Conservative government had created a theoretical ladder from the elementary school to university, the Liberals – thanks to the extension and formalization of the free place scheme – gave the ladder more rungs. By way of contrast, Simon (1965) has claimed that since its inception the most progressive elements in the Labour movement were against a divided educational system and for the common school, which clearly implied different basic educational principles from those which actually prevailed. It is fair to say, however, that education was not a prominent concern of the political left at this time and when the Labour party exercised political power, at either national or local levels, it concentrated upon making the ladder longer, wider and sturdier. Under the guidance of Tawney (1922; see

Barker 1972:36ff.) the commitment to a secondary education for all
was to be fulfilled within the framework of a differentiated system of
secondary education. It was firmly believed that given greater equality
of social conditions, and a fair test, working-class children were
capable of competing effectively with middle-class children.

In his influential *Social Progress and Educational Waste* Lindsay
(1926:17–24) demonstrated how local practices and social conditions
affected the educational opportunities of working-class children. The
answer was to improve the terms on which the working class
competed rather than to change the game. For Lindsay this meant the
provision of adequate maintenance grants in addition to free places.
Many working-class families were still dependent for economic
survival upon the incomes of their children, so they could scarcely
meet the extra costs involved in keeping their children in school.
Maintenance grants, he felt, would lead to increased working-class
participation in the free place examinations, to a higher acceptance of
free places on the part of successful candidates, and to a lower
working-class dropout rate from the secondary schools. It was
pragmatic issues of this nature, rather than the deeper questions of
principle, that dominated Labour party thinking.

Probably the work of Sidney Webb illustrates as well as anything
this strand of thinking. Webb had manoeuvred skilfully to ensure that
the provisions of the 1902 Education Act would subsequently be
applied to the London County Council in the London Education Bill
of 1903 (Maclure 1970:76). In his *Secondary Education* he went so
far as to attack the idea of common school and to claim that a
differentiated educational system was more in tune with the spirit of
democracy for it enabled the individual school to fit better 'the needs
of a particular section of children' (Brennan 1975:132). He saw the
need for a 'capacity-catching scholarship' which would permit every
child to develop his potential to the full and felt that his own efforts in
the capital city had helped to provide for 'the cleverest children of the
London wage-earners a more genuinely accessible ladder than is open
to the corresponding class in any American, French, or German city'
(Webb 1904:26). The subsequent work of Lindsay demonstrated the
hollowness of Webb's claim for there were large variations in the
number of scholarship winners from borough to borough, and even
from school to school, with the virtual exclusion of certain segments
of the working class (ibid.:55–116). But such evidence did not
undermine Webb's educational principles; what was required was a

programme which would bring them to fruition and it was to this that the Labour party was committed.

The above discussion suggests that intelligence testing within the British educational system developed in response to a precise educational problem, how to preserve the status of the traditional secondary schools. The problem was compounded in the interwar years by a demand that constantly outran the supply of this scarce resource. The situation could have been mitigated if the established form of high status knowledge, which the traditional secondary schools represented, had been seriously challenged. Whether fundamental change was possible is more problematic as it is difficult to conceive of a rapid collapse in the status of knowledge areas. However, no sustained attack was forthcoming for the dominant political response was to promote intensified competition for the available resource whilst eventually creating alternative forms of secondary education without providing the means which would erode status differentials. What we are suggesting, therefore, is that intelligence testing was a response to the retention of a traditional educational legacy within a changed political climate. The emerging political forces had neither the power nor the will to bring about sweeping educational changes which would make the introduction of intelligence testing unnecessary. On the contrary, the political pressure – encapsulated in the demand for equality of educational opportunity – was just sufficiently potent to make its emergence more likely.

2   *The administrative dimension*

The evidence that Sutherland has collated, demonstrating the very parsimonious use of intelligence testing in the British educational system up to 1940, is conclusive. If one wishes to see intelligence testing as the expression of meritocratic ideology then the point needs to be made that it ran up against institutions and processes which reflected a well-entrenched value system. So a protracted and confused struggle was bound to follow. The most evident resistance to the new ideology was the continued existence, if not well-being, of the public schools. The public school values were not confined to the private sector, for the official commitment to maintaining the links between the public and grammar schools was strong. The Report of the Consultative Committee on Secondary Education in 1939 called for the steady elimination of all fee-payers from the grammar schools, but with a view to retaining the links between the state and private sectors the direct grant grammar schools were to be excluded, at least temporarily, from this proposal. In addition it was recommended that only 50 per cent of the special places (as the free places were now known) should be allocated solely on the basis of individual performance in the selective entrance examination. A wider range of criteria, including character assessments, were to determine the selection of the remaining pupils. Again this was with a view to maintaining that 'real unity' of which 'all schools giving a "grammar school" education are conscious' (Board of Education 1939: 327–9).

Even Sutherland's evidence, however, points to a steady, if limited extension in the use of intelligence tests for the purposes of secondary school selection in the interwar years. As their expanding number of free place pupils suggested, entry into secondary schools was determined increasingly by formal examinations, whether they contained an intelligence testing component or not. Furthermore, regardless of what the situation may have been prior to 1939 one can fairly refer to the universal employment of intelligence testing in secondary school selection after 1945. The essence of their growing attraction was that they resolved an administrative problem in a simple and direct fashion, and the very manner in which they achieved this contained both political and educational defences of their dissemination.

The administrative convenience of intelligence testing flows out of the resolution of two interrelated problems: (1) What do intelligence tests measure? (2) What are the factors that determine the development of this entity measured by intelligence tests? Fortunately we can pass rather quickly over the massive controversies that have surrounded these questions. More pertinent is how they were resolved with specific reference to the introduction of intelligence testing in the process of secondary school selection. Burt (1955: 176) consistently defined intelligence as 'innate, general, cognitive ability' and it is thus that factor which 'enters into all we say or do or think' (Burt 1950: 542). (The argument is that the general factor 'g' is innate but this is only one of the factors that any test measures.) Burt, therefore, had answered the two questions most succinctly and so great was his influence that, whilst intelligence testing was taking root, the accompanying intellectual controversies scarcely appeared to penetrate official circles. Burt's biographer, Hearnshaw (1979: 32), has noted – quite correctly – that, 'The meritocratic principle was not, therefore, the brainchild of psychologists and intelligence testers; it was embedded in the foundations of the new scheme of secondary education which the 1902 Act established.' But the unanswerable question is whether the principle would have been operationalized in the fashion that it was if Burt's view of intelligence had not been officially sanctioned. It is still something of a mystery as to why Burt's view should prevail – his intellectual ability notwithstanding. Hearnshaw's biography does not deal with this precise point, but he does portray a gifted man with considerable energy and ruthlessness; the right personal ingredients to ensure the predominance of his point of view. One suspects, but cannot prove, that it is precisely because his answers to the questions promised most administrative efficiency. This is speculation, but what is not, as Hearnshaw (ibid.: ch. 7) shows, is the influence he wielded on various consultative committees of the Board of Education in the interwar years. Moreover with his appointment as a part-time psychologist to the London County Council in 1913 he could also bring his influence to bear rather more directly upon the education of the capital's children.

If intelligence is innate then it goes without saying that not only are the ultimate test scores comparatively unblemished by environmental factors but also they are relatively static – though this does not mean that children had to be separated educationally at the age of 11 (see Burt 1959:102). Besides providing the fairest means of selection, in the sense that it was the best measure of the individual's *potential* ability, secondary school allocations could be made at a specified point in time. This may not have been what any psychologist, let alone Burt, intended but this was the policy that emerged. That point in time was deemed to be the age of 11, which – not surprisingly – was the established dividing line between elementary and secondary education in the state sector. Reflecting a temporary fall from grace, Burt (1943) attacked this as administratively convenient rather than psychologically justifiable. But it is surprising that he should have overlooked his own much repeated claim, most clearly seen in his contribution to the 1931 report (258; see also Hearnshaw 1979:117–18) on 'The Primary School', that by the age of 11 the mental ages of children were so divergent that they should be subdivided into at least three groups if they were to be effectively taught.

If intelligence was general, with very specialized abilities developing in most cases only after the age of 11, this greatly simplified the process of secondary school selection. It meant that group, rather than individual tests could be conducted, and it should not be forgotten that Burt himself had done much of the pioneer work in developing group tests. These were easy to administer because large numbers could be examined in a comparatively short space of time, no special expertise was required to conduct them, supervision of their administration was comparatively cheap, and they could be readily scored by a few trained experts. The tests were constructed by reputable bodies like Moray House and the National Foundation for Educational Research, both flourishing as part of a growth industry.

The standardized scoring of intelligence testing, Binet's big breakthrough, had immense ramifications. The accumulation of information could be boiled down to hierarchically ranked scores which certainly increased the scientific aura surrounding intelligence testing. More importantly, the apparently definitive nature of the ranking enabled the local education authorities to allocate with precision their available number of grammar school places. Obviously the rank order could be modified by other forms of evaluation but this would be part of a conscious decision to adopt a mixed pattern of assessment. What could be avoided was the pressure upon secondary school places that the prewar qualifying free-place examination exerted. After 1945 the local education authorities could eliminate the embarrassment of failing to provide secondary school places for large numbers of children who had been evaluated as capable of profiting from secondary education.

A very powerful supplementary reason for the administrative appeal of intelligence testing was that judgements were being made about individual capacities. It was individuals and not social groups that were being assessed, 'success' or 'failure' was personalized so helping to diffuse the potential opposition. This was a judgement upon the individual which had the aura of being scientific so that not only was it allegedly fair but also grievances could be seen as expressions of self-interest. Furthermore, the assessments, and this is especially true in the context of the educational system which emerged after the 1944 Education Act, were made – so the official argument went – in the best interests of the individual's future schooling needs. So the purpose was not to 'fail' or 'pass' children but to ensure that they received a secondary education commensurate with their age, aptitude and ability. So this was an assessment of individuals from which *all* would supposedly benefit. Intelligence testing was, therefore, an incisive and defensible means of tackling a delicate and potentially explosive social task.

3 *The economic dimension*

Some social scientists have argued that the introduction of intelligence testing for educational purposes was in direct response to capitalism's changing social relations of production. It could be claimed that this explanation does not contradict the previous arguments we have forwarded but they may in fact complement one another. Although this may be so, there are good reasons for thinking otherwise. At least with reference to Britain the economic arguments have not been presented in much detail. For example Levidow (1979:15) has written, 'My approach tends ultimately to suggest that IQ testing, seen in historical perspective, was less a matter of justifying an existing capitalist society than of constructing a new stage of capitalism' (see Henderson 1976; Esland 1977). The evidence Levidow uses to substantiate his claim is a general reference to Edwardian liberalism and American progressivism as parallel periods in which the individual was recast as a citizen-producer who contributed to the national good, and as a consumer who needed to be serviced. Such vague generalizations must be replaced by detailed statements as to the precise changes in the character of the economy, and equally significantly how these were translated into pedagogic action and what form this took. Much the same cavalier attitude to historical analysis is found in Hilary and Steven Rose's interpretation (1979:86) of the more contemporary intelligence testing debate. Their critique of those who are seen as proponents of intelligence testing may be legitimate but then to see the debate as a product of the present-day crisis of capitalism requires an act of faith that many of us – without careful evaluation – are probably unprepared to make. At the moment we have slogans instead of research.

Sutherland (1977:147–9) has shown that the use of intelligence testing by English educational authorities was limited up to the Second World War. The means of secondary school selection varied considerably from one place to the next; some employed the most 'advanced' techniques while others remained very 'backward'. At the same time the Board of Education remained tentative in its support for intelligence testing. Like Cyril Burt, the Board's official line was that factors other than individual scores in general intelligence tests should be taken into consideration when awarding free places. Burt (1947:66) argued that ideally the local education authorities should allocate secondary school places on the basis of the physical health of the child, his character, his sociological background, teacher's records, an interview in borderline cases, as well as tests of general intelligence. If capitalism's social relations of production in some sense or other needed an educational system centred around the intelligence testing of its pupils, then how is this tentative support to be explained? It is impossible to escape the feeling that the almost universal employment of intelligence testing in the secondary school selection process *after* 1945 was a direct consequence of how the 1944 Education Act was implemented rather than any dramatic change in the character of capitalism as a result of the war years. Moreover, how is the haphazard introduction of intelligence testing to be interpreted? Were those authorities who used them in the early days in tune with the needs of capitalism or simply swayed by dominant economic forces? It seems more probable that those authorities employing educational psychologists were in the van of the testing movement. One suspects that these were the educationally progressive local goverments (or at least influenced by one or more far-sighted individuals), committed to expanding schooling opportunities rather than serving capitalism's alleged needs.

We would suggest that economic factors affected the testing movement in a very restricted fashion i.e. by regulating the competition for free places. In spite of a gradual, if erratic expansion of the free-place scheme, so that by 1937 46 per cent of pupils in maintained secondary schools received full remission of fees, and 7.4 per cent received partial remission, demand continuously outran supply (Board of Education 1939:94–5; see Bernbaum 1967:76–7). The supply shortage, plus the limited and patchy provision of maintenance grants, was inimical to the interests of working-class children. Initially many grammar school teachers were sceptical as to the potential quality of their free-place entrants but this was dispelled by their subsequent academic performance which was, on average, better than that of the fee-paying pupils. Over time, therefore, the status of the free-place pupil improved which was accompanied by the elementary school becoming the dominant route for entry into the maintained secondary schools. By 1937 77 per cent of all maintained secondary school pupils were former elementary school pupils, pointing to considerable middle-class inroads into the elementary school (Board of Education 1939:95). The evidence is that competition for free places increased with at least segments of the middle class following the same path as working-class children into the secondary schools. Given the economic circumstances this is precisely what one would expect; middle-class parents take advantage of state schooling and educational grants as long as there is no negative social price to pay. The losers in these circumstances are those working-class children who would have obtained the educational resources if there had been no competition from the middle classes.

It would have been more plausible to argue that the extension of intelligence testing that followed on from the interpretation of the 1944 Education Act was a response to capitalism's needs if the variously streamed pupils were then exposed to educational experiences which served the nation's long term manpower requirements. However, according to many critics, this is precisely what did *not* happen. The 1944 Education Act said nothing about the content of the schools' curricula. Indeed the influential 1943 Report entitled 'Curriculum and Examinations in the Secondary Schools' (known as the Norwood Report, after its chairman Cyril Norwood) reaffirmed that the kind of pupil educated in grammar and public schools was best served by an academically biased curriculum. It could be argued that this is clear evidence of the ability of the educational system to resist the demands of the economy. Differentiation and labelling are unlikely to be helpful to the economy if the labels are inappropriate and the wrong values are inculcated.

The most judicious, if most unoriginal conclusion is that educational, political and economic pressures complemented one another to form the social context of intelligence testing. The political climate demanded not an attack upon the established educational hierarchy but an extension of educational opportunities to a wider range of citizens. Basing selection for secondary education increasingly upon supposed meritocratic criteria not only satisfied a powerful political demand but also helped to preserve the status quo of schooling. The grammar schools received increased state funding which enabled the more precarious of them to stay in business; after an initial period of concern they were satisfied as to both the academic and the social quality of the free-place pupils; and they were left to carry on with their day-to-day teaching in much the same way as before. If the educational system was failing to meet the long-term needs of the economy this was disguised in the short term by the fact that individual talent was selected by apparently meritocratic criteria and then given the commensurate educational experience, thus making the best use of the nation's human resources. Whether this was a sufficiently powerful, or even necessary theme with which to legitimate existing or future economic inequalities is another matter, but it undoubtedly formed a significant consensus of educational principles that was to last until the 1960s.

The destruction of an educational ideology

Given the potent combination of variables that explain the emergence of intelligence testing as an instrument of social policy within the field of education, how then is one to account for the steady removal of its influence? Much of the initial critique consisted of a piecemeal attack upon various technical aspects of intelligence testing, while the *coup de grâce*, at least with respect to secondary school selection, came with the arrival of the comprehensive secondary schools. With the coming of comprehensive education the need for intelligence testing for secondary school selection disappeared.

A sustained attack upon some of the technical aspects of intelligence testing helped to destroy their credibility. For example, it was admitted that quite sizeable errors of misplacement occurred, even with the use of the very best selection techniques (see Vernon 1960:186; Burt 1959:112). The problem was compounded by the fact that individual test scores could fluctuate according to the predisposition of the candidate on the day the 11 + examination was sat, and that preparation such as coaching and practising helped to boost scores (Watts *et al.* 1952:23–33). The amount of variation does not appear to be great but given the reality of a limited number of grammar school places it could be sufficient to make the difference between receiving a place or not. If one adds to this the fact that some secondary modern school pupils performed better than some of their grammar school counterparts in the General Certificate of Education examination, an examination initially seen as beyond their capabilities, then the whole basis of selection seemed absurd. These quibbles may in retrospect sound trivial but they were accumulating quibbles with wide social implications.

It must be stressed that we are not suggesting that these attacks upon the technical aspects of intelligence testing caused a decline in the ideological underpinnings of the testing movement. In a powerful attack upon this rationalist strategy Nikolas Rose (1972:10) has argued that to assume an ideology will relinquish its hold through such an attack is naive, for what needs to be destroyed is the cause that the ideology serves (see also Demaine 1979:211). Of course by speaking reason and exposing lies the ideology was not destroyed, or at least not as simply as that. What was called into question was *the use* of intelligence tests for a specific social purpose. One can justly ask what use is an ideology if its social instruments can no longer be employed? What is perhaps more significant is that these accumulating quibbles, as we have referred to them, were useful ammunition in a power struggle. They could be used to attack the enemy who in the case of secondary school selection could be defeated politically even if his ideological base remained firm. It was not for nothing that the absolute need for selection techniques was seen as the Achilles heel of any differentiated system of state education.

Rose (ibid.) goes on to argue that 'a rationalist doctrine which fails to recognisze that if ideologies have effects this is only because it is in and through them that the effect of truth is constituted, by means of operations which are not dependent upon rational or causal principles for their actions.' With respect to mental measurement, to use Rose's choice of phrases, this claim is – at first sight – appealing. The bulk of Rose's article (16–57) demonstrates quite skilfully that the measurement of individual intelligence emerged within a particular social context that shaped the understanding of its meaning. Burt himself (1962:261–2) referred to such pressures, and more significantly, implied his willingness to bend to them:

Throughout the country there is urgent need for a practical mental test – for a handy method which can be immediately applied by teachers, doctors and social workers; for a pocket rule which will furnish diagnostic measurements in terms of some plain concept, like the mental year; obvious, exact, and instantly intelligible to a magistrate or a jury, to whom the technicalities of percentiles and standard deviations would be esoteric gibberish. To satisfy such a demand, scientific exactitude may be pardonably postponed for the prompt delivery of a workable substitute. And such a substitute, provisional yet ready-made, is to be found in the Binet-Simon scale.

In view of the contemporary revelations about the quality of Burt's research, and the deceit he used to defend his cause, such words have an ironical ring. However, in spite of what the social context may have required, in spite of how scientific exploration may have been tailored to fit its demands, and in spite of the emergence of an officially sponsored theoretical consensus, the debates were never as controlled as Rose implies, and presumably Burt would have liked. In fact the rationalist attack may be more than 'the confrontation of the falsities of ideology' with reason and truth for the critique may also contain the elements of a counter ideology. For example, the very technical, but equally bitter conflict between the nature and nurture interpretations of how intelligence is formed is obviously an ideological as well as a scientific conflict. And this particular debate has erupted spasmodically throughout the history of intelligence testing so that even if 'the effect of truth is constituted' only in and through ideologies nevertheless continuous ideological conflict, albeit not between equal parties, has raged.

Rose (1979:12) sets himself the objective of developing 'an effective strategy of transformation' with a view to casting 'some light on certain questions of the form and functioning of psychological discourse in the present'. The essence of this strategy is to discover 'the constitution of a "regime of truth" (Foucault) which will establish, in any given discourse, the conditions which statements will have to fulfill if they are to count as truths, and the means and consequences of the production in discourse of the effect of truth' (ibid.:11). However, he never makes it clear why the analysis of the social context in which the discourse emerged (in this case mental measurement) should improve the chances of intervention which then institutes change. More critically, from our perspective, it provides no clues as to what the actual forces are that have been responsible for change. Initially psychology may have been shaped to suit the interests of efficient social administration but this could not have lasted for long unless it was also sustained politically by the dominant interested parties. Selective secondary education was a legacy of the peculiar English definition of high status knowledge, whilst intelligence testing was a convenient device to maintain this state of affairs by restricting access to that which was valued, partly to enable it to retain its value. The initial parties in the construction of this edifice may have been confined but they were regulating the lives of masses of individuals and without a relatively all-encompassing political consensus this was not going to succeed for very long. For all his awareness of 'the political', what Rose ignores is the political basis of ideology, much of which is constructed *between* 'discourse in the present' and 'the constituion of a 'regime of truth' in the past.

The critical key to change, therefore, is how to destroy this supportive political consensus. Within itself this may not undermine meritocratic ideology, of which intelligence testing is a manifestation, but it will result in a very different expression of that ideology. Indeed it could result in breaking the relationship between intelligence testing and the social problem, with attempts to resolve the latter within at least a different institutional context if not by means of entirely different processes.

As we have already indictated the use of intelligence testing to resolve educational problems was initially limited and an increasingly confident sanctioning of them by the Board of Education (even so, remaining quite tentative to the very end) was not readily taken up at the local level. But given a differentiated state system of secondary education, entry to which was to be determined universally by meritocratic criteria, what was the viable alternative? This was the dilemma facing the local education authorities after the 1944 Education Act. Without a comprehensive system of secondary education no alternative in fact was viable. The attack upon the fragile consensus that supported selection could have been made at the ideological level i.e. new structures and processes were needed to educate people for a different kind of social order. Some were prepared to conduct the debate in such terms but the weight of the attack centred around a piecemeal 'rationalist' strategy. Basic to this was the undermining of the 11 + examination, with its heavy reliance upon intelligence testing, as a legitimate instrument of selection. The contradictions, confusions and uncertainties were all political ammunition with which to attack the political consensus, although it is equally certain that this provided few clues as to what should replace the established order.

This process of disintegration occurred at different levels, and within various arenas, with a mutually reinforcing effect. The theoretical challenge was led by an emerging group of 'traditional' intellectuals, the sociologists. Partially in response to this challenge the psychologists established a working party of the British Psychological Association whose results are to be found in Vernon's *Secondary School Selection* published in 1957. The theoretical confusions inevitably were not resolved but simply made more

public. We have already referred to some of the technical criticisms
which did much to undermine the faith of the layman. It was no good
the beleagured educational psychologist claiming – as so often they
did – that the tests were serving the wrong ends for such a posture
merely increased uncertainty.

In 1951 the Labour party formally committed itself to a policy of
comprehensive secondary education, not as Barker (1972 : 83) reflects,
because of a deep-seated desire to rectify 'the inequitable social
structure of Britain' but more as a result of 'the educational
disadvantage of the modern school and the unsatisfied demand for
grammar school education'. What the theoretical and technical
morass accomplished was a reinforcement of this commitment, for it
is a long way from party resolutions to government policy. The cause
of comprehensive secondary education became respectable. Although
elements within the Labour party still looked upon the grammar
schools with affection, it was impossible for the party to continue its
support for an educational system that discriminated so blatantly
against working-class children. At the same time not all middle-class
parents were happy with the fact that private education was usually
the only alternative to the secondary modern school if their child
'failed' the 11 + examination. An expanding birth rate, with restricted
grammar school entry, increased this possibility. The teaching
profession had always been split over selection; the Labour party
commitment crystallized the divisions. Of growing concern was the
pressure the 11 + examination exerted over both the organization and
curriculum of the junior schools. There was a feeling, and not just
amongst teachers, that it was time to liberate the junior school (see
Plowden 1967 : 153; Jackson 1964).

The concerted attack upon the theoretical and technical basis of
intelligence testing made its administrative convenience decidedly
suspect, while the implementation of a comprehensive system of
secondary education would remove the necessity for it. These
developments – actual and impending – were reflected in a rapid
change in official attitudes as exemplified by all the major educational
reports of the 1960s (CHE 1963 : 49; CACE 1963 : 6). Such rapidity
contrasts sharply with the long and tentative creation of official
sponsorship. Kamin (1974 : 12) has argued that the spread of
intelligence testing to resolve social problems in the United States was
stimulated by a conducive political climate – it was an idea whose
time had come. By the 1960s support for the use of intelligence testing

for secondary school selection was dwindling fast – it was a device to be placed in cold storage, if not the morgue. Even a Tory minister of education could write of the need for all children 'to have an equal opportunity of *acquiring* intelligence, and of developing their talents and abilities to the full' (CACE 1963: Foreword; our stress).

We have, therefore, devalued *somewhat* the significance of intelligence testing. It was slow to acquire an educational purpose, was of critical importance for approximately a mere twenty years, and declined rapidly in response to a vigorous, if disparate, political campaign. The dominant reason for the expansion of intelligence testing was the need to retain a narrow definition of high status knowledge within particular institutions while widening, but controlling, the range of social access to that educational experience. Once the political assault upon such educational exclusiveness had succeeded the administrative convenience of intelligence testing was irrelevant for its essential purpose was at an end.

Intelligence testing: its ideological weaknesses

The sociological interpretations of intelligence testing have stressed its ideological importance but surprisingly no analysis of its actual strength as an educational ideology is to be found. With respect to public school education we will argue that one of the central reasons why the public schools were capable of resisting change was the solidity of the ideological foundations they forged for themselves in Victorian England. The rapid erosion of intelligence testing suggests weak ideological foundations. We have already commented upon the confusions that surround the meaning of meritocratic ideology. It is now appropriate to consider further shortcomings.

Intelligence testing can be used to reinforce the belief that each society contains only a limited number of individuals with high ability. Indeed, the purpose of testing was to discover the full extent of this available pool of ability, and one of the advantages of using intelligence tests to select pupils for a grammar school education was that it discriminated *less* against working-class children than other means of selection. So the ideological implications of intelligence testing were conservative in the fundamental sense that it assumed a limit on what the individual was capable of achieving and on the size of the overall pool of ability.

In view of this it was to be expected that Burt (1959: 31) would write, 'Nevertheless, in a highly technological age the genius is equally needed to aid and supplement the comparative ineptitude of the general public; and, among nations, success in the struggle for survival is bound to depend more and more on the achievements of a small handful of individuals who are endowed by nature with outstanding gifts of ability and character.' This was the old education for leadership principle in a new guise and it was propagated in much the same spirit: without the right leaders the natural incompetence of the masses would result in ruin. The logical consequence was a stratified educational system with as much differentiation as possible to match the capabilities of pupils. A critical weakness, however, was the lack of a precise view of the educated man, other than one who had developed his talents to the full. In this peculiar sense intelligence testing was supportive of a liberal theory of education. The emphasis was upon developing the talents of individuals, as if this would automatically maximize the greatest happiness of the greatest number. There is no notion that in order to achieve the social good of the community some talents were more worthy than others. It may well be that the alleged general intelligence supposedly measured by the tests was central to the development of all talents. However, if the main concern is how to relate schooling more precisely to a particular definition of the needs of the economy, perhaps a firmer guidance — that is than the measurement of 'g' — is required.

It is our contention that this failure to spell out in more detail the model of the educated man was reinforced by two interrelated problems. Burt argued that the advanced technological society required its 'talented tenth' if it was to function smoothly and thus a stratified educational system was an economic neccesity. Others, working with a similar premise, reached the diametrically opposite conclusion. They maintained that early secondary school selection, because of its inevitable inaccuracy in at least a minority of cases, led to a loss of talent. In the name of national efficiency therefore, selection should be delayed. Others were prepared to launch a more radical attack. They disliked the fact that intelligence testing helped to legitimate social inequality, no matter how deep and wide the pool of ability was perceived to be. Some felt that society had a growing, perhaps infinite need for talent and it was, therefore, necessary to think in terms of the individual's capacity for self-improvement rather than of a finite pool of ability.

Even if this first problem — whether secondary school selection was necessary for the development of scarce human resources – were resolved, then the second problem – whether the prevailing organization of schooling accomplished this efficiently – still remained. Here a clear distinction between intelligence testing and the meritocratic ideology must be drawn. Putting an end to intelligence testing for the purpose of secondary school selection does not bring about the automatic demise of meritocratic ideology. In fact it may be better fulfilled within a different institutional context; perhaps, for example, within the comprehensive secondary school or the public school. To this end more detailed manifestations of the ideology could be constructed, and implementing them could be more rigorously applied over a continuous period of time. In other words a more complete definition of meritocratic ideology might emerge within a different institutional context.

Within the context of the present-day redefining of the social purposes of schooling we may see the emergence of just such a definition of meritocratic ideology. This would necessitate a continuous assessment of the development of various pupil attributes. The desired characteristics would be more closely scrutinized as to their social utility, in direct contrast to the measurement of individual intelligence which was a personal possession for private use. So a wide differentiation of educational experiences, monitored by carefully devised testing techniques would occur within the educational system regardless of its structural characteristics. Furthermore, there are a number of tentative straws in the wind. The creation of the Assessment of Performance Unit (APU), located within the Department of Education and Science, is a significant development. Not only could this institution help to formulate a universal definition of the desired standards but also it could act as a centralized monitoring body (Vernon 1955:214–5). (However the future of the APU is apparently in doubt, partially because it has proved incapable of meeting all the Department's expectations of it (Doe 1981:3); the question is whether it will be replaced by another body which can meet those demands.) Regardless of the control mechanism such a development would fulfil one of the long-term dreams of many educational psychologists, that all testing should be used for diagnostic purposes. The consequence would still be an inegalitarian distribution of educational resources but, as a process which occurs within the school, this is less politically visible and can be defended more readily on educational grounds. But, in deference to

Rose's analysis, such an outcome would represent the ultimate failure of the successful rationalist attack on intelligence testing! One technique of differentiation would merely be replaced by a more sophisticated batch of techniques but the underlying ideology of testing would remain intact.

[handwritten annotation:] Not clear what C. doing if IL term wear with C600 but meritocratic ideology remains, why not assessment for all?

8

Redefining the Ideology of Public School Education

The gloom that pervades the contemporary British educational scene is by no means universal. Whilst the state sector, operating with a shrinking budget, is forced into a painful redefinition of its purpose so the independent schools continue to hold their own – if not prosper (see ISIS 1978: table 1 ; ISIS 1980: table 7). The Conservative government has not only taken the sting out of the ritualistic threats of recent Labour governments but has also provided positive financial support; indirectly by lowering substantially the income taxes of the schools' potential clients, and directly by proposals to aid selected pupils with the payment of their school fees. (However, if the Labour party is returned to power it is possible that this state of affairs could change rapidly (NEC 1980)). The change is remarkable, for not ten years ago the independent schools were on the defensive: their pupils were a declining percentage of the total school population, some of the smaller establishments were on the verge of closing, and they were subjected to the less than sympathetic gaze of the Public Schools Commission (see 1968a; 1970). (Of course, not all the individual members were hostile and it should be noted that between the two reports there was a considerable change in the membership.) A good symbol of the new-found confidence is the willingness of the schools to expose themselves to the media, of which the 1980 television series on Radley College is the most notable example. This contrasts sharply with the *Manual of Guidance* published by the Headmasters' Conference which notes (para. 21, p. 6) that 'Experience shows that Headmasters can be too trusting in regard to enquiries made by researchers and sociologists. Evidence obtained in so-called confidence may be used several years later, in ways totally different from those intimated at the time of original approach.'

We have claimed that ideological struggles accompany the process of educational change; that new conceptions of the educated man reshape the relationship between schooling and the social order (see pp. 62–5). The traditional public school created, through clearly identifiable educational experiences, a particular model of the educated man who fitted his niche within the established order. This chapter, therefore, will enable us to examine the content of a particular educational ideology, the pressures that have been brought to bear upon it, and how it is changing in response to those pressures. Furthermore, many social scientists have argued that the class structure of British society is legitimated by a dominant ideology which is perpetuated by institutions such as the public schools (Miliband 1969:239 ff.; Parkin 1967:280). To examine ideological change should enable us to understand better what is happening to the class structure of Britain.

In the previous chapter we analysed the political attack upon the use of intelligence testing for secondary school selection. The success of this attack brought to an end the liberal consensus that underlay the post-war expansion of the British educational system. The search was now on for new ideological themes to justify the distribution of educational resources, to guide the character of the curriculum, and to determine the nature of the educated man and how he is to relate to society at large. It is our contention that the independent schools are creating an educational ideology which is gaining dominance, the essence of which is a judicious combination of some of their traditional expressive values (e.g. integrity, hard work, discipline, and – on carefully selected occasions – initiative) with a more recent concern for formally certified academic competence. In pursuing its goal this chapter has three specific tasks: first, to describe the main changes that have taken place in public school education during approximately the past two decades, second, to assess the impact of these changes on the ideology of public school education, and, third, to explain why the public schools have been forced to change.

Our analysis of the public schools is different from that of other interested social scientists. Most sociological attention has been directed at the internal dynamics of the schools, how they are organized in ways that perpetuate a particular ethos (see Wakeford 1969; Weinberg 1967; Lambert 1975). This focus must undervalue change since its purpose is to demonstrate the conserving functions of the schools. Furthermore, change is invariably considered in a descriptive and *ad hoc* manner. The tendency is to list the changes almost randomly with little discussion of their wider social significance (see Gathorne-Hardy 1977:ch. 17). Change is seen in relation to internal problems, specifically in Royston Lambert's work (1977:67; 1966:xxx) the shifting balance between what he terms instrumental, expressive and organizational goals. The underlying reason for this bias is that the sociologists have worked with a model of the public school as a closed and total institution (Weinberg 1967:53–74; Lambert *et al.* 1968:22). When the schools are related to their social context the analysis is often trivial. For example, it is a much reiterated fact that the vast majority of their pupils are from middle-class families and will subsequently become respectable members of the bourgeoisie, often by way of Oxbridge. What is needed is a greater understanding of how the variables interact, which would make the models of either closed or total institutions more tenuous.

To talk of a public school education is to talk of a variety of different educational experiences, so to make the topic more manageable most attention is directed at those some two hundred institutions whose heads belong to the Headmasters' Conference. Within the Headmasters' Conference, however, the diversity of schools is remarkable, with important lines of cleavage according to status – fluid, but clearly identifiable divisions; the degree of their historical independence from the state – the ex-direct grant grammar schools compared to the traditional independent schools; and the proportion of boarders – ranging from wholly boarding to wholly day schools. In spite of this diversity, membership of the Headmasters' Conference grants all of its members a recognizable position in the educational world. The internal differentiation may be marked but rarely is it as pronounced as the gulf between those who belong and those who do not. The extent of shared interests is illustrated by the response to external political threats. In accordance with the recommendations of the Second Report of the Public Schools Commission (1970:11–18) the then Labour government offered the direct grant grammar schools the choice of either joining the comprehensive system of secondary education or of going independent. Within the Headmasters' Conference the hostility to the proposals was unanimous and eventually, although with some regrets, approximately two-thirds of the direct grant grammar schools went independent (TES 1976:4). Because the independent schools cannot be characterized in a neat and simple fashion it is not easy to undermine them with all-embracing proposals for change and their communality of interests makes it equally difficult to slice off one subsection after another. If the independent sector was declining steadily and catering increasingly for only the wealthiest parents then it would be much more politically vulnerable. The implication is that private schools stand or fall as a whole (Glennerster & Wilson 1970:142).

Although the members of the Headmasters' Conference are united by various bonds, the trends analysed in this chapter do not apply to all of them equally. We argue that the schools are increasingly influenced by an academic ethos, which is best defined as the pursuit of examination success. This is to overstate what is occurring, but we rest our defence on the right to a measure of sociological licence, and on the claim that the evidence supports the heart of our case. For a variety of reasons, that we will consider later, the most prestigious of the public schools have been particularly affected by the academic ethos, but it is our belief that where the first division schools go the others are bound to follow.

Besides finding it difficult to define the object of our interest, the time period during which we are observing the schools is equally elusive. The modern public school system developed from approximately 1840 onwards and it has never been entirely static (see Bamford 1967:ch. 2). If by 1870, under Arnold's influence, the desire to turn out scholarly Christians was commonplace, then by 1914 the demands of muscular Christianity were dominant (Newsome 1961). Jonathan Gathorne-Hardy (1977:chs 14 & 15) has described the interwar years as a period of experimentation and fragmentation, the time during which the old order started to crumble. Since the Second World War the public schools have experienced changes almost as far reaching as those which gave birth to the modern public school system in the mid-nineteenth century. Although few new foundations have been created, the kind of educational experience that the public schools offer has been redefined quite sharply in a comparatively few years.

Yet in the immediate postwar years probably few could have guessed at the radical changes that were about to come. The seeds of change may have been sown – as Gathorne-Hardy believes – before the Second World War, and they may have sprouted in the 1940s and 1950s, but it was not evident until the 1960s what the fruit was to be. James Cobban (1972:22), the former headmaster of Abingdon

School, looking back from 1972, dates the start of 'the new era' quite precisely: 'I should date the beginning of the new era to about 1962 … I still think the Abingdon sixth-former of 1960 would have talked to one of my Dulwich sixth-formers of 1936 more easily than he could to one of my last set of prefects'. So this chapter will focus upon these changes, which if they were not initiated in the 1960s, became so evident in that decade that they could no longer be ignored. It is not simply a question of their visibility but more a matter of their significance – in educational, sociological and political terms.

Tom Brown's contemporary universe

There is a wide measure of agreement as to what changes have occurred in public school education on which John Rae gives an interesting protagonist's point of view (Rae 1981:ch. 6). We will divide these into three main areas: the academic ethos of the schools; their social, cultural and moral activities; and their organizational forms. But it should be remembered that these are interlocking forces. For example, Rupert Wilkinson (1964:64–8; see Campbell 1970:253–6; Honey 1977:126–35), in his study of the public schools during the late-Victorian and Edwardian period, argued that a classical education formed the core of the curriculum because it was believed that it perpetuated certain expressive values. So although a knowledge of the classics may have been considered important in its own right, the fact that a classical education allegedly inculcated gentlemanly virtues was at least equally significant.

The present-day stress on academic success within the public schools is neither new nor entirely all-encompassing. In fact it is a traditional requirement for membership of the Headmasters' Conference that the headmaster's school has a well-established sixth form with a certain percentage of its pupils proceeding regularly to university. In his brilliant portrayal of the late-nineteenth-century public school system ('Tom Brown's Universe') John Honey (1977:244–7) hypothesized that examination success was one possible determinant of public school status. Furthermore, a public school education was not entirely without its vocational merits (even the classics can be defended in these terms), although admittedly many of their pupils found it necessary to spend some time at at crammer (see Best 1975:132–3), or to engage private tutors, in order to fulfil their career aspirations.

In spite of the past academic record, very tentative at some institutions but amounting to a tradition of genuine scholarship at others, the contemporary stress on examination success marks a new and distinctive stage in the history of public school education. In fact it is difficult to escape the impression that academic success is equated with examination success at 'A' Level and, even more particularly, in the entrance scholarships and exhibitions of Oxbridge. Although, according to Mr McCrum, Eton has no intention of following in Winchester's scholastic footsteps; it has raised its entrance requirements. Even Winchester finds it difficult to maintain its scholarly tradition in the face of fierce competition for Oxbridge places. The Oxbridge entrance examinations demand a more broadly-based preparation than the average 'A' Level course and the Headmasters' Conference has defended their retention partly on these grounds (Franks 1965 : 45). However, whether the universities can resist the demand for the abolition in the face of the charge that they constitute an unfair obstacle for pupils in the state secondary schools remains to be seen.

As distinctive as the dominance of the academic ethos is the diversification of its content. Some public schools may still have a healthy classics department but no longer are the public schools bastions of a classical education. In the latter half of the nineteenth century the public schools added a so-called 'modern' side as an alternative to their classical curriculum but this was a sop to reformist pressures and never won the status it perhaps merited (Bamford 1967 : ch. 5). Today it is the classics that are on the defensive with Greek especially on the wane. Towards the end of the 1960s, the headmaster of Charterhouse (1969 : 8) – more in sorrow than anger – wrote: 'The fourth thing we have lost is Greek. Even as late as the early '50s there was one school left where more boys had done some Greek than had done none. That is no longer even remotely possible ... Greek has vanished from the curriculum like the spring out of the year.' Whether many schoolboys would have seen Greek as the spring of the year is another matter, but be that as it may.

Today it is impossible to identify a single body of high status knowledge in the public schools. In the 1950s cooperation between the Headmasters' Conference and industry led to the creation of an industrial Fund for the Promotion of Scientific Education in Schools which upgraded the public schools' science laboratories (Glennerster & Wilson 1968 : 309). More recently it is the provision of facilities for 'design and technology' which have been attracting attention (see Howard 1977:2). Consequently, in the public schools the science courses, pure and applied, coupled with the more traditional appeal of mathematics, are taken by more of today's sixth formers than the arts subjects (Kalton 1966:93). Accompanying the growth of the science subjects is that of the social sciences which also have a strong applied element as seen, for example, in the 'A' Level business studies course which was pioneered at Marlborough College, and the economics courses which have an even wider following. We have stressed the practical nature of these subjects because it is in such contrast with the other-worldly image of the classics. A classical education was very useful for certain professional careers – and it may have helped to develop the faculties in general (Campbell 1970:256–7) but the essence of its attraction was its lack of precise vocational utility and as such formed the basis of an education suitable for gentlemen.

The diversification of high status knowledge is reinforced by the cultural pluralism of the present-day public school. The cult of athleticism is dead, but the arts thrive. In general terms, therefore, we are far removed from that philistine world of the past which coupled a worship of games with a deep suspicion of intellectual and artistic pursuits.

A final aspect of the academic ethos which should be noted is the experiments with the curriculum, both what is taught and how it is taught. Some public schools have either initiated and/or adopted various Nuffield projects or Schools Council courses. The fact that many of their pupils spend more than two years in the sixth form, usually preparing for the Oxbridge scholarships, has meant that the schools can go beyond the confines of the 'A' Level syllabus. Furthermore, the comparatively favourable staff–pupil ratios can be used to create more intimate and vigorous learning situations such as the small group seminar. However, this kind of change should be kept in proportion. Although the independent sector contains several progressive schools, this is not an apt description of the overall membership of the Headmasters' Conference. In fact there is a group of independent schools (e.g. Bedales, Abbotsholme, Rendcomb and Dartington Hall School) which are probably less progressive than they used to be (see Punch 1977:155–69).

The main vehicles for the expression of the schools' values are their social, cultural and moral activities. The pluralism we have commented upon with respect to cultural pursuits is a general phenomenon. Whereas in the past boys invariably had a limited choice of activities, with participation in some compulsory, today the choice is broader and the element of compulsion has been mitigated. In the public schools (as in the state schools) games are still an important part of the daily routine. Given the presence of boarders, and the fact that they are educating adolescents, this is almost inevitable. But gone are the days when rugby, football, cricket, and in some schools rowing, were seen as essential prerequisites for the building of a boy's character. Today headmasters will almost defensively confess that the school doesn't, as yet, have a heated swimming pool, although they plan to have one built in the near future.

Many of the public schools were founded for religious purposes, in most cases to ensure that the children of the middle class received a sound Anglican upbringing (Kirk 1937; Heeney 1969). It was not until the final thirty years of the nineteenth century that most public school masters were lay professionals and it was not until the 1930s that the majority of the headmasters of the leading public boarding schools were laymen (Honey 1977:308). The links between church and school were built on the fundamental assumption that the primary end of education was moral – to create the Christian gentleman. It was presumably both the wide appeal of this ideal, and the latitude it permitted with respect to moral ends, that accounts for the founding of public schools to cater for Nonconformists, and Roman Catholics. It would be grossly misleading to say that all this is now dead for the chapel is still a central institution in the life of a public school. But its dominance is no more. The number of services has declined and the boys have a greater measure of choice as to whether they will attend or not. In view of the secularization of formal education – so that it has a pragmatic pay-off for the individual rather than a moral purpose for a whole class of people – this was to be expected.

After games and chapel the third great pillar of the public school value system was the Combined Cadet Force (CCF). The links between the officer corps of the British armed services, especially the army, and the public schools are well-established. In its simplest form those families which have traditionally prized commissions in the armed forces for their sons have also valued a public school education. This three-way relationship between family, school and the officer class is particularly well-developed at Wellington College which has been noted for its consistently special relationship to the officer corps of the British army (Newsome 1959). It has been argued that the presence of CCF, which in the past was to all intents and purposes compulsory, further enhanced the links between the armed services and the public schools by nurturing a militaristic ethos (Best 1975:133–7). Even if this were true of the past the charge is more tenuous today. Membership of the CCF is invariably a matter of personal choice, in the true sense of the term (Wilkinson 1964:178–9), and various social/community services are available as alternatives to serving in the force.

This diversification in the life of the public schools has been reinforced by noticeable changes in their organizational style. The old structures are basically intact, but the way in which they function is very different. For example, critical to the smooth functioning of the old model was the prefectorial system initiated by Arnold. Besides having formal responsibility for much of the discipline of the school the prefects were obliged, at least in theory, to establish the moral tone of the school. The structure was hierarchical; everyone knowing his place with its designated rights and duties. Naturally one's rights tended to expand as one ascended the hierarchy, thus at one extreme newcomers were fags, while at the other prefects had the right to beat. Today, although prefects still exist they rarely have the same privileges – certainly not the right to beat, and fagging has all but expired. With the proliferation of opportunities for gaining individual status, power is inevitably more diffused. The old hierarchical model, based upon the possession of age-related formal roles has been replaced by numerous, at least partially differentiated, arenas within which status and power is much more closely bound up with individual skill and initiative.

After the prefectorial system, the second most distinctive organizational feature of the public schools has been the house system. As with prefects the school houses are still very much alive. In view of the fact that at any one point in time most schools are responsible for the education of several hundred boys it is difficult to imagine that it could be otherwise, especially in boarding schools. The numbers involved simply require their subdivision into more manageable units. In the past, however, the houses were not mere organizational units, a convenient structure for the more ready management of a large number of boys. For many boys the house was the focus of their school lives, to the point where house loyalty could be more dominant, and certainly more tangible than school loyalty. Over time the house cannot help but become a more functional unit. The houses will continue to provide a basis for many of the activities which compose the life of a school; however, except in the larger and better endowed schools, many present-day activities are likely to cut across house boundaries. Not many schools can sustain more than one orchestra or one drama society, and even the feeding of the boys is not necessarily done in the houses. The strength of the academic ethos makes it more difficult for the houses to nurture peculiar characteristics: they all seek the same standard of excellence and are judged accordingly. Although it is dangerous to be dogmatic about where power lies in the public school, the headmasters have about them the aura of calm and competent executives who are very much in charge. Even that paradigm of the house system, Eton College, witnessed under Mr McCrum's headmastership a period of quiet and steady reform to the point where the housemaster's control over the selection of his boys will be limited to not more than half of them. In an age when boys may be excused from the normal daily routine to prepare for forthcoming examinations, when parents may opt for private education for only a portion of their children's schooldays, and may visit the school most weekends (or even have their children home for the weekend) then the notion of the all-embracing house within the closed and total world of the school is an anachronism.

Although these changes in public school education can be seen by all those who wish to enquire, the failure of some sociologists to come to terms with them is remarkable. It is almost as if the critics of the public schools wished that they had not changed, that the caricatures of yesteryear were still valid. A perfect, if extreme, illustration of this point is the unit on 'The Education of Elites' in the Open University's (1977) Educational Studies course. Although its text discusses some of the changes considered above, the photographs and drawings used to illustrate it are outrageously dated and are clearly designed to establish in the mind of the reader an outmoded stereotype. Besides infuriating the schools by presenting a false picture of them it is also poor social science. It not only presents a false picture of the public schools, but also can lead to misinterpretations in relating them to their contemporary social context. Analysis therefore of either the internal workings of the schools or their social function is not helped by presenting grossly biased images, comforting though these may be to the social scientist.

It is necessary to understand the significance of these changes: in what ways the social purpose of the public schools has changed (if at all), why it has changed, and how these changes have been implemented. Although the Headmasters' Conference is keen to stress that the schools are now very much part of the contemporary world, the reluctance to grapple with these further questions is, not altogether surprisingly, somewhat greater. For their part the sociologists have not been so inhibited, again not altogether surprisingly! The consensus of their opinion is unanimous – nothing of fundamental importance has changed. This judgment is based upon assessing the central purpose of a public school education and then claiming that this remains more or less intact. Thus in 1967 Ian Weinberg wrote, 'It also seems that the schools have not deviated from their Victorian purpose of educating anti-commercial Gentlemanly rulers' (46). Perhaps Weinberg was too specific for in 1975 Lambert, without any subsequent elaboration, claimed that 'as would be expected there were few changes in the implemented goals, those long-term, permanent ends which schools actually pursue' (269). In similar vein Madeleine MacDonald noted in 1977 (OU:29) that 'The fact that the public schools have not fundamentally changed their tone and outlook must surely be a result of their recruitment policy'. In view of all that has gone before the only surprise about MacDonald's statement is her simplistic perception of what is required to retain an institution's 'tone and outlook'.

In the second section of this chapter we will interpret the significance of these changes. To say that nothing fundamental has changed begs the question of what is fundamental, and it is also unclear how those changes that have taken place are to be understood, other than in the simple-minded fashion that they are less than fundamental as they do not affect the goals of the schools. In view of the fact that we believe that educational change is accompanied by an ideological struggle, our main purpose is to evaluate the impact of these changes upon the ideology of a public school education. Although this will not enable us to consider all the ramifications of the changes, it should enable us to throw some light on the questions raised above, a process to be completed in the final section of the chapter.

Ideology and change

The consistent, central purpose of the public schools has been to provide an education suitable for those who are destined to become the nation's leaders in practically every field. This does not mean that every future leader passes through their hands, or that all of their pupils are assured of a place in the sun. The ability to survive, however, has been dependent upon the absorption of the rich and powerful, and without such success the public schools would have perished long ago (see Coleman 1973). In view of the prestige, if not the power, that accompanies this it means the schools inherit a past which it is difficult for them to disclaim, no matter how insistently others may demand it of them (see Dancy 1963:145–52; Wilson 1962:118–38). As we will have cause to consider later, the schools are in the marketplace which makes their survival very much dependent upon the belief that they offer an education which leads to future leadership roles. Whether this is true or not is immaterial, but whether it is believed or not is critical to their survival.

Although we agree therefore with other sociologists that the public schools do have the continuing, dominant function of educating the nation's leaders, we believe that this is little more than a statement of the obvious. The performance of this general objective can be accomplished in many ways encompassing different educational experiences designed to train very different kinds of citizens. The purposes of a public school education, or all education for that matter, can be generalized at various levels of abstraction. As we noted Weinberg refers to the education of 'anti-commercial Gentlemanly rulers' but the kind of changes we have documented are totally inconsistent with such an objective. It is still possible to dispute the suitability of the contemporary public school for the education of future élites, but Weinberg's conception of the Victorian ideal is certainly dead. It is fair to say, however, that the nineteenth-century absorption of the bourgeoisie did not result in a radical revamping of all aspects of a public school education. Although the schools educated the ruling class, whether it was a suitable education is a contentious issue. The contemporary public school retains the commitment to the education of élites but it endeavours to provide a different educational experience, one more in tune with the contemporary needs of its clientele.

As equally important as the fact that goals can be expressed at different levels of abstraction is their translation into classroom practice. If the latter is altered then one suspects the goals themselves are also changing. This may not mean a change in goals at the very highest level of abstraction (although even this may be modified or simply confused) but it will almost certainly mean changes in how those goals are to be achieved. In terms of the public schools it may be possible for them to retain the notion of providing an education to suit the needs of a future ruling class but they have to come to terms with the fact that the needs of the ruling class are now different. In what sense the educational experience is less fundamental than the overall goal is a fruitless query for it is the attempt to define the goal in concrete educational forms that gives it substance, one without the other is meaningless. It is our contention that the contemporary public schools now face a dilemma. On the one hand they have retained the idea that their essential purpose is to educate the nation's future élites, and on the other hand they have successfully transformed their educational practices to fulfil this task in today's world. What they have lost, or rather are struggling to rediscover, is a coherent and identifiable educational ideology.

In chapter three we maintained that an educational ideology consisted of three main components: 1 an idea of the educated man; 2 an idea of the social order into which such an individual would fit; and 3 the kinds of educational experiences which were necessary to marry the individual to the social order. Whatever one may feel about the public schools, from approximately 1870 to 1914 (the classical period of public school education) they did at least have a very well-developed ideology. In fact both the criticism and defence of them were so heated because it was self-evident where they stood — educationally, socially and politically (see Wilkinson 1970). The detractors hated what they saw, the defenders admired it, so praise and denigration followed accordingly. It was impossible to sit on the fence.

It is very evident that one of the primary functions of the nineteenth-century public school was to establish a common normative framework for élite groups. For all his emphasis on the divisions within the public school community even Honey (1977:291) concludes that the schools were *a community*, and at least within the divisions showed a degree of mutual recognition which could be very beneficial in furthering the individual's career. Increasingly one's status was more dependent upon education than upon kinship and a precondition for the realization of this was that the schools inculcate a comparatively narrow set of values. As we have already noted the schools exercised an important social homogenizing effect, embracing an expanding range of the bourgeoisie along with the aristocracy, and encompassing Roman Catholic, Nonconformist and Jewish schools as well as the Anglican foundations.

D. C. Coleman (1973:97) has described this process of social accommodation as a mutual coming-to-terms of gentlemen and players: 'In one sense the industrial revolution was a revolution of those who were not gentlemen. And, as is usual in partial revolutions, sooner or later the values of the revolutionaries succumb to those of the surviving élite who, in turn modify their own standards to fit the new situation.' It is within this context that the nineteenth-century public school evolved and one can see the outcome as a 'rather rapid and self-interested change in response to the prevailing social climate' (O'Connor 1979:20). But a further issue is on whose terms the accommodation took place, where was the line drawn between players and gentlemen? It would be difficult to deny that the gentlemen won, and won handsomely, notwithstanding the fact that Coleman discerns some modification of their own standards. The perception was of a social order divided into a rigid class hierarchy, headed by the aristocracy and underpinned by the Anglican church. Interclass obligations were accepted but this was the *noblesse oblige* of the superior to the inferior. The public schools aimed to make 'synthetic gentlemen' of the bourgeoisie (Wilkinson 1964:4). The class accommodation, therefore, took place on terms which denied the central bourgeois value of aggressive entrepreneuralism. Public service, frequently in some remote corner of the empire, was the ultimate goal while the pursuit of private profit, especially through trade or industry, was held in the lowest esteem.

To characterize the kind of individual who was meant to fit into this social order is more difficult and controversial, if only because the generalizations are inevitably so great. In spite of this some points have been widely agreed. The Victorian public schools stressed the importance of leadership qualities but it was a tempered form of leadership, forged in the communal world of a boarding school, acquired after an extended apprenticeship in subordinate roles, and infused with Christian morality. This was a class of leaders rather than individual leadership, assured of its moral superiority but equally determined to lead responsibly. The personalities who manifested these qualities were equally lacking in individuality. Self-restraint could become 'the stiff-upper-lip' while 'fair play' could mean a pedantic following of the rules with a willingness to accept second place. The end product is a gentlemanly style marked by its speech, mannerisms and modes of thinking and acting (King 1961). The Fleming Report summarized its view in these less-than-flattering terms: '(they also) tended to encourage the production of a recognised type, loyal, honest and self-confident but liable to undervalue the qualities of imagination, sensibility and critical ability' (Board of Education 1944:29).

It is vital to remember that the late-nineteenth-century changes in public school education were *not* simply a self-interested response on the part of the schools to the changing social climate of Britain. Powerful individuals within the school system, none more so than Thomas Arnold, were determining what the response to the social climate would be. They were not simply translating forces greater than themselves into educational practice. Of course it was within the schools themselves — how they conducted their daily business — that the reforming headmasters of the nineteenth century could exercise their greatest influence. But it does not end there for they were men who had clear conceptions of what the social order should look like, and how their schools could best educate the boys who would be the nation's leaders. By the turn of the century the end result was the chapel, CCF, athleticism and prefects. One of the consequences of this is that the public schools undoubtedly aided the cause of social and political harmony by bringing segments of the middle class and upper class closer together. But equally they must take some of the responsibility for the social divisiveness that follows from a system of education divided along class lines. Consider the following extract from evidence given to the Public Schools Commission by the Joint Working Party of the Governing Bodies' Association and Headmasters' Conference:

... we hardly think that we can reasonably be supposed to be the cause of the class system as it exists in this country: ... What is presumably meant by the charge against us is that some features of the social groupings in this country are undesirable and that we make them worse. We are at least entitled to ask how we do this ...' (1968b:153)

Some have extended the argument by tracing the nation's economic woes to the anticommercial bias of the nineteenth-century public schools but this is a more debatable contention.

In his study of 'Tom Brown's Universe' Honey (1977:247–95) came to the conclusion that the best criteria for defining a public school, and discovering its ranking order, was one of mutual recognition. It was the willingness to engage in various activities with other schools, most significantly on the sports field, that formed the public school system and its internal hierarchy. The public schools, therefore, defined themselves by the criteria that *they* considered to be relevant. The definition was not imposed upon them, rather they formed it. If one adds to this the fact that the nineteenth-century public schools created their own model of the educated man, the full awareness of their power is evident.

What does today's public school education offer in place of this model? Over a long period of time the main political thrust of their opponents has been directed at the schools' alleged social divisiveness — i.e. they bear much of the responsibility for the perpetuation of Britain's class structure, with its concomitant undesirable social effects. Partly because the proponents of this charge have periodic access to political power, and partly because some who are sympathetic to the cause of independent schooling also believe it to be true, it is a charge that has to be taken seriously. The consequence is that the advocates of private education have ambivalent perceptions of what the social order should be, and how the public schools should relate to that. Periodically the schools have expressed their disquiet at their social exclusiveness and have sought the assistance of the state to remedy this. The Headmasters' Conference welcomed the recommendations of the Fleming Report which suggested that all public schools, more or less along the lines of the old direct grant grammar schools, should accept 25 per cent of their pupils from elementary schools with the cost to be met by the state (Board of Education 1944:62–9). At a later date the reception of the First Report of the Public Schools Commission (1968 i:8–14) was more cautious, but the recommendation that eventually each should be composed of at least 50 per cent of assisted place pupils who would encompass approximately the top three-quarters of the ability range was not rejected outright.

In spite of the goodwill of individual schools, and the existence of some general scholarship funds, it is evident that the class composition of the public schools will not change significantly without an influx of state money. Successive governments, however, have refused to commit the resources – either money is too tight or they have lacked the political will to overcome the obstacles. But when the will and money are forthcoming the problems seem merely to grow as is illustrated perfectly by the present government's assisted places scheme. It has not been wholly welcomed by the independent schools themselves – with John Rae, headmaster of Westminster School, leading the public opposition – and the opponents of private education have, to some effect, made political capital out of it. And all this for a scheme that will barely scratch the surface of the problem, and perhaps by selecting pupils according to academic criteria, simply exacerbate it. How to select state-aided pupils demonstrates the schools' ambivalence towards the nature of the social order. On the one hand it is accepted that only by taking more pupils from the state sector can they hope to widen their social intake, and that this is a desirable objective. On the other hand they want to decide what kind of person is selected, so retaining ultimate control of their social intake. They have shown a willingness to accept pupils from the state sector who are in need of boarding education, but the level of commitment must inevitably be limited if the schools are to remain financially solvent. There is certainly no desire, quite naturally, to have the total character of their schools altered by a sudden large influx of assisted place pupils, whether they need a boarding education or not. The qualms of those who fear that in token schemes of integration the character of public school education will not change are recognized, but there is a reluctance on the part of the schools to risk the destruction of what they cherish. When this is coupled with a continuous reiteration of the claim that fee-paying heightens both the parents' and pupils' commitment to schooling, and the pride in the academic standard of many of their schools, then not surprisingly a suspicion as to how far they can widen their social intake – given these guidelines – is fostered. Finally, few headmasters would be prepared to accept pupils unless they had the final say on selection which inevitably arouses the suspicion – whatever goodwill there may be – that those whom it is thought will not fit in will be weeded out (see Stagg & Lambert 1968).

The problem facing the proponents of independent schooling is that it is politically unwise, and perhaps personally repugnant to favour social privilege and divisiveness and yet they have to support the rights of fee-paying parents. The Victorian public schools were not hedged in by such uncertainties. They existed in a social context in which the division of society into different classes was considered as natural, and they were not, therefore, constantly on the political defensive with respect to this issue. A perfect illustration of this point is the perpetration of a snobbish public school image in the mass circulation weekly comics that were created at the turn of the century. Orwell (1958) implied that these comics, with their cosy view of social reality, successfully sapped the potential political militancy of their large working-class readership. Be this as it may, it is equally hard to believe that such an image could be presented in the first place unless the privileged class position of the public schools was already very secure. Today the schools require legitimations of their privileged position (and thus of fee-paying) which can be defended both in their own eyes and in the eyes of significant others.

Their embracing of the academic ethos serves these purposes admirably. In the first place it has been firmly implanted in the state system thanks to the grammar schools. As such it has an established body of support, stretching over a long period of time, amongst all those with an interest in schooling. Secondly, thanks to its promotion of individual achievement through personalized examination success, it is an effective disguise of the social reproduction process. It thus helps the public schools to achieve one of their traditional goals, class reproduction, through much more acceptable means. Thirdly, as we have already noted, it is not entirely alien to traditional public school values. Although in the past some schools saw themselves as centres of intellectual excellence, it is not too great a step to translate this into academic success measured by examination results. In fact it is possible to see the schools' defence of 'intellectual standards' as their main rationale. John Vaizey (now Lord Vaizey and once a scourge of the public schools) has written (1971:8):

My view, in short, is that the key issue is not fee-paying or parental choice. It is that some schools – not all schools, but some – set before their pupils a respect for the intellect, standards of common decency and endurance which, whatever their other drawbacks, are invaluable ... I rest my case – and I hope you would rest your case – on intellectual standards.

But whether Vaizey meant by this more than the pursuit of 'A' Levels and university scholarships, he refrains from saying.

The fourth reason for advocating the academic ethos – that it is needed by present-day society – sheds more revealing insights into one contemporary public school perspective as to what the character of the social order should be. The two foremost proponents of this viewpoint are John Rae (1977), the headmaster of Westminster School, and Lord James (1951; 1968), the ex-high master of Manchester Grammar School. James has argued that as leadership is an inevitable requirement of society the central purpose of schooling should be 'education for leadership'. Although leadership qualities are a product of the individual's intellect as well as his temperamental and moral qualities, it is the former that the schools should concentrate their energies upon developing. The ultimate goal is to produce an 'élite of merit'. The element of *noblesse oblige*, however, is not forgotten: the strengthening of economic prosperity depends upon the talented few and without this the chances of 'greater equality and a better life for the poor' are slim (James 1968:9). Rae rounds out James's rather narrow concerns; he stresses the need for a competitive individuality which is directed towards industry and trade. He dislikes the government service bias of the public schools and universities, and seeks government-sponsored initiatives in curriculum innovation to counteract this. He is not optimistic, however, for he draws a close parallel between the expressive concerns of today's comprehensive secondary schools and the Victorian public schools. This rather heady stuff represents the viewpoints of only two particular individuals but it does illustrate the kinds of links that can be drawn between the academic ethos and a meritocratically based social order in pursuit of the specific economic goal of growth.

Rae and James are influential figures and they may well be the forerunners of a new public school view of the social order. Neither man may be much enamoured of the idea but their influence could be boosted by the wave of 'new conservatism' which was so strongly reinforced by the election of a Conservative government in 1979. The time is appropriate for the trumpeting of personal initiative and competitiveness, concentrating resources upon the education of the talented few, defining schooling as an experience geared primarily to the goal of economic growth, and pursuing these ends within a narrow definition of the national interest. The basic contradiction, however, still remains – the independent schools may embrace these ends but their very existence is a symbol of the fact that such aims cannot be fully realized. For the moment we remain in a state of suspended animation with political discretion more in evidence than ideological valour as the mixed reaction to the present government's assisted places scheme admirably illustrates.

The fifth, and final strength of the academic ethos is its broad political appeal. It is much easier to defend schools politically if they fall within a well-established and popular educational tradition and they are seen to be serving the contemporary needs of society rather than just the interests of their own clientele. The conscious attempt to portray themselves as the last bastion of academic standards has reaped its rewards in the recent expansion of their numbers. To see this as mainly middle-class parents escaping their perception of the likely consequences of comprehensive secondary education is too easy a diagnosis. Not all the escapees are firmly ensconced members of the bourgeoisie, and the respect for examination success runs deep and wide – not surprising in view of the perceived importance of schooling as a mobility route for the British working class.

If there is no positive view of what the social order should be then it is impossible to state concisely and clearly what is the desired product of the educational process and how the schooling experience is to be structured to achieve it. We have already commented upon the diversification of school life i.e. the increase in social, cultural and academic pluralism. But this has been accompanied by considerable confusion as to what values the individual is supposed to embrace by the end of his schooldays. Again the schools have been placed on the defensive by the ebb and flow of broad currents in the wider society. More rigid academic standards have gone hand-in-glove with a much laxer moral code. Not even the public schools were so 'total' and 'closed' that they could entirely resist the repercussions of the burgeoning youth culture movements of the 1960s. As Gathorne-Hardy (1977:400) notes the 1970s have seen a mild reaction to this, a reaffirmation of some of the traditional values. The outcome is invariably a reiteration of a commitment to certain basic standards – with an inevitable reference to the Christian legacy – usually accompanied by the contention that the schools will adjust to changing realities (see Howarth 1972; Woodhouse 1975; Thorn 1978). This begs more questions than it answers but it is preferable to the presentation of a checklist of value items which it is assumed that all reasonable men will agree upon, and that the schools will defend to the last. Thus we read:

True standards and values are not relative; they are absolute and unchanging. Mercifully for our country the public schools have no monopoly on virtue but at their best, in the training which they give, they have stood for integrity, responsibility, intellectual guts, respect for others, good manners, honesty, tolerance, ordinary human decency, above all compassion. These virtues are most easily inculcated in an ordered and disciplined society. I believe that the permissive age has been both inevitable, and to a large extent sound, but I also believe that we have gone far enough and that many of our parents are looking to us to give a lead which they seem unable to give themselves (Headmasters' Conference: 1968: 5).

Except for minor quibbles these are probably sentiments with which few could disagree and this is their very problem for they give no indication that a *distinctively* worthwhile public school ethos is thriving.

The essence of our argument, therefore, is that the public schools have changed, and changed very successfully. They are now flourishing institutions, no longer on the defensive but making out a case for themselves which appeals where it counts most – in the market-place i.e. to the parents of their potential customers. The public schools are still training their pupils for leadership roles, although the Public Schools Commission (1968a: 61) naively believed differently. The stress now is upon the attainment of examination success which is seen as the key to future individual promotion in today's meritocratically ordered society. But with the exceptions we have considered, there is no general view of the desired social order. Their internal catholicism, again one of their strongest selling points as far as parents are concerned, is matched by not so much a vacuum with respect to values but rather timidity (the advocacy of a 'middle way') and blandness (the reiteration of slogans with which few could disagree). The present-day public school lacks the ideological self-confidence of its Victorian predecessor. But perhaps in view of the rapidity of change, the collapse of the old public school world in somewhat less than two decades, this is not so surprising.

It could be argued, in the light of the pressures that the public schools faced about a decade ago, that survival was the name of the game and in this respect few could deny they have done surprisingly well. In the next decade we may see a fuller redefinition of their educational ideology, an attempt to combine their internal pluralism with a more developed view of the social order and how their pupils should relate to it. Even in the nineteenth century the relationship between internal processes and perceptions of the social order was never entirely static. These interacted with one another, coming to fruition in the late-Victorian/Edwardian period. What is different today is the social context in which the schools find themselves. Whereas the Victorian public schools were highly influential in drawing the line between 'gentlemen' and 'players', the schools now have far less room to manoeuvre. In view of this it could suit them better *not* to redefine their role – to be most things to some men and to survive, rather than to be specific things to all men and to perish.

The process of change

A revealing mystery is why some schools have bothered to change at all. The very cream of the 'first division' schools have experienced few problems in attracting more than the desired number of pupils. And yet they have often been in the very forefront of change. This could be explained in terms of their headmasters. As they are the more prestigious schools they attract the most talented individuals, who in Machiavellian fashion introduce changes both because over the long run these help to maintain the status of the school and because in the meantime they undermine the opposition to independent education. Alternatively, perhaps the headmasters of the great schools are simply more liberal and reformist in outlook and thus their changes are a result of personal predispositions i.e. they are simply good educationalists. As must be obvious from the tone of this chapter we do not devalue the importance of individual action to the process of change. However, in line with our general theoretical position we would stress the importance of the pressures emanating from the institutional context in which the schools are located as the most critical stimulant of change. Ironically, for all their popularity with wealthy parents, it is in fact the prestigious schools which are most firmly enmeshed in a web of institutional relationships and thus, in spite of the considerable power this gives them, it also severely constrains their freedom of action. Some of the analysis which follows considers other stimulants of change which do not readily fit into this line of argument. Although important, they are essentially supplementary to the main pressure of institutional interaction.

Independent schools are in the marketplace in the sense that parents can choose to have their children educated elsewhere if they should so desire – in a state school or another private school of their choice. Ultimately it is parents who decide the well-being of a public school. If sufficient of them decide to remove their children – or as is more probable not to send them in the first place – then the school will either close, or change in ways that will overcome the crisis. In this very real sense independent schools can be held accountable to the parents of their pupils in a way that state schools can not. Headmasters do see themselves as responsive to the demands of parents and there is little doubt that they have picked up, loud and clear from them, the message of the importance of examination success. The sparse evidence on the attitudes of the parents of public school-children draws a broad distinction between 'conventional' parents who think *only* in terms of independent schools for the education of their children and 'pragmatic' parents who make a positive choice between the state and independent sectors and favour the latter because of perceived specific payoffs (see Bridgeman & Fox 1978). One important payoff as far as most of the pragmatic parents are concerned is that they believe – no matter what the reasons may be – academic standards are higher in the private schools (ibid.: 704).

Although the great public schools are still national, indeed international, institutions the trend is towards parents selecting a school within a fifty mile radius of their home – a comfortable day's return journey by car. The principle of boarding, at least any stringent definition of it, is thus slowly being eroded. Parents make more frequent trips to the school and children return home for at least the occasional weekend. Another trend to emerge in the past decade is the steady movement away from boarding, no matter how flexibly organized, towards day school education (see Rae 1978:16). The schools, therefore, are subjected to at least the gaze of concerned and inquisitive parents. This is a good example of a changed relationship between institutions (the family and the school) that results from new social trends. As the parents of children in the independent sector are less organized than are some of their counterparts with children in the state sector (i.e. in PTAs), so their power is directly dependent upon the personal resources they command (in particular their payment of the fees!) and decisions as to how they will conduct their private lives (giving more direct and continuous attention to the upbringing of their children).

The apparently greater interest of parents in the education of their children should influence the relationship of pupils to the school. If parents are concerned overwhelmingly with the academic aspects of the school's work it would presumably strengthen the pupils' commitment in that respect and lessen it in others. Furthermore, it would be foolish to deny the impact of the burgeoning youth culture movement. The culture of the young may be socially fragmented but it would be difficult to identify a distinctive public schoolboy ethos. The intrusiveness of the outside world is far too strong and pervasive to tolerate the presence of such esoteric islands of resistance. Change has also been encouraged by the introduction of girls, initially at Marlborough College, but today in a number of schools. Middle-class girls may fit in very comfortably with the academic values and with the established curriculum, but few are likely to sympathize with many of the traditional expressive values or with those activities through which they were manifested. At the same time the diversification of the new life of the public school has helped to undermine the stereotypical image of the public schoolboy. The element of competition in a variety of spheres is intense and much of this competition is of a highly personalized nature. The irony is that as school life becomes more open and less hierarchically organized it could also possibly become less communal with a vaguer individual sense of its meaning. We make this point tentatively. Clearly varying social forces are at work and how they resolve themselves will depend upon the strength of the pressures and personalities involved.

The temptation to portray masters in public schools as an isolated segment of their profession is great – they are Oxbridge graduates, lack a teacher's training qualification, and have taught only in public schools (Kalton 1966:47, 52, 78). The gradual change with respect to all these variables has meant the emergence of a new type of public school master, one who is not as closely wedded to the public school world as the master of old. This is not to question the commitment of today's teacher but to suggest that he is subjected to a wider range of influences. The very prominence of the academic ethos has helped to reinforce this change. If a teacher's success is to be measured in terms of the scholarship performance of his pupils then this will inevitably be one of his dominant concerns. The gravity of his attention is likely to shift away from the school's more general goals to the furtherance of his specific subject interests. Of course this is less true of those teachers who have greater responsibility for the organization of the school, especially headmasters and housemasters, but it is doubtful if they can do little more – or even want to – than control the excesses of this movement. Indeed in the case of some headmasters they have done much to encourage it. School governors and old boys (who are sometimes also governors) are other internal bodies that are part of the process of change. Very little is known about their attitudes but conventional wisdom suggests they are conservative forces.

Because the data on the attitudes of parents, pupils and teachers is so sparse we have been forced to make commonsense inferences. Although the specifics may be disputed, the overall direction of our argument is widely supported. We claimed earlier that the model of the public school as a closed and total institution drew attention away from the schools' relationships to their social context. What has been happening is a broadening of the context within which the schools are located. Social forces intrude through a whole range of channels to reshape the character of the school; to employ Weinberg's (1967:xiv) terminology, role conflict is endemic. The external pressures have become more powerful and insidious over time, the needs – and therefore the demands – of parents, masters and pupils are now more clearly formulated and strident, and the schools are far less certain as to their social role. Once the pressures of the marketplace have succeeded in undermining an institution's ideological foundations then almost any change can be contemplated.

The reason why public schools flourish is because they continue to educate most of the nation's élite groups. Parents pay the fees because they value the education their children will receive. It is impossible to believe that the two statements are not related i.e. parents value a public school education because these are literally schools for top people. The schools, therefore, have to maintain the following links if they are to prosper: 1 Attract parents who can afford the fees; 2 Offer an education which is deemed suitable for the children of those parents; and 3 Be seen to ensure that in post-school life their pupils occupy those positions which command a disproportionate share of status, income and power. The latter is central to what we have termed the tightening institutional bonds.

The links the public schools have established with the universities, and the colleges of Oxford and Cambridge in particular, are vital to their continued well-being. Increasingly the passage into élite membership is funnelled through the universities so that today it is more difficult to obtain élite membership with a public school education alone (Bishop & Wilkinson 1967; Boyd 1973; Glennerster & Pryke 1973). Furthermore, the academic ethos cements the ties between school and university for the latter are its formal institutional culmination. At one time there were few problems in maintaining this connection as the competition for university places was restricted, and both the formal and informal ties between public schools and Oxbridge were strong. Certain colleges were founded for the express purpose of taking boys from a particular public school, many closed scholarships were established, Oxbridge dons were school governors, it was common for dons to become schoolmasters, the classical curriculum dominated both schools and universities, and the colleges were accustomed to receiving public schoolboys – it was simply the done thing. Gradually these advantages have been whittled away. The ties of a common classical education were eroded by the growth of science, engineering and the social sciences. When Oxford decided to accept undergraduates without an 'O' Level pass in Latin, the final symbol of this particular link went. A career line which goes from university don to schoolmaster or vice versa is now exceptional. Although students from the public schools still make up a disproportionate percentage of the Oxbridge student population, both universities are now tuned to receiving undergraduates from other sources (see Franks 1966 ii : 47 ; Oxford University 1979 ; Cambridge University 1980). The established order has been modified.

The retention of some closed scholarships and of college entrance examinations have helped to keep the links tighter than they might be otherwise. Oxford's own commission, the Franks Commission (1966 i : 413), recommended the abolition of all closed scholarships which was finally implemented in 1980. Although it should be remembered that the academic qualifications of their recipients were sufficient to ensure their entry by other means (ibid. : 89/90). Nonetheless the entrance examinations of the various Oxbridge colleges still give the public school applicants a clear advantage for it is hard to succeed without more than two years in the sixth form which is much commoner in the public schools than in the state schools. However, the number of candidates gaining entry through the fourth term examinations (i.e. the candidate sits the examination in the fourth term of their sixth form course) has climbed steadily. So it is fair to conclude that the formal rules governing the struggle for Oxbridge places discriminate less and less in favour of students in the private sector which is reflected now in the educational backgrounds of the successful candidates. Periodically there is a debate in the quality press to the effect that Oxford and Cambridge Universities should join UCCA and recruit their students in a similar fashion to the other British universities. Regardless of what the barriers against applicants from state schools may have been in the past (either confused admissions procedures, or the failure to apply because they believed – rightly or wrongly – they would not be accepted) it is our contention that the competition has been made slowly more equitable. Clearly the final step in this process has to be the acceptance of all applicants on the basis of their 'A' Level results.

With the removal of some of their past privileges in the competition for Oxbridge places, and the threat to those few that still remain, the public schools have been forced to renew the old bond through different means. They can no longer depend upon an historical legacy which bestowed privilege on them alone; today the ties are nourished by the ability of the schools to achieve consistently high examination success. As irksome as their remaining competitive advantages may be, it cannot disguise this simple, fundamental fact. Ironically, therefore, as the colleges of Oxford and Cambridge have become increasingly important for the public schools so their formal links with them have been weakened. It is quite clearly Oxbridge which is dictating to the public schools what the basis of the future relationship must be. The schools have little choice in the matter because if they fail to go along with it their well-being, if not existence, is threatened.

The pivotal position that Oxford and Cambridge universities occupy in the formation of élite groups in this country means that it is the prestigious public schools that are most dependent upon their demands. The reputation of these schools is bound up with their apparent ability to produce leaders, and to maintain this reputation, therefore, they have to nurture their links with Oxford and Cambridge. The dominance of the academic ethos that this entails does not command, however, a universal respect. Undoubtedly a unique school like Eton College can withstand its pressures somewhat; its ex-pupils are still very heavily represented in those few élite groups which are not – at least for the time being – organized meritocratically. Some of the headmasters of the smaller public schools have voiced their opposition to the over-dominance of the demands of the universities (Hodgkinson 1966), preferring to emphasize some of the more traditional expressive values in their schools. But these are exceptions to the general rule, the public schools have been ensnared by their own central purpose, educating élites.

Over the years public schoolboys have entered, and dominated a range of professional occupations. Law, medicine, and the Church of England make up the traditional areas of employment which are predominantly in the private sector of the economy. With the rapid expansion of the state apparatus in the nineteenth century various other careers assumed a wider importance: the armed services, the foreign and colonial office, and the home civil service. The one distinctive feature of all these occupations is the gradual rationalization of their recruitment patterns. This is a process commenced in earnest in the last century and refined ever since (Carr-Saunders & Wilson 1964:307–18), so that entrance is now determined by the individual's ability to satisfy academic standards which have been defined more precisely over time by demanding a higher level of specialized – job related – knowledge. Control of the social and personal characteristics of recruits has been increasingly regulated by their academic training rather than monitored by a separate examination i.e. an interview. Interviews still take place but their function has changed – they weed out the obviously unacceptable candidate rather than select the successful applicants.

The nineteenth-century spread of industry was accompanied by the growth of a wide range of financial services which created further employment opportunities for public schoolboys in fields such as accountancy, insurance, the actuarial profession, banking and the stock exchange. Some of these fields are very highly professionalized (e.g. accountancy), while others are less so (e.g. the stock exchange).

The rationalization of the professional ethic – of which the civil service presents an excellent model – have influenced the public schools in much the same fashion as the contemporary pressures emanating from the universities. Even those careers which it is still possible to enter without a university degree are now dominated by meritocratic values and few of today's parents will want to send their children on to a crammer in order to ensure a professional career for them. Where personal connections ('the old school tie') and money are still as, if not more, important than certified expertise – as may be the case with the stock exchange – then the academic ethos can be resisted and traditional expressive values retain their significance (honesty, integrity, and a masterful smoothness with clients are apparently necessary virtues for stock brokers) (see Sampson 1962:ch. 21). The propensity for old Etonians to dominate these less professionalized careers (including, of course, politics) may reflect the fact that the school still attracts some boys who can make their way in the world without relying unduly upon examination success. This point should not be overstressed. Information from an interview with the then headmaster Michael McCrum on the careers chosen by those who left Eton College in the period 1967–73 reveals three highly professional occupations at the top of the list: chartered accountants, officers in the armed services and lawyers. This raises the question of what sets the tone of a school and how different its social composition must be before this is affected.

In spite of their official ethos, most clearly exemplified by the curriculum, the public schools since the latter half of the nineteenth century have sent a significant proportion of their pupils into industry (Reader 1966: 212-5; Coleman 1973: 106; Bishop & Wilkinson 1967: chs 6 & 7). What is more uncertain is whether the education received was appropriate for their subsequent employment, and what particular branches of industry they entered. The popular image is that their education was inappropriate in the extreme, and they invariably returned to the family firm to perpetuate its inefficient management (see Coleman: ibid.). The contemporary public school has done much to change this image. The curriculum, with its strong applied element in both the sciences and social sciences, is attuned to the needs of industry and many, if not most, of its pupils think in terms of careers in industry (Campbell 1978: 13). There is still some dispute as to whether sufficient numbers are so motivated, and whether the selected employment areas chosen are those where they are most needed. According to some commentators industrial management is favoured more than applied fields such as engineering. As important as these reservations may be they cannot disguise the fact that a very significant change in attitudes towards industry has taken place.

However, although the very acceptability of a career in industry represents a remarkable change for the public schools, the constraints this imposes upon them are perhaps less than those demanded by either the professions or Oxbridge. This is most true of the field of industrial management and less true where the job requires very specialized expertise. This is because management, although groping towards professional status, still apparently requires rather nebulous qualities for its successful performance. As Dancy (1963: 95–6) notes, 'whatever industry is thought to *need*, what it in fact *wants* is the public school product', and the irony of the fact that 'many of the qualities of personality that the critics object to in public schools are

those which are most sought after in modern industry' does not
escape Dancy. In its evidence to the Public Schools Commission
(1968 ii: 228) the Confederation of British Industry stated that 'the
public school tends to bring out at an early age the qualities of
leadership, self-reliance, self-confidence and self-discipline'. The
parallel between the Confederation's stress upon these expressive
values and the evidence of a firm of stockbrokers is remarkable. The
latter firm claimed that a 'Public school education is of no significance
as a qualification for partnership in a firm of stockbrokers; but the
high degree of probity, the capacity for prolonged hard work and
personal discipline and the personal connections required to obtain
access to business are less frequently found in men who have not
attended public schools' (ibid.: 228–9). Again it is not our interest to
question the validity of such sentiments, but what is striking is the
similarity of outlook on the part of two very different segments of
British capitalism. Such beliefs permit the public schools a degree of
latitude which a more tightly defined standard of desirable individual
qualities would not. It certainly enables them to continue stressing the
importance of their traditional forms of character training.

In spite of the less precise demands that industry makes of the
public schools, the schools must define themselves within an
environment which allows them decreasing room for manoeuvre.
There is little doubt, moreover, that the whole range of acceptable job
opportunities in industry will be gradually rationalized. The price the
schools pay, therefore, for educating future élites is that the terms on
which they accomplish this are dictated by forces beyond their
control. Whereas Honey argued that the nineteenth-century schools
identified themselves according to the criteria they themselves judged
to be important, it is our contention that today precisely the opposite is
true for the criteria are imposed upon them. Some, like John Rae
(1977: 16–17), may welcome this as the recognition of the inevitable,
but no one should mistake its implications for the character of public
school education and for the social role of public schools.

Obstacles to the formation of a new ideology

The structure of public school education in this country is ideal for
controlled innovation. The heterogeneity of the Headmasters'
Conference, with its various segments holding somewhat different
interests and facing different kinds of problems, encourages the

intrusion of new ideas while preventing a rapid sell-out to fads and fashions. The Headmasters' Conference is a means for monitoring change. Individual innovations can be chewed over within the various forums it has created – the regional meetings, the formal meetings of recognized subgroups (e.g. the ex-direct grant grammar schools hold separate sessions), the more informal cabals (e.g. The Twenty-Seven Club and The Gang: each consists of approximately twenty-five headmasters who meet regularly, and informally, to discuss educational issues), the open sessions of the annual general meetings, and the permanent committees. Moreover the house journal – *Conference* – is a good medium for transmitting new ideas and innovative practice. The incremental pattern of innovation commences with experiments in one or two schools which then appear to filter slowly through the independent sector.

The consequences of this accumulated incrementalism is a public school system which has a healthy number of pupils, is financially sound, narrow in its educational goals, and ideologically vague. With respect to all four characteristics the schools are probably more than satisfied. The student numbers and financial soundness, in the absence of direct political intervention, guarantee their survival. The schools have retained the favour of sufficient middle-class parents, and with respect to the independent sector in general their class appeal appears to be on the increase. The narrowness of their educational goals is a direct result of the growing dominance of the academic ethos. As this is so important for attracting prospective parents, and for maintaining the institutional ties that have established their reputation as educators of the future ruling class, this has to be reinforced. Furthermore, in view of the wider educational climate it probably gives them a considerable amount of self-satisfaction; the public schools have moved from the political defensive to the educational offensive.

No matter how much their headmasters may regret it the independent schools can educate only a very select segment of the nation's children. This can be mitigated somewhat by state intervention but the individuals who benefit – unless the whole character of private education is to change beyond recognition – will be few in number, almost certainly academically superior to their peers, and equally certainly (means tests notwithstanding) socially unrepresentative of the population at large. It is this fact which makes it so difficult for today's public school system to develop a new coherent ideology. What is required is a firm philosophical basis for educational privilege, but besides the political dangers of creating and advocating such a perspective it would offend many of those most sympathetic to the cause of private education. Stalemate and confusion would seem to be the order of the day.

Although we have argued in this chapter that the public schools are increasingly influenced by an academic ethos, which is defined in terms of the examination success of their pupils, it should not be forgotten that they are still committed to many of their traditional expressive values. In our second chapter we made the rather obvious point that one of the stimulants for educational change is the attempt to forge closer links between schooling and the needs of the labour market, in particular the needs of manufacturing industry (see pp. 31–40). What many employers appear to be demanding of their prospective employees is precisely the qualities that today's public schools are inculcating. This therefore suggests that the independent sector may in the future be able to legitimate its privileged educational position on the grounds that its schools offer an experience which fits the dominant understanding of the nation's needs. In other words public schools present a model of the experience of schooling which others would do well to follow. Ironically, therefore, although the two systems of schooling may be formally further apart than ever before (that is with the abolition of the direct grant grammar schools), in terms of the experience of schooling they offer they may be about to travel along the same path with the state schools being forced (some more willingly than others) to follow in the steps of the private sector.

9

The Great Debate and Its Aftermath

4 fnrlkin
Debate
1968, 70, 8

Introduction

As a piece of theatre, the portentously labelled 'Great Debate' on education lacked that vital spark needed to set the audience alight. In a way this was to be expected. The stage management, the DES, is rather inexperienced (this was their first full-blown production), the scriptwriters, HMI, are still learning their new trade and the actors were never entirely sure as to who had the leading and supporting parts. As for the chorus, the media, they were obviously bored throughout. The question which concerns us as theorists of educational change, however, is does it matter? Does it matter that the production could have been slicker, the audience more appreciative and the reviews more laudatory? What, after all, was it designed to achieve? Perhaps its very amateurism was a contrivance.

In this chapter we examine the Great Debate with the objective of answering these questions while drawing together the different threads of the analysis of educational change developed in the preceding chapters. As a vehicle for elucidating our framework the debate has obvious advantages: it was a highly visible series of events, the data on it is plentiful, it was seen as highly significant by most educational commentators, and the wheels it set in motion are still turning. Our central concerns in investigating what the Great Debate can tell us about the bureaucratization of educational power and the process of educational change are these. Firstly, what are the sources of the dynamic in the situation? Secondly, how is this dynamic expressed and/or constrained in institutional terms? – i.e. what structural changes does it demand and cause? Thirdly, what ramifications do these institutional shifts have for the power of other groups involved in the education system? Fourthly, what ideological changes are necessary to legitimize both the immediate and the future redistribution of educational power? Fifthly, what are the implications of these ideological changes for education's role as legitimizer of social inequalities? As these questions indicate, we do not view either the Great Debate in particular, or educational change in general, as accidental events responding to the whim of capricious public opinion. But neither do we assume that the dynamic in the situation is easily identified or that the links between cause and effect are readily drawn.

In placing the Great Debate in the context of broader educational trends, we will be arguing that the Debate illustrates particular aspects of the political logic behind DES development. The problem with identifying general trends is that this exercise must, if it is to avoid becoming bogged down in a welter of detailed institutional features, ignore the lower level conflicts and inconsistencies. Yet at the same time, the analysis has to remain sensitive to those internal divisions which have a genuine impact on the overall direction of an institution's development. A balance has to be struck. So in the case of the DES we would be the first to admit that it is not monolithic and that it is as tribal as any other government department: these are essential working assumptions. What is more important, however, is that above and beyond the normal round of internal dissensions and bickering, general bureaucratic movements are taking place. It is to these we address ourselves.

Before launching into the analysis proper it is well to set the scene by briefly recalling the main public events around which the Debate was centred. Although the prime minister, Mr Callaghan, formally inaugurated the Debate with his speech at Ruskin College, Oxford, in October 1976, much speculation and some nascent political posturing had already been evoked in the preceding weeks by the thoughtful and fairly comprehensive leaking of a confidential report from the DES to the prime minister. This report, known as the 'Yellow Book', had been requested by Callaghan earlier that year in May. Following the prime minister's speech, the DES organised a public discussion of the issues it deemed central to the debate in the form of eight regional conferences in February and March of 1977. Four months later came the publication of the government's Green Paper 'Education in Schools', supposedly summarizing the results of the discussions. These were hectic times indeed. In September, while the teacher unions were still sorting out their written responses to the Green

Paper, the Taylor Report on school government was published, opening up yet another flank which the teaching profession rushed to defend. But that was where the Great Debate, in the sense of the government dangling a variety of educational issues before an interested public, came to an end. No one officially announced that the road show was over but 1978 was much more prosaic with the discussion document 'Education into the 1990s', the Oakes Report (1978) on the management of higher education in the maintained sector, the White Paper 'The Composition of School Governing Bodies' (1977f) and the subsequent Education Bill belonging more to the normal round of government activity than to the cultivated populism of the Great Debate. These then are the more visible bare bones of the matter and we turn now to the question of why the debate happened at all.

The nature of the dynamic

1   *One way of looking at it*

Although it is not the primary purpose of this book to lampoon certain Marxist approaches to education the temptation is nevertheless at times severe if only on account of the innocent, and apparently unshakable certainty they display in the face of complex issues. This is not a frivolous point since it has considerable implications for the way in which educational change is viewed. At the height of the Great Debate in the summer of 1977 an editorial in *Radical Education* announced that 'the ruling class intend to achieve a major historic victory on education'. It continued:

In effect the purpose is to obtain a new educational settlement, which will redefine the content and the terms of access to education, an educational settlement which will be historically equivalent to the 1944 Education Act, in redetermining the political function of education in reproducing and justifying the existing social order.

Similar sentiments were expressed at the Politics of Education Conference, organized by the Socialist Teachers Alliance in April 1978. One paper (Frith 1978:1) saw the Great Debate as concealing a much wider process of reorganizing the roles of state and individual in the preparation of young workers while another (Holloway & Picciotto 1978:10) decided that the most important point to be made about the Taylor Report was its part in 'the more general attempt by the bourgeoisie to reassert bourgeois relations of control over an educational process shaken by the crisis of capitalism'. The paradigm on which these statements rest is no doubt familiar: the economy develops fresh needs, the ruling class recognizes that these needs will have to be satisfied for it to survive, it therefore ensures that the state apparatus responds by translating these needs into new forms of social relations and new types of social control.

The implication of this analysis is that the dynamic of educational change originates from the capitalist economy–ruling class axis which is of course external to the education system itself. Educational institutions are therefore cast in an essentially passive and responsive role: they may be able to resist and divert this dynamic but it is highly unlikely that they themselves can initiate change. While no doubt comforting in its simplicity, this reflex action interpretation of what lay behind the Great Debate offers little specific prediction as to what the future will hold beyond that of 'more state manipulation of educational ideology'. The absence of detailed institutional analysis means that generalizations become the stock in trade ensuring that all subsequent government actions can be readily slotted into the existing framework as further proof of the grand capitalist conspiracy. They do not have to be measured against precise institutional predictions. We are less confident that educational change can be viewed solely as the by-product of the social reproduction of class relations.

Nevertheless, if we begin by listing the objective factors which could have precipitated a debate on education, the external pressures for change appear considerable. First of all, as the downturn in the economy continued in the mid-1970s, youth unemployment assumed alarming proportions. For the 16- to 17-year-old age group, the estimated unemployment rate increased from 12.1 per cent in July 1975 to 26.2 per cent a year later (TES 1977: 7). Secondly, the innate lack of accountability (so far as the centre is concerned) of a decentralized education system, which in 1977 consumed more than £7,300 million (15 per cent of government spending and 50 per cent higher in real terms than a decade earlier), could not continue indefinitely (Wilby 1977: 16). Thirdly, the fact that live births in England fell from 830,000 in 1964 to under 540,000 in 1977 (DES 1978b: 13) meant that in its 1977 Annual Report the DES (1977b: 1) was predicting a decline in the school population (primary and secondary) from 8.4 million in that year to 7.5 million in 1983 and perhaps 6.5 million in 1989. Fourthly, a series of studies were published by Start and Wells (1972), Bullock (1975), and Bennett (1976) which raised serious questions about the standards of literacy and numeracy in schools. And last but not least, the party political dimension: Callaghan could recognize a burgeoning political issue when he saw one and the consequent need to outmanoeuvre the Conservatives.

These are generally the factors mentioned in any more immediate explanation of why the Great Debate was initiated when it was. Glancing through the jumble of facts, no particular pattern readily emerges: the pressures span the economic, political, demographic and educational spheres; no one factor is obviously more important than another in precipitating the Debate and any suggested connection is bound to be descriptive and speculative. If there is a dynamic present then it is well hidden. But perhaps we and the Marxists are being over-optimistic and over-theoretical in searching for a dynamic in educational change. Perhaps change occurs when a largely accidental aggregation of external pressures reaches a level which forces the education system to adapt itself accordingly. Alternatively, perhaps the assumption which regards educational institutions as the passive recipients of outside pressures is itself false. It could just be that the pressure is two way and that the relationship between institution and environment is, to use a piece of sociological argot, causally interactive.

2   *The institutional context*

It will be remembered that in our discussion of ideology in chapter three we agreed with Gramsci that tension exists not only between the economic base and the superstructure but also within the superstructure between the state and civil society. Furthermore, that given the bureaucratic nature of what Althusser has called the Ideological State Apparatuses (ISAs), notably education, it is perfectly possible for an institution to develop its own course of action in line with its internal needs as a bureaucracy but possibly out of line with its role as an ISA. Our subsequent chapter on educational policy-making then indicated that it is precisely professionalized bureaucratic concerns which are leading to the encapsulation of the policy-making process by the DES with its increasing emphasis on rationality, efficiency and technical expertise as the main criteria in policy construction. Given this, the question which concerns us here is how far these institutional considerations provide insights into the dynamic behind the Great Debate. Putting it simply, why did the DES need the debate at all? Why did the Department decide to 'go public' when it did?

By 1975 something of a gap had developed between the implications of the DES's internal planning arrangements and the reality of its external power, or lack of it. By then the continuing trend towards the internalization of the policy-making process had been further manifested in the form of the Departmental Planning Organization (DPO), established in 1971, which confined its membership to DES staff alone. As the Expenditure Committee report on policy making in the DES pointed out,

This has the advantage for the DES that discussions within the planning group can be unconstrained by tactical considerations about relationships with and between outside interest groups, with the disadvantage that local authorities, teachers' organisations and others having a legitimate interest in the development of educational plans are not associated at first hand with 'the actual planning process'. (Tenth Report 1976:xvii)

Similarly, the committee observed (ibid.:xxx) that although interests are consulted on a wide range of decisions within their zones of concern 'the DES does not encourage interest groups, or indeed the wide public, to participate in discussion of long-range planning of the overall purposes and shape of the education service.' By 1975 the Department was also in the position of being able to decide on patterns of resource allocation within LEAs on the basis of DES priorities i.e. on policy implementation as well as policy formation. Reflecting on what this meant for local authority freedom to spend its educational budget as it wished, the chairman of the Expenditure Committee (ibid.:22) commented: 'It does sound rather like telling a goldfish "You may swim anywhere you like within your bowl".'

However, while the Department was becoming increasingly more sophisticated in its formulation of the details of educational policy, it still lacked the power either to monitor systematically the effects of its decisions or to ensure that its policies were put into effect. Even recognizing the work of HMI, its national information network was limited and finance for local authority educational spending was allocated as part of the total rate support grant – a block grant for all local authority services which could be divided up and spent as each local authority deems fit. (It remains to be seen what effect the 1980 Local Government Planning and Land (No. 2) Act, which replaces the single block grant with one awarded on a service by service basis, will have on the DES-LEA relationship.) This 'discontinuity', as the Expenditure Committee called it, between central intentions and the extent of local authority implementation or avoidance of these intentions led Sir William Pile, then Permanent Secretary at the DES, to admit that he would prefer an alternative system of allocation (ibid.:25). As a developing bureaucracy the DES had undoubtedly reached a point where its frustration with this discontinuity was on the verge of becoming manifest. The institutional pressures for change were mounting.

To cast the LEAs in the role of unwilling recipients of central directives is to underestimate the identity of interest which, as we argued earlier (see pp. 93–100), exists between bureaucracies charged with the common task of managing education. In *Management in the Education Service* published in 1975, for example, the Society of Education Officers (local authority based) maintained that output measurement is needed as a tool of management to assist decision making. The significance of this is that, in order to be put into effect, the measurement of educational output would require a more rigorous definition of educational objectives as well as the development and imposition of new measurement techniques for pupil testing. Accountability and monitoring are issues with which any manager of the education service interested in its efficiency, centrally or locally, is bound to be concerned. For that reason it is not surprising to find that in their evidence to the Expenditure Committee (Tenth Report 1976:90) both the Association of Metropolitan Authorities (AMA) and the Association of County Councils (ACC) indicated that they would not be opposed to a more active DES involvement in curricular matters. Nor should it be seen as entirley unexpected that two months after the Prime Minister's Ruskin College speech, and ostensibly in response to that speech, Lancashire education committee approved a plan to introduce testing of children at 9 and 13. The chief education officer justified these and other measures in the following terms:

The problem is knowing how to deploy resources, where to put additional staff, where to allow in-service training, and you cannot respond unless you have the information. The real advantage of countrywide testing is that the authority will have *far more information* on which to base its decisions. When money is scarce you need a much more careful analysis. (Vaughan 1976:1; our stress)

If a bureaucracy is to expand the interventionist side of its operation then it has to develop the procedures necessary to acquire the information on which to base this intervention. Without an increase in the flow of information it receives, a bureaucracy cannot justify to itself, or anyone else, that an expansion of its decision-making capacity is a rational development. Furthermore, this information flow has to occur on a routinized and predictable basis in order that it can be smoothly incorporated into the normal operation of the bureaucracy.

In a crude sense it can be stated that for an ambitious bureaucracy, an increase in its standardized information flow is a necessary prerequisite of any increase in its power. Neither the DES nor the LEAs could be expected to attempt to extend their control over education without an improvement in their information gathering techniques. Equally, both were likely to benefit from a public discussion which approved the introduction of such techniques. So although there may be centre–local tensions in the DES–LEA relationship there are also sound motives for mutual support in circumstances likely to bolster the efficiency of their operation as bureaucracies. The DES was well aware that its own frustration was almost certainly replicated in many instances at the local level and could therefore feel reasonably confident that the LEAs would not oppose a central initiative aimed at improving the position of education's management in general. Always providing, that is that the initiative is handled with some delicacy and due allowance is made for the genuine differences that exist between the values of central and local educational administrators: values which are in turn reinforced by quite distinct types of career structures. For while the local administrator specializes early on in his career and usually follows a fairly consistent educational path, the DES administrator is still expected to be a generalist and, in accordance with civil service tradition, is duly moved on once he has become familiar with one particular field of education. The result is that the two types of administrators do not necessarily share the same view of the educational world even though they may share a common desire to manage it more efficiently.

If it is claimed that the dynamic for educational change which produced the Great Debate lay within the education system's dominant bureaucracy as well as in its environment, then it should be possible to identify changes within that organization signalling the direction it was about to try to take. Two such indications can be cited: the changing role of HMI and the birth of the Assessment of Performance Unit (APU), both concerned with information collection and dissemination. Between 1975 and 1976 plans were drawn up to reorganize HMI with the object of making it a more centralized, national and efficient body. Roughly a quarter of the total force was to be withdrawn from the general, local and subject specialist work to be employed instead on national surveys and studies (see Stevens 1977:1). Two major national studies of primary and secondary education were in any case begun well before the details of the reorganization were finalized. As the field taskforce of the DES, HMI was the obvious starting point for any rationalization of the information gathering process. Up to this time, the Department had relied mainly on returns from LEAs for its data on what was happening in the education system, a fairly inflexible procedure, but now it required not only more data but also more control over the means of its acquisition. This does not deny that the appointment of a new senior chief inspector, Sheila Browne, in 1975 with her own ideas on the reorganization of HMI had an individual impact but rather that the logic of the DES's development as a bureaucracy allowed these ideas their full expression.

The setting up of the APU was announced in 1974 in the White Paper on Educational Disadvantage and its terms of reference were: 'To promote the development of methods of assessing and monitoring the achievement of children at school, and to seek to identify the incidence of under-achievement' (DES 1978c:1). In its early days it was not at all clear to anyone, including probably the DES, as to how its function was to relate to that of HMI once it got properly off the ground. What is clear, nevertheless, is that its commissioning of the National Foundation for Educational Research (NFER) to explore the feasibility of the national monitoring of schools (DES 1977e:48) was directly in line with the DES's need for standardized information flows.

Later in this chapter we will discuss how the roles of HMI and the APU have become complementary in the post-Great Debate situation rather than competitive as appeared a possibility in 1975-76. For the moment suffice it to say that at this point they can be seen as heralds of more substantial changes to come, as structural indications of a bureaucracy in transition. But although there is sound evidence to support the thesis that a strong institutional dynamic for change had developed in the DES by the early and mid-1970s, this does not of itself explain why a public debate on education would be in the service of that dynamic.

Ideology to the rescue

1   *Legitimate or lose*
We have argued earlier that for a group to mount a serious bid for power with any chance of success at the national level it has to do so equipped with a well-developed ideology capable of challenging the dominant set of values which are already ensconced. Without such an ideology, the group would be unable to legitimate its new position and its authority would be dependent solely on whatever coercive means it had at its disposal. Now whatever one may think of the DES it has to be admitted that it is not strong on coercion. The corridors of Elizabeth House are not exactly lined with hit men. Any expansion of the department's interventionist role, any upgrading of its authority and control has, therefore, to be accompanied by ideological legitimation of this change. Otherwise it is doomed to failure.

The traditional method employed by the DES to legitimate fresh policy directions was the well-publicized report from a prestigious body – generally one of the Central Advisory Councils (CACs) or occasionally a royal commission (see pp. 111–14). The problem with this method, however, was that it was both inefficient (from the DES point of view) and at times unpredictable. In his evidence to the Expenditure Committee (Tenth Report 1976:104), Sir William Pile argued that with events moving fast and a shortage of resources it was a drawback to have to stop policy development in order to wait for the results of an inquiry. Also, there was a need to strike the relative priorities between programmes, a need which a committee examining just one sector was likely to ignore. It is ironic that in its move to rationalize its policy-making process the DES felt obliged to do away with the instrument, the externally-based inquiry, which rendered these policies credible and acceptable to the general public. Nevertheless, having decided largely, though not entirely, against inquiries the Department was then in the position of having to find other methods of endowing its policies with status. In the event, it concluded that it would itself enter the business of the sponsorship of values rather than rely on members of the existing élite of educational status (generally the universities) to carry out that task on the Department's behalf.

To use Gramsci's distinction, it can be said that it was at this point in its development that the DES was obliged to encourage the growth of its own, organic intellectuals to carry out the task of justifying its interest. The parting of the ways between itself and the traditional intellectuals, prestigious academic and cultural figures, has come because the Department is no longer prepared to accept the dominance of values which it senses are outmoded, which clash with the rationalizing tenets of its *modus operandi* and which deny it the autonomy its enclosed policy making demands. This does not mean that it is not prepared to utilize the legitimating capacities of traditional intellectuals: it is, but on its own terms. The DES is still part of the ideological state apparatus but it has its own ideas as to how that apparatus should be run.

The DES's need to take a more activist stance on what values it promoted and when it promoted them coincided with its need to become more interventionist with regard to its methods of resource allocation and data collection. All three requirements for more control over its environment arose from its burgeoning confidence in its ability to perform its allotted task efficiently through the application of 'objective' planning techniques. It was no longer prepared to tolerate the oft-quoted remark that it had 'responsibility without power' particularly since the way it exercised this responsibility had lately come under fire. Both the OECD (1975) and Expenditure Committee reports on DES policy making had criticized the Department for being too secretive, the Expenditure Committee (Tenth Report 1976:xxi) making the additional point that 'the planning machinery in the DES would acquire increased public confidence from greater openness', thus emphasizing the conflict between the effects of the Department's drive towards enclosure of policy making and its need for legitimation. Although the Department's reply to this criticism was dismissive, it must have felt that it deserved a little more ideological protection.

2   *Making an ideology – background*

The 'natural' ideology of the DES is embedded in its decision-making
and planning procedures, its search for the optimum rational mode of
operation and the controls it considers necessary for ensuring that its
bureaucratic techniques perform efficiently. But to the outsider, who
perceives the Department as an institution which should be concerned
primarily with educational issues rather than with bureaucratic
niceties, it is not a 'natural' ideology. Thus the Expenditure
Committee (Tenth Report 1976 : xxi) criticized the DES for an over-
emphasis on resource allocation, quoting the DES's own evidence
which stated that 'DES planning, as undertaken by the Departmental
Planning Organization ... is ... resource-oriented, being concerned
primarily with options of scale, organization and cost *rather than
educational content*' [our stress]. Unimpressed by this preoccupation,
the committee recommended (ibid.) that the 'DPO should make
arrangements for *broader educational objectives* to be kept under
review as regularly as the resource implications of objectives through
the Public Expenditure Surveys' [our stress]. The lesson to be drawn
from this is that what makes sense to a bureaucracy does not
necessarily make sense to the audience it is supposed to serve. To
justify itself, to endow itself with authority, the Department is obliged
to translate its bureaucratic needs into the language and ideas of
education. It could not expect its requirements for more efficient
resource manipulation within, and more influence over the education
system to carry much political weight if expressed literally : the
capacity to manage the system had to be given legitimacy under the
cloak of educational ideology.

It would be doing the DES an injustice to maintain that it was
entirely a novice in the art of ideology promotion. In *Education and
the Political Order* (Tapper & Salter 1978 : ch. 7) we have traced the
rise of the economic ideology of higher education and demonstrated
the convenient links which exist between an ideology which stresses
education's role as the servant of the national economy and the
output–budgeting planning techniques of the DES. In ideal terms, the
individual is portrayed as making rational decisions based on his
awareness of employment opportunities to acquire the knowledge and
credentials appropriate to his future occupation. This means that the
economy gains the manpower it needs, educational planners manage
the system in order to produce the appropriate numbers of different
vocational outputs and the Robbins principle of educational response

to individual demand is conveniently integrated with the principle of educational response to economic demand via the concept of the rational and fully-informed student. However, while it was one thing for the DES to be explicit about higher education's function as servant of the economy, as it was in *Education: A Framework for Expansion* for example (1972:34), it was quite another to apply the same argument to the primary and secondary sectors in a formal and obvious manner and in a short space of time rather than over a number of years. This necessitated a much more total and conscious approach to ideology formation than had been the DES's style in higher education. Higher education had been resistant enough to attempts to erode its autonomy, though the University Grants Committee (UGC) had wilted considerably over the years (see Tapper & Salter 1978:168–71), and primary and secondary education were likely to prove even more so. Despite this, in June 1976, four months before Mr Callaghan's speech, we find Mr James Hamilton, Permanent Secretary at the DES, saying to the annual conference of the Association of Education Committees: 'I believe that the so-called secret garden of the curriculum cannot be allowed to remain so secret after all, and that the key to the door must be found and turned (Devlin & Warnock 1977:13). Intervention was the intention and was already on the way.

The opportunity for the DES to take the ideological initiative came with the request by the Prime Minister in May 1976 for a memorandum from the then Education Secretary, Fred Mulley, on what he discerned as four major areas of public concern: the basic approach in primary schools to the teaching of the three 'Rs'; the curriculum for older children in comprehensives; the exam system; and the problems of 16- to 19-year-olds who have no prospect of going on to higher education yet who seem ill-equipped even for the jobs they find. This was clearly a broad enough brief to provide a platform for the initial stimulus at the governmental level of a substantial reappraisal of the education system.

The selection of items for inclusion in the supposedly confidential 'Yellow Book', as the memorandum was called, had to take into account the political environment of the day. If the DES was to harness the motley collection of external pressures for change (see pp. 192–3) to the direction indicated by its internal dynamic towards greater educational managerialism, the balance had to be struck correctly. It could not commit itself too soon. There was certainly no guarantee that, in initiating a debate on education, it would succeed in establishing an ideology which gave itself more authority. Bearing in mind that the intended audience of the Yellow Book was, at least ostensibly, the higher echelons of government, the document can best be seen as a kite-flying exercise which did not try to develop a detailed ideological position. Themes are raised but not fully elaborated. Hence the diagnosis of the problem includes the standard of basic skills (literacy and numeracy), the balance in the curriculum (is there enough science and maths teaching for the country's needs?), the inadequate supply of maths teachers, the need that 'education and training must be planned in a unified way' and the weakness that 'some teachers and some schools may have overemphasized the importance of preparing boys and girls for their roles in society compared with the need to prepare them for their economic role' (TES 1976:2–3). The links with the economic ideology of education are clearly present but not fully enunciated.

If the diagnosis of the problem lacks coherence, the proposed solutions do not. They are based firmly on the premise that what is good for the DES and all its works is good for education as a whole: more control is therefore essential. This conviction emerges in a number of recommendations. Firstly, the Yellow Book argues that 'the time has probably come to establish generally accepted principles for the composition of the secondary curriculum for all pupils, that is to say a "core curriculum".' And it just so happens that HMI is already working on models of such core curricula as well as on particular areas of the curriculum that need attention. Secondly, it is no good centralizing the curriculum if the means are not available to check on the efficiency of this move through the appropriate monitoring arrangements. The report therefore recommends an increase in the work of the APU and the acceleration of its programme. Thirdly, it is no good monitoring the system and its deficiencies if the means for remedying them are not available: so the report maintains that HMI's involvement in both initial and inservice teacher training should be strengthened. Fourthly, the vital control from the Department's immediate point of view is the financial one. Several times the report contrasts its own position regarding financial controls with that of the Training Services Agency (TSA) of the Manpower Services Commission (MSC), in their mutual efforts to help the 16 to 19 age group. 'At present', it says 'there is some risk of distortion [of the relationship] because the existing statutory and administrative provisions make it much easier for MSC and TSA than for DES to channel resources quickly and selectively where they are needed.' Consequently, 'if the Department is to play as constructive a role as it could wish, then serious thought needs to be given to some extension of its powers in this direction' (ibid.) To put it another way, give us the tools and we will finish the job.

As an internal government document the Yellow Book did not need to have a well-developed public face and could afford to concentrate on what it regarded as the key issues without too many educational ideological trimmings. For that reason, its importance for us lies in the attention it gives to the capacity to *manage* educational change rather than to the *content* of educational change. Explicit in it is the notion that change can no longer be allowed to occur in a random, disorganized fashion: education must be controlled for its own good. Given this emphasis, it is amusing to note this protestation of innocence from HMI: 'No exercise of power is involved in this search for improvement; the Inspectorate, by tradition and by choice, exerts influence by the presentation of evidence and by advice.' Be that as it may, the report was sufficiently aware of the power politics of the situation to raise some of the strategic issues concerning the implementation of its recommendations. In particular it mentioned the problem of securing the acceptance by local authorities of its ideas, the timing of the necessary review of the Schools Council's functions and constitution ('a move may be precipitated by the examination issue'), and the usefulness of an authoritative pronouncement from the Prime Minister which would both suggest that the Department should give a firmer lead on what goes on in schools and refute the argument that no one except teachers has any right to such a say. It concluded: 'The climate for such a declaration on these lines may in fact now be relatively favourable. Nor need there be any inhibition for fear that the Department could not make use of enhanced opportunity to exercise influence over curriculum and teaching methods: the Inspectorate would have a leading role to play in bringing forward ideas in these areas and is ready to fulfil that responsibility' (ibid.)

The 'climate of opinion' may well have been favourable but it was another question altogether as to whether it could be harnessed and directed in a way which suited the DES's need for self-legitimation. The dynamic within the bureaucracy of the Department may have wrought internal changes but how far these changes could be externalized in ideological guise was problematic. The Yellow Book has provided us with clear indications of the direction the Department preferred the debate to take in its own ideological interests and our analysis now will deal with how far that ambition was realized.

3   *Making an ideology – content*

If the ideological content of the Great Debate was to be of any use to the DES then it had to serve other interests apart from those of the Department alone. As well as being the expression in educational values of the DES's bureaucratic needs, it had to assist the aspirations of other powerful groups. Otherwise the Department was likely to find itself ideologically isolated with no possibility of ideological overlap and alliances. For this reason therefore, and because it had already been tested in the field of higher education, the economic ideology of education was a prime candidate. Not only had it already demonstrated its ready ability to be integrated with the quantitative, output–budgeting techniques coming into vogue in the Department but it also provided what was rapidly becoming an essential defence against competition from the MSC. Set up in 1974 to oversee the work of the Employment Services Agency (ESA) and the TSA, the MSC was increasingly presenting itself as the organization with the answers so far as the training needs of the nation were concerned: a not unuseful claim in a period of mounting youth unemployment. Obviously this placed it in direct competition with the traditional training role of the further education sector though this competition was mitigated somewhat by the MSC's need for further education to run courses on its behalf. So an ideology which emphasized education's responsiveness to the economic needs of the nation would clearly afford the DES both protection from the encroachments of the MSC as well as a strong platform for launching cooperative ventures. In addition, and not to be underestimated, the ideology guaranteed the backing of both employers and trade unions.

We argued earlier that for an aspiring educational ideology to be able to mount a serious challenge at the national level it has to link three concepts coherently together: the desired society, the type or types of educated individual necessary for that society, and the educational means required to fulfil these two ends (see pp. 62–5). Now although most of the elements of an economic ideology of education capable of meeting these three criteria had been around for decades, they had never before been brought together in the crucible of an officially sponsored debate. Here was the opportunity to forge permanent links between them. The desired society of the economic ideology is a more rationalized and efficient version of the industrialized society we have already. As the influential government White Paper *An Approach to Industrial Strategy* (frequently referred to in subsequent DES publications) pointed out in 1975, a high wage, high output, high employment economy requires that industrial objectives 'be given priority over other policy aims, and that policy in other areas, *including education*, will need to be influenced by our industrial needs' (DI 1977:2; our stress), particularly in an era of economic stagnation. Such a society cannot operate successfully without appropriate supporting values and their associated status systems: applied and more vocational skills are upgraded to promote a technical culture with the esteem it already holds in continental society (ibid.:1–2). Elite groups are defined much more in terms of their managerial and professional expertise acquired through a rational and explicit career hierarchy of training and credentialling rather than in terms of more informal criteria.

The individuals necessary for this desired society must accept that education's purpose is primarily to prepare them for their economic role. Mr Callaghan (1976:72) made this point in his Ruskin speech when he argued: 'There is no virtue in [education] producing socially well adjusted members of society who are unemployed because they do not have the skills.' (Though, to be fair, he continued: 'Nor at the other extreme must they be technically efficient robots.') At the more sophisticated end of the scale this means that we have the image of rationally economic and educational man moving effortlessly through the education system and gliding into the appropriate (for the economy) industrial niche:

One aim of school education is to ensure that, as pupils progress through school, they develop an understanding about the role of industry in society, the challenges and breadth of employment it offers and the education and training necessary for a successful industrial career. In this way they can come to a more informed choice about which subjects at school and which discipline to follow in further and higher education. Pupils and their parents need to have the information early enough to ensure that their curricular choices in school will be appropriate for their further education and for the career they wish to follow. (DI 1977:21)

Some have higher niches than others, of course, and for those lower down, this elegant and informed passage through the educational system is not really appropriate. For those less fortunate it is most important to attain the basic standards of literacy and numeracy which many employers claimed, and claim, are lacking in those presently entering the nation's industrial workforce. Nevertheless what both of these desired products of education have in common is a mutual understanding and acceptance of the contribution that industry makes to the well-being of the country.

Just as the desired society of the economic ideology of education requires a rearrangement of existing status systems to improve the position of professional and technical cultures, so the parallel definitions of educated individuals include particular ideas regarding the types of knowledge they should possess. 'Applied' rather than 'pure' knowledge is preferred though this insistence wavers when it comes to a conflict over whether engineers or scientists best serve the nation's interest partly because the 'pure' scientist lobby of the late 1960s still retained considerable influence in the 1970s (see Garnicot & Blaug 1973). On the whole, though, the Great Debate saw the new ideology embracing the engineer and technologist, the embodiments of applied knowledge, as its favourite sons. This is illustrated by the UGC's decision in 1977 to promote a small number of very high quality first degree courses in engineering with a pronounced orientation towards manufacturing industry (UGC 1978).

To a large extent, these first two components of the new ideology (desired society and desired individual characteristics) could be left to their natural sponsors to promote – employers, trade unions, Department of Industry, private interest groups such as the Industry Society etc. Once the public vehicle for their expression was provided in the form of the Great Debate they could emerge as they had done on numerous occasions in the past. In 1928, for example, the Malcolm Committee produced its report *Education and Industry* to a barrage of complaints in the press and from employers about standards of literacy and numeracy in schools. And in the postwar years the Federation of British Industries (FBI) regularly bemoaned the lack of liaison between education and industry writing at least four reports on the topic in the period up to 1965. Similarly, in more scholarly circles there is a well-established school of thought which attributes Britain's economic decline at least partly to the Victorians' failure to develop the education system essential for national efficiency, comparing us unfavourably with our continental rivals in this respect (see Gowing 1976; Sanderson 1972; Simon 1965: ch. 6). There was no lack of forces prepared to push the first two components once the opportunity arose. However, specifying the educational means necessary for realizing these societal and individual goals of education was a complex task which only the DES itself could undertake. The trick so far as the Department was concerned was to integrate its ambition for more comprehensive lines of educational management with the other two components of the ideology.

In both the background paper for the regional conferences of early 1977, *Educating Our Children* (DES 1977c), and the Green Paper of July 1977, *Education in Schools* (DES 1977d), summarizing the results of the Debate and making proposals for the future, many of the ideas contained in the Yellow Book re-emerge – albeit in more diplomatic form. *Educating Our Children* argues for a common core curriculum: the Green Paper echoes this call but within a broader strategic perspective which proposes, first of all, that local authorities carry out a review of curricular arrangements in their own schools. Following on from this,

They [the Secretaries of State for Education] will in the light of the review seek to establish a broad agreement with their partners in the education service on a framework for the curriculum, and on whether part of the curriculum should be protected because there are aims common to all schools and pupils at certain stages. These aims must include the achievement of basic literacy and numeracy at the primary stage. (TES 1977: 5)

The subtlety of this statement lies in its implication that the DES is seeking control through cooperation, that it is still in the business of reflecting the educational consensus. As we shall see, the increasing dominance of the Department in terms of both information and value supply in education renders the word 'cooperation' little more than an imaginative political device.

On the question of the most effective means of monitoring an education system geared to economic goals, *Educating Our Children* is less shy about the importance of controlling information flows. Referring to the assessment of standards, it states that the aim is:

to measure, in terms of selected aspects of performance, the effectiveness of the education system as a whole, or local parts of it ... Better information on standards should improve the quality of rationally-based discussion of educational issues; its provision should assist those making policy decisions at central and local government level and also teachers and teacher trainees. At the local level it could help to indicate schools with a particular need for extra measures or help from the local education authority. (DES 1977:7)

Once national or local needs are identified the issue then arises of how they are to be met and, in particular, how the teaching force can best be deployed to meet those needs. Hence it is no surprise to find the Green Paper arguing for more systematic approaches to the recruitment, career development, training and deployment of the teacher force and for more information about it (TES 1977:8).

In terms of the coherence and staying power of the economic ideology of education, it was important that the educational means for the realization of individual and societal goals should be linked to the latter two components of the ideology: a bare statement of the DES's interventionist intentions would have been impolitic to say the least. This tying together of educational means and economic goals occurred at a number of levels. Within the school it was argued that room should be made for the cultivation of an improved understanding of productive industry and an improved position for careers guidance in the curriculum. 'Local education authorities, schools and industry must work much more closely together', maintained the Green Paper (ibid.:8) and continued: 'Industry, the trades unions and commerce should be involved in curriculum planning processes'. Similarly, at the level of teacher training the case was frequently made (ibid.:5) that 'more attention should be given ... to the national importance of industry and commerce, to helping them [teachers] in their responsibility for conveying this to their pupils.' The age of the independent teacher, justifying his autonomy and control over the curriculum in terms of his professional competence, was, according to this line of reasoning, at an end. But if it was at an end, how did the teachers' unions react to this assault on their power and how did the emerging ideology cope with their reaction?

Nails in the coffin

Throughout the Great Debate the teachers' unions were run ragged by an opposition which had seized the ideological initiative, controlled the manner and timing of its expression, manipulated its agenda and commanded a huge advantage of resources in terms of strategic know-how, information supply and manpower. Take the initial union reaction to the Yellow Book for example. Mr Fred Jarvis, general secretary of the National Union of Teachers (NUT), told Mr Callaghan not to take it seriously, whilst the NUT's executive committee called it an 'ill informed, superficial and biased tract'. Three months later we find feelings unassuaged with Mr Sam Fisher (TES 1977:13), chairman of the NUT's education committee, telling the conference that the Yellow Book was 'misinformed, overtly biased and malicious'. Mention of the 'common core curriculum' produced an even more Pavlovian reaction: Mr Robert Cook, general secretary of the National Association of Head Teachers, said, 'I was teaching in Nazi Germany in the thirties and saw what happened where the curriculum was nationally controlled.' (TES 1977:3) Not all teachers heard the steady tramp of DES jackboots in the street at the mention of 'core curriculum'. Mr Pat Martin, president of the Head Masters' Association welcomed the suggestion: 'It repeats exactly what I called for in my presidential address' (ibid.), he said. We see here the sorts of reactions that were to characterize teacher participation in the debate: surprise, chagrin, paranoia and qualified welcome. Teachers were both divided and unprepared for the ideological campaign the DES was about to wage. Hence their response was bound to be uncoordinated, personalized and, in the long run, ineffective.

It was key to the Department's legitimation of more centralized power through the propagation of a new ideology that this ideology should, at one and the same time, render illegitimate the decentralized power of the teacher. Although in the short term it could rely on the political incompetence of the teachers' unions to win its arguments on its behalf, in the long term the Department required a justification for the erosion of teacher power capable of standing the test of time. This was duly found in the doctrine of 'education's accountability to the community' which was tacked on to the other social and individual goals of the economic ideology of education already discussed. The attraction of the concept of 'community' is that it is both very difficult to attack directly and, at the same time, broad enough to allow the DES plenty of room for manoeuvre – as the teachers were to discover to their cost. In the Great Debate, it was used to erode teacher power at two levels: firstly, school management and, secondly, the Schools Council.

Coming as it did shortly after the Green Paper, and its fairly general recommendations, the publication of the Taylor Report on school government in September 1977, with its specific proposals on power sharing between school staff, LEA representatives, parents and local community representatives, did very little for the teachers' union morale. Although the 1944 Education Act had theoretically given LEAs the power to supervise the curriculum through delegation to a board of governors, in practice it was teachers, particularly headteachers, who decided on curriculum content. So here was a straight challenge to teacher autonomy. And it was not just with regard to the curriculum. The Taylor Report stated (TES 1977:8), 'Except where we specifically say so, we do not intend that *any* part of a school's activity should remain outside the governors' concern', (our stress) and included in the purview of governors: behaviour in schools; finance; appointments and dismissals of staff; admissions, suspensions and expulsions of pupils; school premises and holidays. Governor control of all these areas could be justified, the report felt, in terms of the school's responsibility to the wider community, not merely because the school was founded by the community, but because (ibid.:7) 'if we want all the things we care about to be carried on after we are gone, our schools must be the home of our hopes and of our values'.

Regardless of how far the Taylor Report was, or was not, implemented, its significance from the teachers' union perspective was that it completely outflanked them ideologically in that it helped to legitimate external interference in the classroom. No matter that the report did not seek to justify direct DES influence. The point was that an ideological breach had been made in the professional autonomy of the teaching profession and it was not going to be easily repaired. Reactions of the teachers' unions to the report reflected a sense of their own importance which was rapidly becoming anachronistic. Fred Jarvis called it a 'busybodies charter' (Vaughan 1977:1) while the National Association of Schoolmasters–Union of Women Teachers said the report offered a 'bogus partnership' because it was impossible for lay people 'intelligently to share in the management of the education system' (ibid.). Neither appeared to realize that the DES was making ideological alliances with everyone (industry, trade unions, LEAs, parents etc.) while they further isolated themselves by insisting on the peculiar territorial rights of the teacher.

However, at a different level, some parts of the teaching profession were more inclined to accept the idea that they should be more responsive to the needs of the community and to wince at Fred Jarvis's inflexible assertion that 'there are points at which the teacher as a professional has to tell the layman that it is his job to know and to decide.' (Cohen and Lodge 1977:6) As we saw in chapter six, the Schools Council, all of whose committees bar one were previously dominated by teachers' union representatives, has seen fit to adapt its structure considerably. This was in the face of direct government pressure. Despite the announcement by the Council of a constitutional review in late 1976, Shirley Williams, then Secretary of State for Education and Science, announced her own proposals for reforming the Council a month later. There was no attempt to disguise the intention of establishing DES control: the changes would bring 'the secretary of state's views to bear more effectively at the formative stages of the Council's work', so 'its eventual recommendations are likely to be acceptable to the Secretary of State'. (Doe 1977) Moreover, the justification for this increased intervention presented the government as the arbiter of community need for it was stated that although the government intended no detailed control over the curriculum nevertheless they were 'entitled to be satisfied that curricula meet, and are responsive to, *the needs of society*' (our stress). Not entirely surprisingly, the Council's own constitutional review bowed to the needs of *realpolitik* and in late 1978 gave responsibility for overall policy decisions to a 'finance and priorities' committee on which teachers were outnumbered by DES and LEA representatives.

Despite the teachers' unions' subsequent written replies to the Department's initiatives, such as the NUT's *Education in Schools* (reply to the Green Paper) and *Partnership in Education* (reply to the Taylor Report), by late 1977 it was pretty obvious that they were on the defensive. Nevertheless, this did not necessarily mean that all was lost. As we remarked earlier, attacks on education for failing to meet the needs of the economy have been periodic rather than unique and previous attempts to make education accountable to the nation had not had any noticeable effect. So even though it can be said, as Brian Simon (1977:18) has stated, that 'the Green Paper marks a new phase in its clear assertion of an active (leadership) role for the DES' with the CAC's prerogative on important educational advice now in abeyance; and that 'there is here a very clear bid, if not for central control, at least for the assertion of the central authority as the leading force or power in the determination of educational procedures' – it is another question altogether whether this assertion of authority through the sponsorship of a particular ideology could be translated into specific forms of structural change. Indeed, it has to be continually borne in mind that although the new ideology suits the bureaucratic aspirations of the DES, nevertheless the status of the ideology remains a fragile one: not least because of the tensions within it. For although an overall ideological commitment to the economic functions of education may fit the DES's managerial ambitions, the details of the ideology have to rely on educational values which remain essentially traditional in their concern with individual development. So at the subjective level of the individual official, it is inevitable that ambiguities will arise where it is not clear how educational values contribute to the economic functions of education. It is only where educational values are subjectively perceived as contingent upon that economic function that the economic ideology of education retains its coherence. In the case of the Inspectorate, in particular, which traditionally sees itself as the custodian of educational quality, such ambiguities are bound to be present. Thus although the Great Debate had acted as a vehicle for the economic ideology of education, the question it leads to is how far could the DES exploit the ideological capital it had established to effect important educational change?

The aftermath

1   *Information and value control*

To an extent this is an unfair question in that even with the legitimacy for more positive management afforded it by the ideology cultivated in the Great Debate, the DES could not take advantage of that legitimacy until its still embryonic lines of control over education had been systematized further. As we stressed earlier, the logic of the DES's bureaucratic development means that it is interested, not in change *per se*, but in the capacity to manage change. What we can expect to find in the post-Debate situation, therefore, is the more rapid development of those features of the Department's activity which we have already identified as being indicative of its desire both to encapsulate the policy-making process and to control more closely the process of policy implementation.

A central indicator is the mushrooming activities of HMI. Prior to 1976 HMI received scanty mention in the annual reports of the

Department: a bare statement of their current strength was the custom. But from 1976 onwards, HMI have a separate, and increasingly lengthy section of their own detailing a broadening range of activities and publications. In the DES *Annual Report* of 1977, for example, HMI is reported as having conducted two surveys in further education, three in the area of teacher training, two in Wales, whilst at the same time producing ten publications on various issues (none the previous year). Parallel to this rapid expansion of HMI's role of marshalling DES information, structural changes have occurred to coordinate the effects of the increased information flows. In 1977 an HMI was given the specific responsibility for coordinating the Department's research programme as well as a more general role in linking HMI work with the planning process (DES 1977b: 36). In the following year HMI further rationalized its own internal operation. Three inspectors were given responsibilities for the 'collection of information and the planning of exercises involving all seven inspectorate divisions' and HMIs attached to the steering groups of projects sponsored by the DES 'were now ensuring that there was a better flow of information about the progress of projects and about any interim findings that might emerge' (DES 1978a: 41). Meanwhile many inspectors continued to act as observers on professional associations, education, training and research bodies and the Schools Council.

In assessing the significance of these changes within HMI one has to bear in mind that HMI is naturally very sensitive to its image and position in the Department as a whole and anxious to present itself as the paragon of efficiency when contributing to its section of the annual report. Even so, it is difficult to avoid the impression that it is becoming much more directly responsive to the Department's policy-making needs and much more alive to providing the right information at the right time. This is true of its local as well as its national work. In monitoring the effects of LEA expenditure patterns HMIs have recently systematized their observations so that these can be fed into a central team of inspectors which, in turn, contibutes to the department's forward planning. Furthermore, the 1978 *Annual Report* (ibid.) comments that 'In the annual cycle of Rate Support Grant discussions [about local authorities] HMI were able to provide illustrative evidence which helped in the interpretation of outturn figures, and to offer qualitative comments on trends, future priorities and patterns of expenditure.'

None of this expanded and centrally oriented activity by HMI is so much sinister as it is obvious. Any bureaucracy requires that decisions be taken rationally in the light of the available information. Therefore he who controls the information flow controls the nature of the rational decision. According to the bureaucratic rules of conduct, information domination is power unless, and it is a big 'unless', these rules allow the introduction of values into the decision-making process at certain points – as theoretically occurs via the role of the Secretary of State for Education. He is supposed to express the 'democratic will' and inject the appropriate educational values into DES decision making. Although this aspect of his role is in any case severely curtailed (see pp. 104–106) it is nevertheless in the bureaucracy's best interests to be able to dominate, or at least sponsor the production of educational values, not only on the grand scale of the Great Debate but also right down to the classroom level. This is another way of saying that aspirant bureaucracies require their own organic intellectuals.

Not surprisingly HMI has shown some hesitancy in taking on this task of organizing the details of DES ideology. In part this is due to the traditional independence of the Inspectorate from the Department which, although now being eroded, nevertheless means that HMI is resistant to being too obviously a slave of DES needs. So rather than be the reluctant handmaiden to the department, HMI has taken a more promotional path in publicly sponsoring those educational values which previously it had mainly encouraged informally. This is just as well since the wheels were soon to be set in motion which would force a change in the Inspectorate's role regardless. As predicted in the Green Paper, circular 14/77 was issued in November 1977 (DES 1978a: 44), inviting local education authorities to review and report on the position in their areas with reference to six main curricular aspects: local arrangements for carrying out functions in relation to the school curriculum; steps taken to encourage appropriate balance and breadth in the curriculum of schools; policies and arrangements for particular subject areas; transition between schools; school records; and preparation for working life. The importance of this move should not be underestimated: effectively it has set into motion the machinery necessary for the DES to intervene directly in the curriculum with the cooperation of the LEAs. In the report which is to follow 'It was intended that this would form the basis for further consultations within and outside the education service in the course of which agreement would be sought on the nature of further action that might be necessary *to develop curriculum policies and to meet national needs more effectively*' (ibid; our stress). Naturally the teachers' unions were opposed to what the NUT described as an 'interventionist' move designed to shift responsibility away from the schools towards more control at national and local authority levels. (Doe 1978) However NUT's request for LEAs not to cooperate except in conjunction with teacher representatives has had little effect, demonstrating once again the exclusion of teachers' unions from the formative stages of policy making.

The significance of circular 14/77 for HM Inspectorate is that if it is to carry out the function of organic intellectuals effectively then it must provide a ready and detailed framework of ideas which can be used to 'guide' future consultations on the curriculum with LEAs. Dominating ideas' production without appearing to do so is no easy task even though HMI has more resources available than any other group involved in education. One rule is to keep up a supply of publications and advice to try and establish the climate within which discussion takes place. HMI's recent series Matters for Discussion, for example, takes each subject area in turn with the objective of stimulating professional discussion. Ostensibly, as each publication declares, 'It is hoped that they will promote debate at all levels so that they can be given due weight when educational developments are being assessed or discussed' (cf. the Schools Council's problems of legitimacy; see pp. 121–32). This is as may be. What is equally apparent is that the later issues in this series are becoming much more directive in tone than the earlier ones, indicating HMI's growing confidence in, firstly, its capacity to assert positively certain educational values and, secondly, the receptiveness of the educational world to such assertions. This latter point represents a critical stage in the implementation of any ideology since the preparedness of teachers to accept the validity of what HMI's have to say is an indication of how far HMIs and the ideology they are propagating are regarded as legitimate and therefore authoritative.

Parallel to the expanding activities of HMI has been the growth of the other means available to the DES for the collection of information: the Assessment of Performance Unit (APU). Originally set up to monitor national standards in maths, language and science, the APU has now widened its brief to include all areas of the curriculum – though so far tests have only been developed for the original three. In the post-Debate situation, the DES has been far less reticent about the APU's function, maintaining that at both national and local government levels 'information about the effectiveness of the school system is essential for the development of educational policy and the allocation of resources' (DES 1978c: 1). The differences between HMI and the APU as data-handling agents for the DES's policy making are two-fold ensuring that their individual operations are complementary rather than competitive. Firstly, the APU is taking over HMI's transitional function of gathering large amounts of quantitative information on a one-off basis and placing it within a permanent and routinized system of on-going monitoring. This then releases HMI for the task of assembling the much more qualitative data necessary for its servicing of DES ideology. Secondly, elaborating on this latter point, HMI is in any case as much concerned with information output as input. As the organic intellectuals of the Department HMIs have the responsibility for ensuring that its policies are legitimized in advance by the presentation of the appropriate evidence and arguments. This means that the APU's reports are almost certainly tailored by the guiding hand of the Inspectorate. It can be no coincidence that not only is the head of the APU an HMI but so also are the chairmen of all its working groups and committees.

To an extent, depending on how visible it is, this domination of the APU by HMI undermines the third distinction between the two: that through its complex and assiduously cultivated consultative arrangements the APU becomes less of an integral part of the DES and hence more acceptable to the teaching profession; and also, that in constructing its method of inquiry into standards of pupil attainment it is reflecting a broad range of non-DES educational opinion. From the point of view of the Department, the status of the information collected by the APU's monitoring procedures is related to HMI's capacity to use that information for policy legitimating purposes. The more that APU data is seen as 'scientific', 'objective' and the product of thorough consultative arrangements, the more authority it will carry when employed in the service of inspectorate arguments, be these arguments advanced under the HMI or the APU banner.

2   *Not so straightforward*

The Department's unfaltering pursuit of the means for information and value control could be taken as a sound indication of its conviction that the Great Debate had firmly established the ideological prerequisites for the expansion of its managerial power. So also could its explicit presentation of managerial needs couched in the language of output budgeting and rational planning. Since the end of the Debate, the Department has become much less reticent in its use of both phraseology and concepts which plainly derive from the style of thinking current in its internal planning procedures. The Oakes Report on the management of higher education in the maintained sector (1978:10), for example, defined its objective as 'the creation of a management system which would make most effective use of the available resources to meet demand from students who qualify for higher education and, in so far as they can be assessed, future needs for qualified manpower.' This, it maintained, would be a rational system with the functions of, firstly, intelligence – that is the collection of information on the demand for, and supply of higher education; secondly, the planning of changes to meet the demand; thirdly, within limits set by the government, determining necessary provision and where it should be made and allocating resources accordingly; fourthly, overseeing the implementation of agreed plans and the cost-effectiveness of the system as a whole (ibid.). If the slick planning jargon of this report is compared to the rather ponderous academic phrasing of the Robbins Report on higher education fifteen years earlier, the shift of emphasis and concern from educational to organizational needs in the intervening period is vividly illustrated.

Nevertheless, despite the Department's apparent confidence in its ability both to introduce the new mechanisms necessary for more efficient management of educational change and to use the language appropriate to the task, in other respects the legitimacy accorded its interventionist ambitions has severe limitations. This is particularly true in the area of training where the Department is frequently in direct competition with the Training Services Division (TSD) of the Manpower Services Commission (MSC). According to the perspective which sees education as the automatic servant of underlying economic shifts, competition between institutions to perform a certain educational function is unlikely, to say the least. Employing that perspective, one could be forgiven for predicting that the demand from a rapidly changing economy for a more sophisticated and flexible training function, particularly in a period of high youth unemployment, would have been met by an extension and adaptation of the structure presently performing that function: that is, further

education. Instead, the demand has prompted the creation of the MSC
and substantial institutional inefficiencies in the form of continual
vying between the DES and the TSD for the same educational market.
Such dysfunctions within the superstructure are regarded as
inevitable according to our own perspective which emphasizes the
capacity of institutions to pursue, and be constrained by the
implications of their bureaucratic development.

The constraints faced by the DES in this situation are two-fold.
Firstly, the traditional ideological division between 'education' and
'training', as with the division between 'school' and 'work', has to be
eroded if the Department is to lay convincing and legitimate claim to
an area presently on the fringes of its activity. Secondly, as the
Department often complains, the TSD can innovate much faster than
the DES because its central–local lines of control are more specific
and efficient. The initiative in the situation was seized by the MSC in
1977 with its publication of the Holland Report and the subsequent
adoption of its recommendations by the government in the form of
the Youth Opportunities Programme (YOP). Since then the
Department has been fighting a rearguard action on both the
ideological and political fronts to protect its interests at the education–
industry interface. Hence we find it continually restating its support
for the government's industrial strategy and advertizing the measures
it is taking relevant to the country's industrial needs. In the 1978
Annual Report, for instance, the DES (1978:xii) stresses how in 'its
efforts to expand educational opportunity and participation the
Department concentrated on the 16- to 18-year-old age group, with
the aim of producing a much more coherent approach to the central
question of giving young people a better start in working life' – a
statement directly rivalling the objectives of YOP. Similarly, in
Progress in Education (1978), it is careful to have a section expressly
concerned with the relationship between education and the
government's industrial strategy, where it lists in detail all the
measures it has taken to contribute 'to the need of the education
service as a whole to underpin the foundations of a modern industrial
society' (DES 1978:39). But rhetoric aside, the DES has not had
conspicuous success in implementing this part of its new ideology.
The Unified Vocational Preparation scheme (UVP) is a case in point.
Jointly sponsored with the TSD (then the Training Services Agency)
as a scheme to help 16- to 19-year-olds already in jobs to cope more
effectively with adult life and work, UVP flopped largely because of

employer antipathy towards it (see Jackson 1977:4). It is clearly one thing for employers to call for closer links between industry and education and quite another for them readily to accept the specific changes which the DES then initiates. In other words although the Department may be working hard to legitimize its activities in this field, it still has a long way to go.

What Great Debate?

More recent publications pursuing the themes initiated by the Great Debate, such as the DES's *A Framework for the School Curriculum* (1980) and *The School Curriculum* (1980) and HMI's *A View of the Curriculum* (1980), as well as the difficulties faced by the universities, are discussed in the next and final chapter where we raise the issue of where this is all leading. But in concluding the present chapter we deal first with the view expressed by the more sceptical observers that the Great Debate was not 'really' a debate, that it was stage-managed in order to exclude certain policy options, that most of the participants did not engage each other in meaningful argument but assumed predictable political postures, that most of the participants sooner or later realized what they were doing and considered the process a sterile one, and that therefore the whole thing was a contrivance and cannot be taken seriously. Apart from the final deduction, we would not disagree with this view. What we deduce instead is that the significance of the Great Debate lies precisely in the fact that individuals participated knowing that it was a contrivance. And the reason they had to participate was that the DES had succeeded in giving the Great Debate the status of an ideological forum where certain battles about the condition and future of education should be fought out. That it was not a fair and balanced exchange of views by rational individuals is of little consequence to its long-term political impact. What is of consequence is that the main educational interests felt obliged to take part, that it was highly visible and that at the public level at least most participants played the game and appeared to take it seriously. That was really all that the Department wanted and, at that point, needed.

The Department needed the debate because the bureaucratization of educational power could not continue under the reigning ideological conditions. If the Department was to increase both its own and local authorities' capacity to manage educational change then a renegotiation of the prevalent educational ideology had to take place. At the same time external economic pressures complemented the internal bureaucratic dynamic by insisting that, in a time of crisis, education should become accountable to the economy. Such accountability could not be achieved, the DES argued, without the introduction of new lines of management planning and control. We have described the ideological result of the harnessing of the economic pressures by the bureaucratic dynamic as the new economic ideology of education. It is an ideology which, if successfully implemented, conveniently legitimizes the ambitions of national and local bureaucracies for more rational means of organizing the education system. The vital questions, of course, are: how far has the new ideology already been implemented (i.e. become authoritative), and what are its chances for success in the future? In that the Great Debate signalled the public unveiling of the new educational ideology, the first steps in its implementation cannot be said to have gone too badly. A procession of documents established the main tenets of the ideology with only token resistance being met from opponents who were largely outgunned and outmanoeuvred. The requisite organizational adjustments to support the new ideology were already in train and continued during and after the Great Debate. Indeed, it was noticeable how the debate effectively paved the way for the expanded HMI and APU activities. If the bureaucratization of educational power is to continue, so also must the process of its legitimation through the appropriate ideological reinforcement. For that reason it is unlikely that we have seen the last of the Great Debate format for the public airing of educational issues by the DES. Until the Department's own organic intellectuals can assume an easy dominance of educational ideas, the elaboration and restating of the new educational ideology must take place on an open and public basis.

(i) all this happened in 5. 20 years earlier

(ii) Br.e5, respond to 'warning' by extending certification; c had one great debates (1968 / 1970)

10

Conclusions and Prospects

There is a severe danger that important educational change will take place in Britain unbeknown to many educational sociologists. Preoccupied as they are with how and why the working class remain working class or the way in which the social relations of capitalist production are reproduced, they deal only indirectly with the political and administrative specifics of educational change. This is not to deny that we must beware of losing sight of broader social movements in a welter of institutional analysis. But grandiose theorizing is of little value unless its treatment of the dynamic of change allows us to understand in concrete terms what is happening around us today and what is likely to happen tomorrow. Nor is it likely to be helped by an exclusive and prior commitment by educational sociologists to certain types of political action as the necessary agents of educational change.

It has been the aim of this book to marry a macro view of the forces behind educational change with their detailed expression in the structural and ideological features of institutions. This has been at times a painstaking task since it has meant, firstly, drawing together theoretical positions normally characterized by a belief in their own exclusiveness and, secondly, illustrating the salient aspects of our own theory through the careful exploration of particular institutional contexts. If we began with the Gramscian suspicion that, in the case of education, tensions exist both between the state and the economic base on the one hand, and between the state and civil society on the other, we end with the conviction that 'tension' may well be too mild a term: 'frequent dysfunction' may be better. There can be no doubt that the objective demand of the dominant economic order for appropriate types of manpower, social relations of production, social control mechanisms and so on is filtered through complex state bureaucracies with needs and minds of their own. For though it is naturally in the interest of major government bureaucracies to respond to the economic order on which their survival ultimately depends, they may also view their interest in terms of the maintenance and extension of their own power. There is no guarantee that the two types of interest, economic and bureaucratic, happily coincide to produce the same policy decisions.

This inherent tension in the state's operation is further complicated in the case of education by its unique ideological role in modern society. Through its command of the formal qualifications necessary for occupational access and mobility, its reinforcement of the different cultural styles which accompany the credentialling hierarchy, and its control of the organization of knowledge appropriate to that hierarchy, education supplies the social inequalities of the dominant political order with a structural rationale overlaid with educational values. Provided that the elements of structure and values interrelate reasonably well, the resulting educational ideology then legitimates the social inequalities.

In developing a theory of educational change, we therefore had to be concerned not only with the negotiations between the economic and bureaucratic dynamics but also with the ideological context in which these negotiations take place. Merely because a dynamic change exists is not a guarantee that an accompanying ideology will be conveniently forthcoming. As our chapter on the public schools demonstrated, it is possible for change to occur where the accompanying ideology does not fully adapt to the new situation, but probably only in that type of privatized circumstance. Where the potential educational change is national in scope the ideological stage is essential before the change can be realized in the form of government policy. So in terms of both dynamic and ideology, educational change is problematic. The detailed studies of particular examples of educational change have convinced us that it is only possible to understand the twists and turns of this problematic by viewing its expression as a process of political negotiation. This does not mean that we are advocating a return to the mechanistic analysis of the interest group approach. It is rather a question of reinterpreting the type of information provided by that level of analysis in the light of an overarching theory. An overarching theory which assumes that statements about educational change can be little more than guesswork unless they include the institutional specifics of the negotiation of dynamic and ideology.

Given this, what does our theory tell us about the likely pattern of British education in the future? In answering this question we raise four issues: firstly, the demographic and economic pressures upon education; secondly, the response of the state apparatus to these pressures in the light of its own needs and its relationship with neighbouring structures; thirdly, the maintenance and extension of state control over education's financial and administrative arrangements and the implications of these changes for the way knowledge is organized; fourthly, the ideological context of educational change.

It does not take a crystal ball to predict that the economic and demographic pressures upon education are unlikely to change greatly for a while yet: the economic recession is too well established to be reversed overnight, youth unemployment is rapidly becoming a structural as opposed to a temporary feature of the economy and falling rolls should ensure a surplus of three million places in primary and secondary schools in England and Wales by 1986 with unpredictable consequences for further and higher education. Economic demands are being placed upon education for it to produce the manpower appropriate to the nation's needs, to remove the distinction between education and training and accept that education is a lifelong process, to provide flexible retraining programmes, and to operate on a more cost-effective basis. As we pointed out earlier, the idea that education should respond more directly to the needs of the economy is of itself nothing new and has been around for at least fifty years. What is new, however, is that education is itself suffering financial cutbacks on an unprecedented scale, that its dominant bureaucracy, the DES, has reached a certain point in its development and now has a rival, the Manpower Services Commission (MSC) – an offshoot of the Department of Employment.

Throughout the 1970s, the DES was engaged on a process of policy enclosure which effectively re-drew the old tripartite partnership of DES, LEAs and teachers' trades unions. As policy making was progressively internalized within the Department's 'rational' planning procedures, the LEAs and teachers' unions were increasingly made aware that they were subordinate, rather than equal partners. The post-1979 Conservative government's education cuts have merely served to accelerate and to justify further the Department's command over policy making: if the cuts are to be made on a rational basis, the argument goes, then there must be some kind of central co-ordination. What the DES has done, therefore, is to harness the economic pressures for educational change in a way which suited its aspirations. In doing so, it was spurred on by the rapid expansion of the MSC in the mid and late 1970s which served as a sharp reminder to the DES that it had only limited control over the education system for which it was responsible. Unlike the MSC, the DES cannot directly implement its policies but has to rely instead on the cooperation of other bodies – notably, the LEAs and the UGC. Whereas the MSC could swiftly respond to the rise in youth unemployment with its Youth Opportunities Programme (YOP) the DES could not (its Unified Vocational Preparation Scheme failed dismally) and so was faced with the galling spectacle of seeing the only really expanding sector of the educational market snapped up by a rival organization. The arrival of the MSC acted as a catalyst to developments already in train in the DES and will continue to do so. It acts as a constant reminder to the Department that being able to claim that it 'serves the needs of the economy' through the efficient organization of education is a very useful political argument in the current climate and one which must remain central to the ideology the DES now sponsors.

As the state apparatus for education gathers the capacity and initiative for policy making unto itself, it has had to rethink its relationship with its previous partners. In the case of the teachers' unions this has increasingly meant ignoring them when at all possible and merely including them in the consultative stage of policy formation. Two examples illustrate the declining power of the teachers' unions in the wake of the Great Debate where they were so thoroughly outgunned and outmanoeuvred by the DES. Firstly, in 1977 when circular 14/77 was issued to local authorities calling for a review of arrangements for the curriculum the NUT called for a policy of non-cooperation: all local authorities with the exception of Kingston-upon-Thames ignored the NUT's request. Secondly, when the Department initiated its ten regional meetings beginning in October 1980 to explain its post-Debate policies, the teachers' unions were given only two representatives per meeting – and those were to be allocated by the LEAs. The unions consequently boycotted the meetings with no effect.

While its relationship with the teachers' unions is of small moment to the Department (the central state) it is unlikely to be able to implement its policies without the cooperation of the local state: the

LEAs. Thus educational change at the central level has to be paralleled by similar shifts at the local level. We speculated earlier on the extent to which the DES and LEA permanent officers can be seen to have common interests as managers of the education system (see pp. 93–100). Unfortunately for the ambitions of the Department, identifying what are objectively-speaking common interests is no guarantee that this commonality will be subjectively appreciated by LEA officers. They may be more concerned with central interference in local affairs than with the advantages of a joint approach to educational management. In the immediate future we can therefore expect that the DES will embark on a concerted effort to woo the local managers of education around to the Department's point on view. For ultimately, the implementation of its own interventionist plans depends on the LEAs adopting similar modes of operation.

The signs are apparent that such a campaign of education and persuasion has already begun. As recommended in the 1977 Green Paper *Education in Schools*, circular 14/77 was sent to LEAs and, as a result of the information collected, a report was compiled arguing in favour of a national framework for the curriculum. Within this argument, local authorities are given a very specific place.

To fulfil their responsibilities effectively within any nationally agreed framework authorities must exercise leadership and interpret national policies and objectives in the light of local needs and circumstances. Moreover, local authorities are concerned with policies for the level and distribution of resources, including staff buildings, equipment and materials which inter-act upon curriculum and standards of achievement. They are also in a position to foster cooperation and complementary provision among their schools, and between schools and further education colleges. It is therefore essential that they should be aware of, and take account of their decisions on such matters for the curricula offered by their schools and colleges. (DES 1979:3)

In 'nudging local authorities into a more active role in curriculum planning', as Bob Doe of the *Times Educational Supplement* put it, the report was at pains to point out that many local authorities 'need to increase their capability to develop and implement more effective approaches to staffing, curriculum development, assessment and their distribution of resources, all of which should be closely related to their curricular policies and the aims of the schools.' (Doe 1979)

Similar statements about the need for LEAs to develop clear policies on the curriculum, the use of resources and future planning also appear in *A Framework for the School Curriculum* supported by the belief that local, as well as national, monitoring of schools is necessary: 'The Secretaries of State consider therefore that authorities should collect information annually from their schools about the curriculum offered, together with school assessments of the extent to which the curriculum matches school aims and objectives.' (DES 1980:4) And the theme occurs again almost exactly word for word in the Department's 1981 pronouncement *The School Curriculum* (1981a:4).

In its leader comment on *The School Curriculum*, the *Times Educational Supplement* (1981b:3) described the document as 'trite', 'a harmless tract' and as representing the 'liquidation of commitments to a core curriculum and a defined framework.' In so doing it entirely missed the political point of the document and overlooked the DES's intention to review local authorities' arrangements for the curriculum two years on. For *The School Curriculum* has to be seen in the context of the Department prodding local authorities into developing more positive lines of management over their schools over a period of time. It also has to be seen in conjunction with parts of the 1980 Education Act now being implemented in detail. In particular, from 1982/83 local authorities will have to provide for parents information about their schools which includes details about the curriculum, discipline, uniforms, arrangements for pastoral care, policy on entry to public examinations and details of past examination results. Dependent as it is at present on persuasion in its relationship with the LEAs, the Department has to adopt a gradualist approach.

However, as an ambitious state bureaucracy the DES is unlikely to tolerate the frustrations of this approach for much longer. It may decide instead to alter the present statutory responsibilities for the education service laid down in the 1944 and subsequent Education Acts. This would not be a substitute for an alliance with local authorities but a complementary tactic designed to increase both central and local administrative powers at one and the same time. Because of the sensitivity of the issue, the Department has frequently been at pains to make its position clear. Thus, in *Local Authority Arrangements for the Curriculum* (1979:2), referring to the partnership between central and local government, school governing bodies and teachers, it states that the 'Secretaries of State do not intend to alter the existing statutory relationship between these various partners'. However, the DES's position on statutory responsibilities is likely to change once it feels that the ideological ground for more intervention has been properly prepared. And the signs are that such a change is already being considered. In *A Framework for the School Curriculum* (1980) it was noted that evidence from both the replies to circular 14/77 and the two HMI surveys (primary and secondary) indicates a need to review the way that the legal responsibilities for education are exercised as laid down in the Education Acts. The document continues: 'There are important differences from school to school and area to area and in some cases *the way in which responsibilities are discharged – or have been allowed to go by default* – does not contribute as it should either to the efficiency of the schools or to their responsiveness to national needs' (p. 1; our stress). But exactly what reallocation of responsibilities the DES is considering is not yet clear, except that whatever it is, it is not going to diminish DES power.

The reaction of local government to a legal change in the central–local state relationship which establishes more detailed national criteria for local education is bound to be ambiguous. While the Association of Metropolitan Authorities (AMA), the Association of County Councils (ACC) and the Council for Local Education Authorities (CLEA) are almost certain to resist such changes, groups such as the Society of Education Officers (SEO), which represents local education officers, may well take a different and more sympathetic line. For example, Dudley Fiske, the chief education officer for Manchester, suggested a strengthening of central government powers and a firmer lead from the DES when he delivered the 1980 William Walker Lecture to the British Educational Administration Society. Behind Mr Fiske's suggestions lay the recognition of the need for basic minimum educational standards in an increasingly mobile society, the fact of 'creeping centralization' anyway and the existing ambiguities over who is accountable for what. To illustrate his point that the position of education officers in the local authority service is often unsatisfactory he quoted the SEO's evidence to the Layfield Committee on Local Government finance. This included the statement: 'We are local government men but not at any price.' (TES 1980: 5) – i.e. education may have to come first.

While the DES has so far adopted a low-key approach to the local authorities over primary and secondary education, it has taken a far

more aggressive stance toward the LEAs' responsibilities for further
and higher education in the public sector and it is here that the most
dramatic changes are likely in the near future. The Green Paper
Higher Education in England outside the Universities (July 1981)
proposes that a quarter of the colleges in this sector (all 30 of the
polytechnics and 60 other colleges) be removed from local authority
control and a central planning body introduced to distribute grants
and rationalize and coordinate courses. The body would be similar to
the University Grants Committee (see also David 1981a:7;
1981b:10). Such a change could represent a massive shift of power
to the DES (the current cost of public sector higher education is
£400 million per year) and indicates that on this issue the Department
is prepared to go ahead despite the opposition of the local authorities.
(The CLEA proposes an alternative model in the Green Paper which
would leave the local authorities in control of the purse strings.) It
knows that it can count on the support of the Committee of Directors
of Polytechnics who, yearning for national status, commented cᴝ the
plan in the familiar rational–economic language of the economic
ideology of education saying that it was 'most likely to lead to a cost-
effective system, capable of responding to the needs of industry and
commerce.' (*Guardian* 1981:3) Tired of the haggle over the pooling
system and the Oakes report and of the local authorities' resistance to
its plans for the 16–19s (the publication of *Higher Education in
England outside the Universities* coincided with £500 million being
awarded for youth training, mainly to the Department of
Employment) the DES has decided to grasp the nettle. In doing so, it
has realized in concrete form one aspect of its development as a state
bureaucracy.

If the DES initiative on this issue succeeds, which it almost
certainly will, it will represent a clear example of the central state
departing publicly from its customary posture of passively
aggregating group interest in the formation of policy (unreal though
this posture may be) and adopting an explicit leadership role. Such a
shift is bound to boost the Department's confidence and encourage it
to take the lead in other fields of education. The most likely one, and
currently the most vulnerable, is the university sector. By creating a
national body for the public sector of higher education the
Department would also be generating the capacity to coordinate *all* of
higher education by linking the work of the new body with that of the
UGC. Mr Richard Bird, DES Deputy Secretary responsible for higher

education, recognized the possibility when the Green Paper was published and said the two bodies could 'be merged under a single umbrella committee or through some other collaborative machinery. (David 1981b:10) Such a merger could include financial and academic planning, particularly course distribution, as well as the rationalization of regional links. (The Department has already persuaded the CLEA and UGC to set up 'transbinary' committees to examine areas of mutual concern though so far these have not got very far.) The implications of such a change for the way in which knowledge is organized and controlled, both in higher education itself and lower down the education hierarchy, are substantial. A decision would have to be made on whether universities should retain their traditional autonomy in the validation of courses or whether a central validating body should be set up to parallel the CNAA and so provide a back-up sanction for the central direction of courses. From the UGC's point of view such a reform would make a great deal of sense: it would enable it to implement the education cuts in a more coherent fashion and would be quite in line with the increasingly dirigiste role of the UGC which we examined in *Education and the Political Order* (Tapper & Salter 1978:ch. 7). Nor is there any legal as opposed to political obstacle in the way of DES intervention. As Robbins prophetically noted in 1964, 'there is no absolute safeguard against interference with the distribution of grants to universities. It is a convention that Government abstains. But it cannot bind its successors: nor is its agreement likely to imply abstention in the face of major difficulties.' (DES 1964:237)

The Department's intention to bring an end to the binary division in higher education was presaged by a reorganization of branches within the DES in 1980. Higher and Further Education Branch 1 (HFE 1), which was responsible for non-university higher and further education, was merged with HFE 3, which handles university policy, to form a new 'super-branch', FHE 1. The clear intention behind the reorganization was to be able to coordinate planning across the binary divide, to restrict the traditional independence of the universities within DES, to allow the Department to 'push ahead more purposively with its policy of course rationalization on a broad transbinary front, and to implement any "broad-steer" to subject balance which manpower forecasts may suggest.' (THES 1980:40) In this context, the 1981 Green Paper on higher education in the public sector is a perfectly logical step for the DES to take.

While the way forward to greater state intervention in higher education is reasonably clear, little progress can be made by the DES in the primary and secondary sectors without the cooperation of the LEAs unless it develops more direct controls over what happens at the local level. While the Department can quite happily exclude the LEAs from policy formation, policy implementation is another matter. There are two main areas in which the Department needs more control: finance and the curriculum. In the 1977 Green Paper *Education in Schools*, and elsewhere, the Department frequently lamented the fact that in its allocation of monies to the local authorities via the Rate Support Grant (RSG) it could recommend, but not ensure, that these allocations should be spent in particular ways. This situation, it was emphasized, compared unfavourably with the direct financing capacity of the Training Services Division of the MSC. It is a situation which has now changed. The 1980 Local Government Planning and Land Act was intended to reshape the system of paying grants to local authorities in a way which replaced local authority responsibility with central government decisions on a service by service basis. This means that the DES should have much more direct control over the spending patterns of individual LEAs. A grant related expenditure assessment (GRE) is made as to what individual authorities should be spending on the education services and authorities are progressively penalized if they spend over 10 per cent more than limits set by the DES. Taken on its own, it is a little alarmist to comment on this measure, as Tony Travers did in the *Guardian* (1980:7), that 'we are witnessing the end of democratic local government and the start of the central state,' but taken together with the structural moves of the DES already detailed, more direct financial control can be regarded as a tightening of the links in the central–local state relationship; though precisely how much they will be tightened remains to be seen.

Although the DES's financial lines of control, where they exist, can be used to implement policies regarding the expansion and contraction of particular parts of the education service, they cannot influence what is taught – i.e. the curriculum. Here local authorities can have an immediate responsibility, and one which the Department is encouraging, but even they must operate within the parameters set by the independent exam boards which administer the secondary education examination system. The responsibility for generating new proposals on exams lies, in turns, with the Schools Council: these proposals are then accepted or rejected by the Secretary of State for Education. At present it is a less than satisfactory system which produces much confusion and little fruitful change. The Schools Council's credibility has lately been eroded by the rejection by the Department of the Council's proposals on 'N' and 'F' level exams and the Certificate of Extended Education and the instigation of the Trenaman inquiry into the fundamentals of the Council's operation. At the same time there have been claims by the teachers' unions that the DES and HMI representatives on the Schools Council have been using 'steamroller tactics' to get their way. (TES 1981a:5) As a quango, the Council is particularly vulnerable given the views of the present Conservative government. There is every likelihood, therefore, that the Department will shortly absorb the Council in order to be able to control the future direction of the curriculum. This is a much softer option than taking on the exam boards directly though the DES may use the reorganization of the CSE and GCE boards required for the new 16 + examination to make some inroads on exam board autonomy.

In expanding its capacity to manage educational change the Department has had to pay due attention to the ideological dimension of change: both its own power and the new structural forms it brings into being have to be seen as legitimate as does their role as avenues to different forms of social inequality. In other words, ideological change must occur to ensure that education's social control function remains obscured and protected. In chapter nine we showed how the economic ideology of education meshes easily with the rationalist-managerial aspirations of the Department: education should be organized more efficiently and centrally in order that it can better serve the needs of the economy. Hence, the Great Debate was not a one-off affair, a momentary upsurge of public concern about the aims and character of our education system: it was a successful experiment by the permanent officials of educational management to generate an ideological platform for subsequent initiatives. There can be no question of the continuity of theme and ambition from the Yellow Book of 1976 through the DES documents for the Great Debate conferences, the Green Paper *Education in Schools* (1977), the circular 14/77 recommended by the Green Paper and the report *Local Authority Arrangements for the Curriculum* (1979) in response to the circular, to most recently, the consultative proposals *A Framework for the School Curriculum* (1980) and the White Paper *The School*

Curriculum (1981). These are not *ad hoc* publications synthesizing current interest group opinion but logical political steps by a bureaucracy bent on establishing its ideological dominance and radically altering the well-known description of the DES as a Department 'with responsibility but without power.' The immediate political effect of the Great Debate and the ideological themes it exploited has been the consolidation of the DES's aim of policy enclosure and the exclusion of 'non-experts' from the rational planning process. Not only were the teachers' unions found badly wanting when faced with the Department's big guns and their mobile cavalry, the HMIs, but it has since become obvious that the political parties themselves have only obsolete equipment at their disposal and are unlikely to mount a fresh attack. As alternative ideological positions, party policies on education are virtually bankrupt and rapidly succumbing to the 'inevitable' and 'economically necessary' components of the Department's new ideology. Even the quixotic Rhodes Boyson, a Parliamentary Under-Secretary of State at the DES, in 1979 justified cuts in university spending in the routine anti-Robbins, manpower language of the economic ideology of education when he argued: 'The way to economic success for Britain is not to go on having an endless supply of people going up – in the most expensive university system in the world – to read whatever course they want. That is the road to an economic Passchendaele' (1979). (Certain courses are economically more important than others and student demand for higher education should be obliged to tailor itself to that reality.) Conversely, it is noticeable how policies beloved of the Conservatives while in opposition, such as pro-grammar school measures and the voucher system, have to all intents and purposes been quietly left on the shelf. Even the Assisted Places Scheme for public schools has been severely whittled down. The decline in the parties' ability to formulate detailed plans for educational change capable of rivalling those of the DES is not entirely surprising while the technical expertise of the Department is regarded as a *sine qua non* of sensible policy making. While the Department retains the initiative in presenting models of educational change justified in quantitative terms (as it did in *Education in the 1990s* for example) and while non-DES sponsored values are downgraded, the political parties will remain essentially responsive and subordinate in the educational field.

The ability of the Department to maintain its ideological dominance will depend primarily on the skills of its organic intellectuals, the

HMIs. So far the Inspectorate has taken up its new, or more accurately expanded, role of publicly recognized educational expert with considerable gusto: its recent publications record is proof enough of that. Furthermore, it has continued to reiterate its traditional independence from the Department itself – an important idea to cultivate since on it rests HMI's reputation as impartial expert and thereby its capacity to legitimize Department policy. Some differences between the DES and HMI view of, say, the content of a core curriculum is therefore to be expected. Where important differences do not occur is in the commonly recognized need by both DES and HMI that there should be more central control over education. In this respect it is interesting to note how the Inspectorate is becoming less reticent about how directive it should be. In the first ten issues of its Matters for Discussion series HMI was at pains to point out how these publications really were only aids for discussion. However, in number eleven, *A View of the Curriculum* (1980), in many ways the most important of the series, the foreword emphasizes that although it is in the Matters for Discussion series, 'there is an urgent need for discussion to lead to agreement about what is desirable and practicable, and to that end the suggestions offered here are positive rather than speculative.' Discussion alone is clearly no longer a sufficient reward for an HMI initiative, though the Inspectorate is hesitant to make too big a point of it.

In the context of more central intervention in education, it is important that the DES–HMI partnership should evolve a mutually recognized division of labour to avoid any unseemly and divisive arguments in public. Such a division of labour is well on the way to being established and can be illustrated by reference to two of the most recent publications on the question of the core curriculum, the aforementioned *A View of the Curriculum* (HMI) and *A Framework for the School Curriculum* (DES), both published in 1980. In the DES document there are detailed arguments in favour of a framework for the curriculum, an explanation of the immediate historical context (including cross-references to previous government publications) and frequent appeals to the guru of 'national need'. It is a document heavily laced with political overtones. *A View of the Curriculum*, on the other hand, seems almost benignly and naively 'educational' by comparison, dealing exclusively with the issue of curriculum content, apparently detached from the hurly-burly of power struggle and machination. And if the partnership is to work, this distinction has to be maintained: while the Department's involvement in the messy business of politics can be excused as inevitable given the duties with which it is charged, the Inspectorate's can not. In a system that trades in knowledge the position of ideological authority has to be attained and guarded with the mantle of impartiality. Just as the universities' place at the top of the knowledge status hierarchy is based principally on their traditional claim to independent thought, so also must the HMI position rest firmly on a just claim to be the wise men of education.

Should the distinction between the Inspectorate and the DES become blurred in the eyes of the public, the role of HMI as the organic intellectuals weaving the appropriate ideological blanket to legitimate future DES policy will be seriously endangered.

As we stressed in the last chapter, now is a critical stage in the Department's development because as it seeks to enlarge its ability to manage educational change, it has to alter both its internal structure and its relationship with surrounding structures at one and the same time. Once the Inspectorate has become accustomed to its new role as the principal shaping force in educational opinion and has fully institutionalized that new role, things will run more smoothly. But at present HMI is in transition as it attempts to organize the ideological stage of the educational change initiated by the Department. A similar point can be made about the Assessment of Performance Unit (APU). As the scientifically respectable monitoring agent of the DES it too is grappling with the implications of the information gathering function it has been given. The difficulty in the case of the APU is that it is also saddled with a cumbersome consultative machinery with major interests which means that each stage in its evolution has to be painfully negotiated internally. Nonetheless, what is important from the point of view of the Department is that the principle of national monitoring has, by and large, been accepted. However, it is also clear that the APU has not come up to the Department's expectations and has failed to gather information in the complexity and depth the DES would have preferred. (Doe 1981:3)

It is perfectly possible that the type of educational change with which we have been concerned in this chapter – large scale, reformist and primarily bureaucratic – can occur without too many ripples disturbing the current life of the classroom. What the DES is interested in is establishing more rational modes of management, more efficient lines of resource and ideology control which do not of themselves involve direct interference in the details of the present curriculum. What they do mean is the establishing of the parameters for change, the promotion of subtle and not so subtle definitions of the desirable content and organization of the curriculum, the emasculation of alternatives by continued ideological dominance and the refinement of the sanctions available. It is the management of the educational future with which the state apparatus is concerned, not the blatant manipulation of the present. Looking at it this way, the apparent double think of the DES statement (1979:1) that 'Secretaries of State do not seek to determine in detail what the schools should teach or how it should be taught; but they have an inescapable duty to satisfy themselves that the work of the schools matches national needs,' becomes rather more comprehensible.

The chances that the bureaucratic dynamic will have its way with the education system are enhanced by convenient linkages between the economic context, the new economic ideology of education and education's role as legitimator of social inequality. The economic problems besetting the country and the consequent cut-backs in educational spending lend a nice authenticity and cutting edge to the DES's clarion calls for more administrative efficiency and greater accountability in the use of scarce educational resources. At the same time, by propagating an educational ideology which explicitly recognizes education's duty to serve the needs of the economy, the Department is supplying itself with strong ideological reasons for more administrative intervention in the running of education. Combining both these factors, one can see that the type of educational change which they are likely to assist is one which will include a more 'efficient' credentialling process and a more 'impartial' distribution of educational inequality. Social inequality can then be legitimated by an education system organized and run along 'rational' meritocratic lines.

The one problem of this scenario so far as the DES is concerned is that it may in time be foisted with the very economic ideology which brings it increased power. For if the Department wins the 'power with responsibility' which it seeks on the back of an ideology which pledges economic results in return for more central intervention in education, it could be in trouble if no such economic improvement occurs as a consequence of that intervention. We may then find ourselves subject to a further ideological barrage on what education should be about!

Bibliography

AGGER, R., GOLDRICH, D. and SWANSON, B. (1964) *The Rulers and the Ruled*. New York: John Wiley.

ALTHUSSER, L. (1977) *Ideology and Ideological State Apparatus*. In B. R. Cosin (ed.) (1977).

APPLE, M. (ed.) (forthcoming) *Cultural and Economic Reproduction in Education*. London: Routledge & Kegan Paul.

ARCHER, M. S. (1979) *The Social Origins of Educational Systems*. London: Sage.

ARMITAGE, P. (1973) *Planning in practice*. In G. Fowler *et al.* (1973).

ASHTON, D. and MAGUIRE, M. (1981) *Employers' Demand for Young Workers* (The Careers Service and Employers' Project). University of Leicester (May).

(Auld Report) Report of the Public Enquiry (1976) *The William Tyndale Junior and Infants Schools*. London: Inner London Education Authority.

(Bains Report) Ministry of Housing and Local Government (1972) *The New Local Authorities: Management and Structure*. London: HMSO.

BAMFORD, T. (1967) *Rise of the Public Schools*. London: Nelson.

BARKER, R. (1972) *Education and Politics, 1900–1951*. Oxford: Clarendon Press.

BATES, T. R. (1975) Gramsci and the theory of hegemony. *Journal of the History of Ideas* 36.

BECHER, T. and MACLURE, J. S. (1978) *The Politics of Curriculum Change*. London: Hutchinson.

BECHER, T. (1971) The dissemination and implementation of educational innovation. *British Association for the Advancement of Science* (Annual Meeting) (September).

BELL, R. and PRESCOTT, W. (eds) (1975) *The Schools Council: A Second Look*. London: Ward Lock Educational.

BENNETT, N. (1976) *Teaching Styles and Pupil Progress*. London: Open Books.

BERGER, P. L. and LUCKMAN, T. (1967) *The Social Construction of Reality*. London: Allen Lane.

BERNBAUM, G. (1967) *Social Change and the Schools, 1919–1944*. London: Routledge & Kegan Paul.

BERNBAUM, G. (1977) *Knowledge and Ideology in the Sociology of Education*. London: Macmillan.

BERNSTEIN, B. (1971) *Class, Codes and Control* (Vol. 1). London: Routledge & Kegan Paul.

BERNSTEIN, B. (1973) *Class, Codes and Control* (Vol. 2). London: Routledge & Kegan Paul.

BERNSTEIN, B. (1975) *Class, Codes and Control* (Vol. 3). London: Routledge & Kegan Paul.

BIRLEY, D. (1970) *The Education Officer and His World*. London: Routledge & Kegan Paul.

BISHOP, T. J. H. and WILKINSON, R. (1967) *Winchester and the Public School Elite*. London: Faber & Faber.

BLACKIE, J. (1970) *Inspecting and the Inspectorate*. London: Routledge & Kegan Paul.

BLACKSTONE, T. (1980) Falling short of meritocracy. *Times Higher Education Supplement*, 18 January: 14.

BLAUG, M. (1968) Cost-benefit analysis of educational expenditures. In M. Blaug (ed.) *Economics of Education* (Vol. 1). Harmondsworth: Penguin.

BLAUG, M. (1970) *An Introduction to the Economics of Education*. Harmondsworth: Penguin.

BOADEN, N. (1971) *Urban Policy-Making: Influences on County Boroughs in England and Wales*. London: Cambridge University Press.

Board of Education (1926) *Report of the Consultative Committee on the Education of the Adolescent* (The Hadow Report). London: HMSO.

Board of Education (1931) *Report of the Consultative Committee on the Primary School*. London: HMSO.

Board of Education (1939) *Report of the Consultative Committee on Secondary Education* (The Spens Report). London: HMSO.

Board of Education, Committee on Public Schools (1944) *The Public*

Schools and the General Education System (The Fleming Report). London: HMSO.

BOGGS, C. (1976) *Gramsci's Marxism.* London: Pluto Press.

BOTTOMORE, T. (1977) Foreword to P. Bourdieu and J. C. Passeron (1977).

BOTTOMORE, T. and RUBEL, M. (eds) (1956) *Karl Marx: Selected Writings in Sociology and Social Philosophy.* London: C. A. Watts.

BOURDIEU, P. and PASSERON, J. C. (1977) *Reproduction in Education, Society and Culture.* London: Sage.

BOWLES, S. and GINTIS, H. (1976) *Schooling in Capitalist America: Educational Reform and the Contradictions of Economic Life.* London: Routledge & Kegan Paul.

BOYD, D. (1973) *Elites and their Education.* Slough, Bucks.: National Foundation for Educational Research.

BOYSON, R. (1979) Degree courses may be reduced. *Guardian,* 22 August: 1.

BRENNAN, E. (1975) *Education for National Efficiency: The Contribution of Sidney and Beatrice Webb.* London: Athlone Press.

BRIDGEMAN, J. M. (1969/1970) Planning, programming, budgeting systems I and II. *O and M Bulletin, Journal of the Government Management Services* (Nov./Feb.).

BRIDGEMAN, T. and FOX, I. (1978) Why people choose private schools. *New Society,* 29 June: 702–5.

(Bullock Report) (1975) *A Language for Life.* London: HMSO.

BURT, C. (1943) Education of the young adolescent: the psychological implications of the Norwood Report. *British Journal of Educational Psychology* 13.

BURT, C. (1947) A general survey. *British Journal of Educational Psychology* 17.

BURT, C. (1950) Testing intelligence. *Listener,* 16 November: 542–3.

BURT, C. (1950) The evidence for the concept of intelligence. *British Journal of Educational Psychology* 25.

BURT, C. (1959) Class differences in intelligence at 11 +. *British Journal of Statistical Psychology* 12.

BURT, C. (1959) The examination at eleven plus. *British Journal of Educational Studies* 7.

BURT, C. (1962) *Mental and Scholastic Tests* (4th edition: 1st edition 1921). London: Staples Press.

BUTT, R. (1972) A Feasibility Study of PPBS in Gloucestershire. *Local Government Studies* 2 (April).

BUTT, R. (1978) The demolition job waiting for Mr. Carlisle. *The Times*, 23 November: 18.

BYRNE, E. (1974) *Planning and Educational Inequality: A Study of the Rationale of Resource Allocation.* Slough, Bucks.: National Foundation for Educational Research.

The Cabinet Office (1970) *The Reorganisation of Central Government* (Cmnd 4506). London: HMSO.

(CACE) Central Advisory Council for Education (England) (1954) *Early Leaving.* London: HMSO.

(CACE) Central Advisory Council for Education (England) (1963) *Half our Future.* London: HMSO.

(CHE) Committee on Higher Education (1963) *Higher Education.* London: HMSO.

(CPRS) Central Policy Review Staff (1980) *Education, Training and Industrial Performance.* London: HMSO.

CALLAGHAN, J. (1976) Ruskin speech. *Times Educational Supplement*, 22 October: 72.

Cambridge University (1980) *Reporter.* Special Issue 16 (August). cx: 15, table 1; 20, table 1.

CAMPBELL, B. (1978) Shortening the odds. *Conference* 15, ii (June).

CAMPBELL, F. (1970) Latin and the élite tradition in education. In P. W. Musgrave (ed.) (1970).

CARR-SAUNDERS, A. M. and WILSON, P. O. (1964) *The Professions.* London: Frank Cass.

Centre for Contemporary Cultural Studies (1981) *Unpopular Education: Schooling and Social Democracy in England since 1944.* London: Hutchinson.

CHIN, R. and BENNE, K. D. (1969) General Strategies for effecting change in human systems. In W. G. Bennis, K. Benne and R. Chin (eds) *The Planning of Change.* London: Holt, Rinehart & Winston.

COBBAN, J. (1972) Looking back, *Conference* 9, i (February).

COHEN, S. and LODGE, B. (1977) 'Blundering intruders' warned (report of Jarvis' speech to NUT Conference). *Times Educational Supplement*, 15 April: 6.

COLEMAN, D. C. (1973) Gentlemen and players. *Economic History Review* (2nd. series) 26, i: 92–116.

COLEMAN, J. S. (1966) *Equality of Educational Opportunity.* Washington DC: US Department of Health, Education and Welfare, Office of Education.

COLLINS, R. (1972) Functional and conflict theories of educational stratification. In B. R. Cosin (ed.) (1972).

CORBETT, A. (1973) The secret door of the curriculum – who should hold the key to the door? *Times Educational Supplement*, 13 July: 4–5.

COSIN, B. R. (ed.) (1977) *Education, Structure and Society*. Harmondsworth: Penguin.

COX, C. B. and DYSON, A. E. (eds) (1969a) *A Black Paper*. London: The Critical Quarterly Society.

COX, C. B. and DYSON, A. E. (eds) (1969b) *Black Paper Two*. London: The Critical Quarterly Society.

COX, C. B. and DYSON, A. E. (eds) (1970) *Black Paper Three*. London: The Critical Quarterly Society.

COX, C. B. and BOYSON, R. (eds) (1975) *Black Paper 1975*. London: Dent.

COX, C. B. and BOYSON, R. (eds) (1977) *Black Paper 1977*. London: Maurice Temple Smith.

CROWTHER-HUNT, Lord and KELLNER, P. (1980) *The Civil Servants: An Inquiry into Britain's Ruling Class*. London: Macdonald & Janes.

(DES) Department of Education and Science. Committee in Higher Education (1964) *Higher Education* London: HMSO.

(DES) Department of Education and Science (1970a) *HMI Today and Tomorrow*. London: HMSO.

(DES) Department of Education and Science. (1970b) *Output Budgeting for the Department of Education and Science: Report of a Feasibility Study* (Education Planning Paper No. 1). London: HMSO.

(DES) Department of Education and Science. (1970c) *Student Numbers in Higher Education in England and Wales* (Educational Planning Paper No. 2). London: HMSO.

(DES) Department of Education and Science. (1972) *Education: A Framework for Expansion*. London: HMSO.

(DES) Department of Education and Science (1974) *Management in the Education Service*. London: HMSO.

(DES) Department of Education and Science (1977a) *Local Education Authority Arrangements for the School Curriculum* (Circular 14/77) (November). London: HMSO.

(DES) Department of Education and Science (1977b) *Annual Report*. London: HMSO.

(DES) Department of Education and Science (1977c) *Educating our Children – Four Subjects for Debate.* London: HMSO.

(DES) Department of Education and Science (1977d) *Education in Schools. A Consultative Document* (Cmnd 6869). London: HMSO.

(DES) Department of Education and Science (1977e) *Education and Science in 1976.* London: HMSO.

(DES) Department of Education and Science (1977f) *The Composition of School Governing Bodies* (Cmnd 7430). London: HMSO.

(DES) Department of Education and Science (1978a) *Annual Report.* London: HMSO.

(DES) Department of Education and Science (1978b) *Progress in Education. A Report on Recent Initiatives* (September). London: HMSO.

(DES) Department of Education and Science (1978c) *Report on Education: Assessing the Performance of Pupils.* London: HMSO.

(DES) Department of Education and Science (1978d) *The Attainment of the School-leaver* (Cmnd 7124). London: HMSO.

(DES) Department of Education and Science (1979) *Local Authority Arrangements for the Curriculum – Report on the Circular 14/77 Review.* London: HMSO.

(DES) Department of Education and Science (1980) *A Framework for the School Curriculum.* London: HMSO.

(DES) Department of Education and Science (1981a) *The School Curriculum.* London: HMSO.

(DES) Department of Education and Science (1981b) *Higher Education in England Outside the Universities: Policy, Funding and Management.* London: HMSO.

(DI) Department of Industry (1977) *Industry, Education and Management, a Discussion Paper.* London: HMSO.

DAHL, R. A. (1962) A critique of the ruling class model. *American Political Science Review* 56, iv.

DALE, R., ESLAND, G. and MACDONALD, M. (eds) (1976) *Schooling and Capitalism.* London: Routledge & Kegan Paul.

DALIN, P. (1978) *Limits to Educational Change.* London: Macmillan.

DANCY, J. C. (1963) *The Public Schools and the Future.* London: Faber & Faber.

DAVID, P. (1981a) Public body politic. *Times Higher Education Supplement*, 7 August: 7.

DAVID, P. (1981b) A surprise package. *Times Higher Education Supplement*, 14 August: 10.

DAVIES, I. (1971) The management of the use of typologies in the sociology of education. In M. F. D. Young (ed.) (1971).

DEMAINE, J. (1979) IQism as ideology and the political economy of education. *Educational Studies* 5.

DEVLIN, T. and WARNOCK, M. (1977) *What Must We Teach?* London: Maurice Temple Smith.

DOE, R. (1977) Minister moving to end union grip on Schools Council. *Times Educational Supplement.* 21 January: 3.

DOE, R. (1978) Dear big brother... *Times Educational Supplement*, 11 August: 5.

DOE, R. (1979) Framework for a common curriculum. *Times Educational Supplement.* November 16:16.

DOE, R. (1981) Performance unit threatened. *Times Educational Supplement.* 17 July: 3.

DURKHEIM, E. (1956) *Education and Sociology.* Glencoe: The Free Press.

DURKHEIM, E. (1977) *The Evolution of Educational Thought.* London: Routledge & Kegan Paul.

EDDISON, T. (1973) *Local Government: Management and Corporate Planning.* Aylesbury: Leonard Hill Books.

EDMONDS, E. L. (1962) *The School Inspector.* London: Routledge & Kegan Paul.

EGGLESTON, J. (1977) *The Sociology of the School Curriculum.* London: Routledge & Kegan Paul.

ELLIS, T., MCWHIRTER, J., MCCOLGAN, D. and HADDOW, B. (1976) *William Tyndale: The Teachers' Story.* London: Writers and Readers Publishing Cooperative.

ESLAND, G. (1977) Diagnosis and testing. In Open University, *Schooling and Society* (E202, Unit 21). Walton Hall, Milton Keynes: Open University Press.

(FBI) Federation of British Industries (1945) *Industry and Education.* London: FBI.

(FBI) Federation of British Industries (1949) *Industry and the Universities.* London: FBI.

(FBI) Federation of British Industries (1965) *Industry and the Schools.* London: FBI.

FISHER, S. (1977) Hands off our syllabus (address to NUT Conference). *Times Educational Supplement.* 21 January: 13.

FISKE, D. (1980) *Education: Going National?* William Walker Lecture. London: British Education Administration Society.

FLEW, A. (1976) *Sociology, Equality and Education.* London: Macmillan.

FLUDE, M. (1974) Sociological accounts of different educational attainment. In M. Flude and J. Ahier (eds) *Educability, Schools and Ideology.* London: Croom Helm.

FOWLER, G., MORRIS, V. and OZGA, J. (eds) (1973) *Decision-Making in British Education.* London: Heinemann.

FOWLER, G. (1974) *Central government of education 1: policy formation.* Unit 2 of OU (1974).

FOWLER, G. (1975) DES, ministers and curriculum. In R. Bell and W. Prescott (eds) (1975).

(FRANKS) University of Oxford (1966) *Commission of Inquiry* (two vols). Oxford: University Press.

(FRANKS) University of Oxford (1965) *Commission of Inquiry, Evidence, Part Three* (evidence received by 31st October, 1964). Oxford: University Press.

FRITH S. (1978) 'Education and Industry' (mimeographed).

GARNICOT, K. G. and BLAUG, M. (1973) Manpower forecasting since Robbins – a science lobby in action. In G. Fowler *et al.* (eds) (1973).

GATHORNE-HARDY, J. (1977) *The Public School Phenomenon.* London: Hodder & Stoughton.

GERTH, H. H. and WRIGHT MILLS, C. (1964) *From Max Weber.* London: Routledge & Kegan Paul.

GLENNERSTER, H. and WILSON, G. (1968) The Finances of public schools. In Public Schools Commission, *First Report* (Vol. 2). London: HMSO.

GLENNERSTER, H. and WILSON, G. (1970) *Paying for Private Schools.* London: Allen Lane.

GLENNERSTER, H. and PRYKE, R. (1973) The contribution of the public schools and Oxbridge: 1 'Born to rule'. In J. Urry and J. Wakeford (eds) *Power in Britain.* London: Heinemann.

GOWING, M. (1976) Lost opportunities in an Age of Imperialism. *Times Higher Educational Supplement*, 26 November: 15.

GRAMSCI, A. (1957) *The Modern Prince and Other Writings.* London: Lawrence & Wishart.

GRACE, G. (1978) *Teachers, Ideology of Control: A Study in Urban Education.* London: Routledge & Kegan Paul.

GRAVES J. (1940) The use of advisory bodies by the Board of Education. In R. V. Vernon and N. Mansergh (eds) *Advisory Bodies*. London: Allen & Unwin.

GREENWOOD, R., NORTON, A. L. and STEWART, J. D. (1969) *Recent Reforms in the Management Arrangements of County Boroughs in England and Wales; Recent Reforms in the Management of Local Authorities – the London Boroughs*; and *Recent Reforms in the Management Structure of Local Authorities – the County Councils* (Occasional Papers Nos. 1, 2 and 3). Birmingham: INLOGOV, University of Birmingham.

GRIEG, C. and REID, W. A. (1978) Proposals and possibilities in curriculum development: a study of the Cambridge School Classics project. *Journal of Curriculum Studies* 10, iv (Oct.–Dec.).

Guardian (1979) Degree courses may be reduced 22 August:1.

(HMI) Select Committee on Education and Science (1968) *Her Majesty's Inspectorate (England and Wales)* (Report Part 1, Session 1967–68, HC 182–1). London: HMSO.

(HMI) Her Majesty's Inspectorate (1977) *Curriculum 11–16* (Series: Matters for Discussion). London: HMSO.

(HMI) Her Majesty's Inspectorate (1980) *A View of the Curriculum* (Series: Matters for Discussion, No. 11). London: HMSO.

HALSEY, A. H., HEATH, A. F. and RIDGE, J. M. (1980) *Origins and Destinations: Family, Class and Education in Modern Britain.* Oxford: Clarendon Press.

HALSEY, A. H. (1972) *Educational Priority, Volume One: Problems and Policies*, London: HMSO.

HALSEY, A. H. (1980) Education can compensate. *New Society*, 24 January: 173.

HARGREAVES, D. (1967) *Social Relations in a Secondary School.* London: Routledge & Kegan Paul.

HARGREAVES, D. (1972) *Interpersonal Relations and Education.* London: Routledge & Kegan Paul.

HAVELOCK, R. G. and HAVELOCK, M. C. (1973) *Training for Change Agents.* Ann Arbor, Michigan: Institute for Social Research, University of Michigan.

Headmasters' Conference (1968) Annual General Meeting. *Conference* 5 iii (October).

Headmasters' Conference (1978) *Manual of Guidance.* London: HMC.

HEARNSHAW, L. (1979) *C. Burt: Psychologist*. London: Hodder & Stoughton.

HECLO, H. H. (1972) Review article: policy analysis. *British Journal of Political Science* 2.

HEENEY, B. (1969) *Mission to the Middle Classes*. London: SPCK.

HENDERSON, P. (1976) Class structure and the concept of intelligence. In R. Dale *et al.* (1976).

HIRST, P. (1974) *Knowledge and the Curriculum*. London: Routledge & Kegan Paul.

HOARE, Q. and NOWELL SMITH, C. (eds) (1971) *Antonio Gramsci, Selections from the Prison Notebooks*. London: Lawrence & Wishart.

HODGKINSON, H. (1966) The smaller public school and its place in Britain. *Conference* 3, ii (July).

HOGBEN, L. (1939) *Nature and Nurture*. London: Allen & Unwin.

HOLLOWAY, J. and PICCIOTTO, S. (1978) 'Education and the crisis of social relations' (mimeographed).

HONEY, J. R. DE S. (1977) *Tom Brown's Universe*. London: Millington.

(Hornsey) The Association of Hornsey College of Art (1969) *The Hornsey Affair*. Harmondsworth: Penguin.

House of Commons, Fifth report from the Education, Science and Arts Committee (1980) *The Funding and Organisation of Courses in Higher Education*. (House of Commons Paper 787-1-i-xiv). London: HMSO.

HOWARD, P. (1977) 'Mother of Schools' gets a new offspring. *The Times*, 5 October: 2.

HOWARTH, A. (1972) Public Schools and the millenium. *Conference* 9, ii (June).

Humanities Curriculum Project (1970) *The Humanities Curriculum Project*. London: Heinemann Educational Books.

HUSSAIN, A. (1976) The economy and the educational system in capitalist societies. *Economy and Society* 5.

(ISIS) Indendent School Information Service (1978) *Statistical Survey of Independent Schools, 1978*. London: ISIS.

(ISIS) Indendent Schools Information Service (1980) *Statistical Survey of Independent Schools, 1980*. London: ISIS.

ILLICH, I. (1973) *Deschooling society*. Harmondsworth: Penguin.

JACKSON, B. (1964) *Streaming: An Educational System in Miniature*. London: Routledge & Kegan Paul.

JACKSON, M. (1977) City and Guilds to the rescue. *Times Educational Supplement*, 12 August: 4.

JACKSON, M. (1980) DES goes 'on the road', to explain policy to select few. *Times Educational Supplement*, 26 September: 6.

JAMES, E. (1951) *Education and Leadership*. London: Harrap.

JAMES, E. (1968) The maintenance of academic standards. *Conference* 5, i (February).

JENCKS, C. and 7 others (1973) *Inequality: A Reassessment of the Effect of Family and Schooling in America*. New York: Basic Books.

JENCKS, C. and 11 others (1979) *Who gets Ahead? The Determinants of Economic Success in America*. New York: Basic Books.

JENKINS, D. and SHIPMAN, M. (1976) *Curriculum: An Introduction* London. Open Books.

JENNINGS, R. E. (1977) *Education and Politics: Policy-Making in Local Education Authorities*. London: Batsford.

JOSEPH, K. (1976) *Stranded on the Middle Ground*. London: Centre for Policy Studies.

KALTON, G. (1966) *The Public Schools: A Factual Survey*. London: Longmans.

KAMIN, I. (1974) *The Science and Politics of IQ*. New York: John Wiley.

KEDDIE, N. (1973) Introduction to N. Keddie (ed.) *Tinker, Tailor ... the Myth of Cultural Deprivation*. Harmondsworth: Penguin.

KEDDIE, N. (1971) Classroom Knowledge. In M. F. D. Young (ed.) (1971).

KERR, C. (1963) *The Uses of the University*. Cambridge, Mass.: Harvard University Press.

KING, E. (1961) The gentleman: the evolution of an English ideal. *The Yearbook of Education*.

KIRK, K. (1937) *The Story of the Woodard Schools*. London: Hodder & Stoughton.

KOGAN, M. (1971) *The Politics of Education*. Harmondsworth: Penguin.

KOGAN, M. (1973) The function of the Central Advisory Council in educational change. In G. Fower *et al.* (1973).

KOGAN, M. (1975) *Educational Policy-Making*. London: Allen & Unwin.

KOGAN, M. (1978) *The Politics of Educational Change*. London: Fontana.

KOGAN, M. and VAN DER EYKEN, W. (1973) *County Hall, The Role of the Chief Education Officer.* Harmondsworth: Penguin.

KOGAN, M. and PACKWOOD, T. (1974) *Advisory Councils and Committees in Education.* London: Routledge & Kegan Paul.

LACEY, C. (1970) *Hightown Grammar.* Manchester: University Press.

LAMBERT, R. (1966) The public schools: a sociological introduction. In G. Kalton (1966).

LAMBERT, R. (1975) *The Chance of a Lifetime?* London: Weidenfeld & Nicolson.

LAMBERT, R. (1977) The public school ethos. In OU (1977).

LAMBERT, R., HIPKIN, J. and STAGG, S. (1962) *New Wine in Old Bottles?* (Occasional Papers on Social Administration, No. 28). London: G. Bell.

LASSWELL, H. D. and KAPLAN, M. (1950) *Power and Society.* New Haven, Conn.: Yale University Press.

LASSWELL, H. (1956) *The Decision Process.* College Park, Md.: Bureau of Government and Research.

LAWTON, D. (1980a) *The Politics of the School Curriculum.* London: Routledge & Kegan Paul.

LAWTON, D. (1980b) Platform: responsible partners. *Times Educational Supplement,* 7 March.

LEES, R. and SMITH, G. (eds) (1975) *Action Research in Community Development.* London: Routledge & Kegan Paul.

LEVIDOW, L. (1979) Towards a materialist theory of ideology: the IQ debate as a case study. *Radical Politics* (Summer).

LIGHT, A. J. (1974) The Schools Council and the development of the secondary curriculum. *Ideas* (October).

LINDSAY, D. (1968) Chairman's address to the annual general meeting of the Headmaster's Conference. *Conference* 5, iii (October).

LINDSAY, K. (1926) *Social Progress and Educational Waste.* London: Routledge & Kegan Paul.

LOCKE, M. (1974) *Power and Politics in the School System: A Guidebook.* London: Routledge & Kegan Paul.

(Lockwood Report) (1964) *Report of the Working Party on School Curriculum and Examinations.* London: HMSO.

MACRAE, D. (1980) Bad taxonomy leads to bad sociology. *Times Educational Supplement,* 18 January: 23.

McINTYRE, D. and BROWN, S. (1979) Science teachers' implementation of two intended innovations. *Scottish Educational Review* II (1).

MACLURE, S. (1970) *One Hundred Years of London Education.* London: Allen Lane.

MACLURE, S. (1975) The Schools Council and examinations. In R. Bell and W. Prescott (eds) (1975).

MANZER, R. (1970) *Teachers and Politics.* Manchester: University Press.

MANZER, R. (1973) The technical power of organised teachers in R. Bell, G. Fowler and I. Little (eds) *Education in Great Britain and Ireland.* London: Routledge & Kegan Paul.

MARX, K. (1965) *The German Ideology.* London: Lawrence & Wishart.

(Maud Report) Ministry of Housing and Local Government. Committee on the Management of Local Government (1967) *Volume I: Report of the Committee.* London: HMSO.

MILIBAND, R. (1969) *The State in Capitalist Society.* London: Weidenfeld & Nicolson.

MUSGRAVE, P. W. (1970a) A model for the analysis of the development of the English educational system from 1860. In P. W. Musgrave (ed.) (1970).

MUSGRAVE, P. W. (1970b) *Sociology, History and Education.* London: Methuen.

(NEC) National Executive Committee, the Labour Party (1980) *Private Schools.* Discussion Document (August).

NEILL, A. S. (1969) *Summerhill: A Radical Approach to Education.* London: Gollancz.

NEWSOME, D. (1959) *A History of Wellington College, 1859–1959.* London: John Murray.

NEWSOME, D. (1961) *Godliness and Good Learning.* London: John Murray.

NISBET, J. (1973) The Schools Council. *Case Studies of Educational Innovation: 1 At the Central Level.* Paris: CERI/OECD.

NORTON, A. L. and STEWART, J. D. (1973) Recommendations to the New Local Authorities 1973. *Local Government Studies* 6 (October).

(OU) Open University (1974) *Decision-Making in British Education Systems,* (E221, Units 5–7). Walton Hall, Milton Keynes: Open University Press.

(OU) Open University (1977) *Schooling and Society* (E202, Unit 29), Walton Hall, Milton Keynes: Open University Press.

OECD (1975) *Educational Development Strategy in England and Wales*. Paris: OECD.

(Oakes Report) (1978) *Report of the Working Group on the Management of Higher Education in the Maintained Sector* (Cmnd 7130). London: HMSO.

O'CONNOR, M. (1979) Apartheid: the British disease. *Guardian*, 28 September: 20.

ORWELL, G. (1958) Boys' weeklies. In *Selected Writings*. London: Heinemann Educational Books.

OWEN, J. (1973) *The Management of Curriculum Development*. Cambridge: University Press.

Oxford University (1979) *Gazette* 3781, Supplement 2 (September). 23: table 1.

PAIGE, G. D. (1968) *The Korean Decision: June 24–30*. New York: The Free Press.

PARKIN, F. (1967) Working-class conservatism: a theory of political deviance. *British Journal of Sociology* 18.

PARKINSON, M. (1970) *The Labour Party and the Organization of Secondary Education, 1918–1965*. London: Routledge & Kegan Paul.

PARRY, I. (1974) The Schools Council and primary education. *Ideas* (June).

PILE, W. (1979) *The Department of Education and Science*. London: George Allen & Unwin.

(Plowden Report) Central Advisory Council for Education (England) (1967) *Children and their Primary Schools*. London: HMSO.

PRING, R. (1975) Integration: official policy or official fashion. In R. Bell and W. Prescott (eds) (1975).

Public Schools Commission (1968a) *First Report* (Vol. 1). London: HMSO.

Public Schools Commission (1968b) *First Report* (Vol. 2). London: HMSO.

Public Schools Commission (1970) *Second Report* (Vol. 1). London: HMSO.

PUNCH, M. (1977) *Progressive Retreat*. Cambridge: University Press.

RADICAL EDUCATION (1977) Editorial: The great diversion. 9 (Summer).

RAE, J. (1977) Our obsolete attitudes. *Encounter* 49, v (November): 10–17.

RAE, J. (1978) What future for independent schools? *Sunday Telegraph*, 2 April.

RAE, J. (1981) *The Public School Revolution*. London: Faber & Faber.

RANSON, S. (1980) Changing relations between centre and locality in education. *Local Government Studies* 5.

READER, W. J. (1966) *Professional Men: The Rise of Professional Classes in Nineteenth Century England*. London: Weidenfeld & Nicolson.

RICHARDS, C. (1974) The Schools Council – a critical examination. *Universities Quarterly* 28, iii.

(Robbins Report) Report of the Committee appointed by the Prime Minister under the chairmanship of Lord Robbins (1963) *Higher Education* (Cmnd 2154). London: HMSO.

ROBINSON, J. (1962) *Congress and Foreign Policy-making*. Homewood, Illinois: Dorsey Press.

ROSE, H. and S. (1979) The IQ Myth. In D. Rubinstein, *Education and Equality*. Harmondsworth: Penguin.

ROSE, N. (1979) The psychologocal complex: mental measurement and social administration. *Ideology and Consciousness* 5 (Spring).

ROSE, R. (1969) *Policy-Making in Britain*. London: Macmillan.

RUSSELL, B. (1926) *On Education*. London: Unwin Brothers.

(SC) Schools Council (1973) *Evaluation in Curriculum Development: Twelve Case Studies*. London: Macmillan Education.

(SC) Schools Council Report of Schools Council Working Party on Dissemination 1972–3 (1974a) *Dissemination and In-Service Training* (SC Pamphlet 14). London: HMSO.

(SC) Schools Council (1974b) *Dissemination and In-Service Training* (SC Pamphlet 14).

(SC) Schools Council (1978a) Constitution of the Schools Council for Curriculum and Examination, London: at 1 September 1978. *Schools Council Report*. London: Evans/Methuen.

(SC) Schools Council (1978b) Constitution of the Schools Council for Curriculum and Examination, as from 1 September 1978. *Schools Council Report*. London: Evans/Methuen.

SAMPSON, A. (1962) *Anatomy of Britain*. London: Hodder & Stoughton.

SANDERSON, M. (1972) *The Universities and British Industry*. London: Routledge & Kegan Paul.

SARAN, R. (1973) *Policy-Making in Secondary Education*. Oxford: Clarendon Press.

SHARP, R. (1980) *Knowledge, Ideology and the Politics of Schooling.* London: Routledge & Kegan Paul.

SHARP, R. and GREEN, A. (1975) *Education and Social Control.* London: Routledge & Kegan Paul.

SHIPMAN, M. (1974) *Inside a Curriculum Project.* London: Methuen.

SIMON, B. (1965) *Studies in the History of Education and the Labour Movement, 1870–1920.* London: Lawrence & Wishart.

SIMON, B. (1977) The Green Paper. *Forum* 20, i (Autumn).

STAGG, S. and LAMBERT, R. (1968) Integration: a pilot scheme. In R. Lambert *et al.* (1968).

START, B. and WELLS, K. (1972) *The Trend of Reading Standards.* Slough, Bucks.: National Foundation for Educational Research.

STEADMAN, S. D., PARSONS, C. and SALTER, B. G. (1980) *A Second Interim Report on the Schools Council.* London: Schools Council.

STENHOUSE, L. (ed.) (1980) *Curriculum Research and Development in Action.* London: Heinemann Educational Books.

STEVENS, A. (1977) Shake-up in the inspectorate: focus switches to centre. *Times Educational Supplement,* 4 February: 1.

STEWART, J. D. (1971) *Management in Local Government: A Viewpoint.* London: Charles Knight.

STEWART, J. D. (1974) Corporate management and the education service. *Educational Administrative Bulletin* 3,i.

SUTHERLAND, G. (1977) The magic of measurement: mental testing and English education 1900–40. *Transactions of the Royal Historical Society* (Fifth Series) 27.

(TES) *Times Educational Supplement* (1976) Extracts from the Yellow Book. 15 October: 2–3.

(TES) *Times Educational Supplement* (1977) Extracts from the Green Paper. 22 July: 5,8.

(TES) *Times Educational Supplement* (1977) A New Partnership, 23 September: 7, 8.

(TES) *Times Educational Supplement* (1977) And the reaction [sc. to the Green Paper]. 15 October: 3.

(TES) *Times Educational Supplement* (1977) Girls overtake boys in the unemployment stakes. 11 November: 7.

(TES) *Times Educational Supplement* (1978) Ring of confidence. 21 July: 1.

(TES) *Times Educational Supplement* (1980) Call to strengthen central power over education service. 7 November: 5.

(TES) *Times Educational Supplement* (1981a) Steamroller tactics used on Schools Council, claim union leaders. 13 February: 5.

(TES) *Times Educational Supplement* (1981b) Cautious DES prefers platitude to prescription. 27 March: 3.

(THES) *Times Higher Education Supplement* (1980) DES re-shuffle to ease binary planning. 23 May: 40.

(TES) *Times Educational Supplement* (1980) Pay panel splits over a Burnham seat for PAT. 14 November: 4.

TAPPER, T. and SALTER, B. (1978) *Education and the Political Order*. London: Macmillan.

TAWNEY, R. H. (1922) *Secondary Education for All*. London: George Allen & Unwin.

TAYLOR, G. and AYRES, N. (1969) *Born and Bred Unequal*. London: Longman.

TAYLOR, P. H., REID, W., HOLLEY, B. and EXON, G. (1974) *Purpose, Power and Constraint in the Primary School Curriculum* (Schools Council Research Studies). London: Macmillan.

(Taylor Report) Department of Education and Science (1977) *A New Partnership for our Schools*. London: HMSO.

Tenth Report from the Expenditure Committee (1976) *Policy Making in the DES* (Sessions 1975–76, Cmnd 6678). London: HMSO.

THOMPSON, E. P. (ed.) (1970) *Warwick University Ltd*. Harmondsworth: Penguin.

THORN, J. (1978) Mind-Forg'd manacles. *Conference* 15, i (February).

TRAVERS, T. (1980) The new block grant will place decision-making in the hands of the DES – or worse, the DOE. *Guardian*, 18 March: 7.

TYLER, W. (1977) *The Sociology of Educational Inequality*. London: Methuen.

(UGC) University Grants Committee (1978) *Annual Survey 1976–77* (Cmnd 7119). London: HMSO.

VAIZEY, J. (1962) *The Economics of Education*. London: Faber & Faber.

VAIZEY, J. (1971) Address to the annual general meeting of the Headmasters' Conference. *Conference* 8, i (February).

VAUGHAN, M. (1976) LEA plans major changes to meet PM's challenge. *Times Educational Supplement*, 17 December: 1.

VAUGHAN, M. (1977) Snub for 'busybodies' charter. *Times Educational Supplement*. September 23: 1.

VAUGHAN, M. C. and ARCHER, M. S. (1971) *Social Change in England and France, 1789–1848*. Cambridge: University Press.

VERNON, P. (1955) Recent trends in mental measurement and statistical analysis. *Studies in Education* 7, (London: Institute of Education, University of London).

VERNON, P. (1960) *Intelligence and Attainment Tests*. London: University of London Press.

WAKEFORD, J. (1969) *The Cloistered Elite*. London: Macmillan.

WATTS, A. F., PIDGEON, D. and YATES, A. (1952) *Secondary School Entrance Examinations*. Slough, Bucks.: National Foundation for Educational Research.

WEBB, S. (1904) *London Education*. London: Longmans, Green.

WEBER, M. (1968a) The types of legitimate domination. In G. Roth and C. Wittich (eds) *Economy and Society* (Vol. 1). New York: Bedminster Press.

WEBER, M. (1968b) Domination and Legitimacy. In G. Roth and C. Wittich (eds) *Economy and Society* (Vol. 3). New York: Bedminster Press.

WEINBERG, I. (1967) *The English Public Schools: The Sociology of Elite Education*. New York: Atherton Press.

WHITTY, G. and YOUNG, M. (eds) (1976) *Explorations in the Politics of School Knowledge*. Nafferton: Nafferton Books.

WILBY, P. (1977) The next exam for Shirley. *Sunday Times*, 27 November: 16.

WILKINSON, R. H. (1964) *The Prefects*. London: Oxford University Press.

WILKINSON, R. H. (1970) The gentleman ideal and the maintenance of a political élite. In P. W. Musgrave (ed.) (1970).

WILLIAMS, R. (1961) *The Long Revolution*. London: Chatto & Windus.

WILLIAMSON, B. (1979) *Education, Social Structure and Development*. London: Macmillan.

WILLIS, P. (1977) *Learning to Labour*. Farnborough, Hants.: Saxon House.

WILSON, J. (1962) *Public Schools and Private Practice*. London: George Allen & Unwin.

WOODHALL, M. (1972) *Economic Aspects of Education*. Slough, Bucks.: National Foundation for Educational Research.

WOODHOUSE, J. (1975) Learning to live with others. *Conference* 12, iii (October).

WOODS, P., and HAMMERSLEY, M. (eds) (1977) *School Experience*. London: Croom Helm.

YOUNG, M. F. D. (1961) *The Rise of the Meritocracy*. Harmondsworth: Penguin.

YOUNG, M. F. D. (ed.) (1971) *Knowledge and Control: New Directions for the Sociology of Education*. London: Collier-Macmillan.

YOUNG, M. F. D. (1976) The rhetoric of curriculum development. In G. Whitty and M. Young (eds) (1976).

YOUNG, M. F. D. and WHITTY, G. (1977) Towards a critical theory. In M. F. D. Young and G. Whitty (eds) *Society, State and Schooling*. Ringmer, Sussex: Falmer Press.

YOUNG, M. F. D. (1973) On the politics of educational knowledge. In R. Bell, G. Fowler and K. Little (eds). *Education in Great Britain and Ireland*. London: Routledge & Kegan Paul.

Subject Index

Name Index